SPIRAL GUIDES

M000121782

CANADA

Contents

Written by Penny Phenix
Magazine section by Paul Waters; The North by Jenni Davis

Updated by Penny Phenix

American editor Tracy Larson

Edited, designed and produced by AA Publishing
© Automobile Association Developments Limited 2005, 2008
Maps © Automobile Association Developments Limited 2005

Published in the United States by AAA Publishing,
1000 AAA Drive, Heathrow, Florida 32746-5063
Published in the United Kingdom by AA Publishing

ISBN 978-1-59508-233-6

Cover design and binding style by permission of AA Publishing
Color separation by Keenes, Andover
Printed and bound in China by Leo Paper Products

10 9 8 7 6 5 4 3 2 1

A03183
Mapping produced from Canada data © Tele Atlas N.V. 2005

the magazine

Best of Canada

Best cities

Canada has three great metropolises: west to east, Vancouver, Toronto and Montréal. All three make the "best-of" charts for different reasons.

Vancouver (► 54–57) wins hands down for setting, framed by the Coastal Mountains to the north and the fertile Fraser River Delta to the south. Its west end fronts on English Bay, and it has both the best urban green space in Canada – Stanley Park – and the best urban ski resort – Grouse Mountain.

Toronto's (► 103–106) surroundings on the other hand are, well, dull (aside from the lake), but no one goes to Toronto for the scenery. In the last 30 years, the city has emerged as the cultural center of Canada and one of the most multicultural cities on Earth. It has Canada's best street market (Kensington), some of its best restaurants and first-rate dance and opera companies. After New York and London, this is also the world's most important center for English-language theater.

Montréal (► 122–125) is something completely different – or, *quelque chose complètement différent*. One of the largest French-speaking cities in the world, it has Canada's most adventurous restaurants, best nightlife, best-dressed street crowds and most magnificent cathedrals and churches. It also has a history that stretches back to 1638 – positively paleolithic by Canadian standards.

Most Unusual Names

Newfoundland wins for the delightful villages of Heart's Desire, Heart's Delight and Heart's Content. Some other place names in the province – Come-by-Chance, Blow-Me-Down and Run-by-Guess, for example – hint mistakenly at a devil-may-care attitude to the art of navigation by local mariners.

Cosmopolitan street life is a great attraction in Montreal

Vancouver's setting between the ocean and the mountains is nothing short of spectacular

Cobblestones and French Colonial architecture in Québec City's Place Royale

Best small town

Following strict orders from back home, colonists in **Lunenburg** (➤ 156), Nova Scotia, ignored the steep landscape and laid out their town of multicolored wooden houses according to a rigid grid. The result is a delightful triumph of order over common sense.

Best walled city

Not only the best, but the *only* walled city (in the whole of North America), **Québec City** (➤ 126–128) is a beautifully preserved piece of New France.

Best wilderness

Canada's wilderness begins just a few miles from some of the country's biggest cities and ends at the edge of the polar ice-cap. It includes soaring mountains, thunderous rivers, endless stretches of lichen-covered tundra and about a quarter of the world's fresh water. And much of it is surprisingly easy to get to.

Mont Tremblant offers year-round activities in easy reach of Montréal

The best wilderness for beginners is Quebec's **Mont Tremblant National Park** (▶ 134). Its 1,510sq km (583 square miles) of mountains, lakes and rushing rivers are just a couple of hours north of Montréal.

Just as dramatic is **Kluane National Park** (▶ 191), a mountainous, 21,980sq km (8,486 square-mile) reserve on the western edge of Yukon territory. Its peaks include Canada's highest – Mount Logan at 5,959m (19,551 feet) and it is home to grizzly bears and sure-footed Dall sheep.

Best road trips

Nothing beats the **Cabot Trail** (▶ 188–190) that wraps around the mountainous northern end of Cape Breton Island, Nova Scotia. In the west, Alberta's **Icefields Parkway** (▶ 180–181) lacks Cape Breton's ocean vistas but makes up for it with bigger mountains, wolves and mountain goats.

In the north, the gravel-surfaced **Dempster Highway** (▶ 173) starts near Dawson City, Yukon and runs 750km (465 miles) to Inuvik on the Beaufort Sea, 200km (125 miles) north of the Arctic Circle (which means 24-hour daylight in summer).

Best ferry ride

No contest: It's the spectacular southbound trip on B. C. Ferries' *Queen of Chilliwack* from **Bella Coola to Port Hardy**.

The Dempster Highway crosses a wild and remote landscape

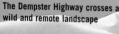

Best music

Natalie MacMaster (below), one of Nova Scotia's world-famous fiddlers, is at the fore-front of the Celtic music revival. Toronto's **Tragically Hip**, inducted into the Canadian Music Hall of Fame in 2005, remain Canada's favorite rock band.

Best beach

On the east coast, long strips of pink and white sand ringed by dunes and wild rose bushes make up much of the 40km (25 miles) of coast-line within the **Prince Edward Island National Park** (▶ 150). The island also claims to have the warmest seawater north of the Carolinas. Out west, the water that breaks ashore on **Vancouver Island's Long Beach** (▶ 53) is decidedly chillier, but both the waves and the surrounding land-scape are far more dramatic.

Just say hockey

It's difficult for outsiders to grasp the true ferocity of Canada's national sport. To begin with, it's played not with a ball or a shuttlecock, but a puck – an inch-thick disc of granite-hard black rubber that can fly at speeds of up to 145kph (90mph) when properly "slapshot." It's one reason why hockey players strap on about 9kg (20 pounds) of plastic armor before they take to the ice, and why goalies wear enough pads to deflect anything short of a scud-missile.

It's also why in the 1950s and 1960s, when helmets were rare even at the high-school level and face-guards unheard of, that Canada was known as the "land of

Fast and furious (literally), hockey is a national obsession

Information
www.hockeycanada.ca and www.nhl.com are the best sites to find out how to see a game.

the toothless forechecker." A well-directed puck can harvest a whole row of incisors and canines in a single, blinding moment of pain. Is it any wonder that legendary goalie Glenn Hall ducked into the bathroom to vomit before every single one of the 764 maskless games he played during his National Hockey League career?

But the puck is the least of it. This is a game, remember, played by guys (and these days, girls) with steel blades attached to their feet and 1.5m (5 feet) sticks in their hands on a cold, hard and unfor-giving surface. And it's perfectly legal – in the men's game anyway – for a 115kg (250 pounds) defenseman to slam a stickhandling forward into the boards that line the rink with enough force to shatter the chassis on a tank. And fight! The guys in the professional leagues drop their gloves and pound at each other with such regularity that it's a favorite joke of sports fans to say: "I went to a boxing match and a hockey game broke out."

But in spite of the brawls, bruises and dental bills, there's not a boy over six (or under 80) who doesn't sometimes fantasize about playing left wing for one of the 30 teams in the National Hockey League.

Kids are as young as six when they begin trying to live that fantasy in thousands of local arenas across the country, padded and helmeted from head to foot so even their

Get the Name Right
Canadians call their game simply hockey, not ice hockey. The game played on the grass in England is referred to as field hockey in North America.

Hockey skills are learned from an early age

parents have to identify them by the numbers on their jerseys. Increasingly the faces behind those masks belong to girls, who often play on the same teams as their male counterparts until their early teens, when the male leagues begin to allow bodychecking.

In summer, the best kids and those with rich parents go to hockey camps to get tips from the pros. The rest play street hockey, a lightly padded version of the real thing, featuring a ball instead of a puck and a lightweight goal that can be moved out of the way whenever a car drives by.

Few of these enthusiasts ever make it into the professional leagues, or even on to the elite junior teams that feed players into the pros. But they all dream a little, including the girls: Canada's senior women's team won eight consecutive world championships between 1990 and 2004.

And the game – despite its ferocity and the expense of the equipment – is fun. How else to explain all the guys in their 30s, 40s and 50s who book time in local arenas – often at midnight or later – to play refereeless games before empty stands. There's more to it all than blood and glory.

National Hockey League
Only six Canadian cities – Montréal, Ottawa, Toronto, Edmonton, Calgary and Vancouver – have teams in the National Hockey League. The other 24 teams are American, but more than half the players are Canadians.

Olympic Triumph
In the 2002 Salt Lake City Winter Olympics, Canada won gold in both men's and women's hockey – which for many Canadians were the only medals that counted.

Origins
There are angry disputes over where hockey started, but most experts agree the first real game with rules and referees was played on Montréal's Victoria Skating Rink on March 3, 1875, between McGill University and a team called the Victorias. McGill won 2–1.

The Cry of the Wild

If Africa's animals are noted for ferocity and Australia's for weirdness, the signal characteristic of Canada's has to be gregariousness. There are exceptions, of course. Few mammals are more solitary (or fiercer) than the polar bear, and his cousin the grizzly is about as sociable as a badger with toothache.

Snow Geese

Among Canada's most social creatures are the snow

Above: the gray wolf is more often heard than seen

Below: orcas are year-round residents off the BC coast

geese. Every spring and fall, great clouds of these graceful white birds descend on the marshy fields along the St. Lawrence River in southern Québec. They spend several days there each season, resting and stocking up on calories before continuing their journey, either to their summer breeding grounds

near Baffin Island or their winter home in the southern United States. By day they search for food, but every evening they gather by the thousands in the fields along the river, squatting in noisy contentment in the damp stubble, chattering and gabbling with gusto.

Caribou

The North American reindeer, the caribou, are perhaps the most outgoing of all Canadian animals. In the summertime they gather in herds that can number into the tens of thousands. They're big travelers, too, migrating sometimes as much as 5,000km (3,000 miles) a year in search of food and breeding grounds. In winter, the caribou manages to live almost entirely on lichens, thanks to a staggeringly efficient digestive system.

Caribou once ranged as far south as the state of Maine, but most of them now live on the tundra or among the sparse woodlands of northern Québec and Ontario. There is, however, a herd of them in Québec's Gaspé Provincial Park, the only place where caribou, deer and moose coexist.

Beavers

The beaver, Canada's national animal, is positively subur-

Main picture: magnificent, and dangerous, polar bears can be seen (safely) in the wild at Churchill, Manitoba

ban in its pursuits, living in tight-knit family groups and spending its days engaged in endless home-improvement projects. It constructs long wooden dams across streams and brooks and then builds its snug wooden lodges in the middle of the ponds that form behind the dams. It's a high-maintenance way of life that requires constant dedication.

Canadians like to think the beaver exemplifies all the best qualities of the the national character: discretion, industriousness and family devotion. The unvarnished truth, however, is that the beaver is a national emblem because slaughtering this toothy little rodent was Canada's first major industry. In fact, some Canadians still make a living trapping beavers and other fur-bearing animals – an economic fact of life that sometimes shocks the sensitive. International protests against the spring seal hunt in the Gulf of St. Lawrence, for example, are a regular event on the enviromentalists' calendar.

the beaver exemplifies all the best qualities of the national character

Marine Mammals
Harp seals – the prey in this enterprise – are a gregarious bunch, too, gathering by the tens of thousands on the icefields to give birth. Sealers prowl among them, clubbing the pups and stripping them of their silvery pelts. It's a gruesome picture, all right, but seals are not an endangered species and to those who kill them to make a living for their families, they're just another marine resource like cod or herring.

Efforts to make the seals a tourist attraction have been only marginally successful. The number of people ready to pay big money to be helicoptered out to an ice floe in March or April is somewhat limited.

Whales, however, have become an unqualified success as a tourist attraction. Fishermen and other entrepreneurs make a tidy extra income taking tourists out to see orcas and grays on the Pacific coast and right whales, minkes, belugas, finbacks and even blues on the Atlantic coast.

It is perhaps fitting that one of Canada's most popular destinations for whale-watchers is the same Gulf of St. Lawrence that is so deadly for the seals.

Klondike Days

Then I ducked my head and the lights went out,

And two guns blazed in the dark;

And a woman screamed, and the lights went up,

And two men lay stiff and stark.

Pitched on his head, and pumped full of lead,

Was Dangerous Dan McGrew,

While the man from the creeks lay clutched to the breast

Of the lady that's known as Lou.

From "The Shooting of Dan McGrew" (1907)
by Robert Service (1874–1958)

Gold Rush

The Klondike Gold Rush began on August 17, 1896, when George Carmack, Tagish Charlie and Skookum Jim struck it rich on Bonanza Creek. At least 35,000 Gold-Rush stampeders descended on the town, making it the largest Canadian city west of Winnipeg. In 1900 the Yukon goldfields produced more than 1,077,500 ounces in nuggets and dust.

Makeshift settlements rose and fell with the fortunes of gold seekers

No hardship seemed too great for those who had caught gold fever

"The Shooting of Dan McGrew" is perhaps the most famous poem ever written in Canada. For many romantics it captures the very spirit of the Klondike Gold Rush that in the early days of the 20th century made the remote Yukon settlement of Dawson City (►168–169) one of the richest towns on Earth. Indeed, the writer – bank clerk Robert Service – knew Yukon well. He lived there in those halcyon days when men were men and women were less than entirely honest.

And his setting was certainly perfect for a shoot-'em-up tale. Even today, Dawson City is an almost perfectly preserved Wild West town of wooden sidewalks, gingerbread architecture and bars with batwing doors. But Service's story was a work of almost pure imagination. Dawson City was, in spite of the gamblers, fast women and criminals it attracted, a law-abiding place.

Robert Service

Robert Service's most famous poem was inspired by an actual shooting – of sorts. One night, he slipped into the bank where he worked to spend a few quiet hours writing. Unfortunately (or fortunately from a poetic point of view), his arrival startled the bank guard who took a shot at him, by mistake.

commander was the aptly named Superintendent Sam Steele, who not only enforced laws rigorously but was not above making up new ones when the old ones were inadequate.

Steele's toughness was legendary. Prospectors landing in Skagway, Alaska, had a hard time making it ashore without being cheated or robbed of nearly everything they'd brought with them. But once across the Canadian border into Yukon, it was said a sourdough (old-time prospector) could leave his pack by the side of the trail for days and return to find it undisturbed.

There were few robberies, no shootings and no murders. In fact, guns weren't even allowed in town.

Credit for the town's probity belongs to a tiny detachment of incorruptible policemen. They were members of the Northwest Mounted Police, the red-coated force that became the modern Royal Canadian Mounted Police. Their

Glittering grains being weighed to pay for provisions

Steele was a firm believer in upholding the Sabbath. Dawson City's bars, brothels and casinos operated full tilt 24 hours a day every day except Sunday. One minute before midnight on Saturday night, the people would clear out of the saloons and casinos. The owners would leave the lights on and a Mountie would walk by each bar to make sure they were all empty. Then they'd turn off the lights and close down until one minute past midnight on Monday morning.

But Steele was more than just an honest cop. He also established and chaired Yukon's first board of health, chaired a board of license commissioners and supervized the winter mail service.

When "the Lion of the North" finally left Yukon, thousands of Dawsonites lined the wharves to bid him farewell. For two years he had been the only law on the very edge of civilization, a position that a more venal man could have used to make himself very rich with a minimum of effort. But when Steele left, he was no richer than when he arrived, save for the purse of gold nuggets the town's leading citizens presented him in appreciation for his services.

Sam Steele

After his Yukon service, Sam Steele (1849–1919) commanded the Strathcona's Horse in the Boer War in South Africa. From 1901 to 1906 he took charge of the South African Constabulary, styled after the Northwest Mounted Police. During World War I he was promoted to Major-General, commanding Canadian forces in England.

The Women of New France

It's not very politically correct to say it, but Montréal (► 122–125) has been described as Canada's most feminine city. People say that largely because it's undeniably romantic, with sidewalk cafés, narrow, cobbled streets and a mountain park smack in the middle that's perfect for springtime courtships.

But the city's femininity goes a lot deeper than a little surface romance. Montréal owes its very existence to a pair of formidable females. The first was Jeanne Mance, the daughter of a French lawyer who for the first

The Musée M. d'Youville honors the founder of the Grey Nuns Hospital

sweeping France. Instead of entering a convent, however, she abandoned her home in Champagne and sailed off across the Atlantic with a group of pious settlers to found a Catholic colony in the Canadian wilderness. This, remember, was in an age when proper young women were expected to learn needlepoint, marry well and have babies, or if they were religiously inclined, to disappear genteely into some cloister and learn to sing hymns. Traipsing halfway round the world to found colonies was not on the list of recommended occupations.

Jeanne and her 53 companions landed in Canada in May 1642 to establish Ville Marie – the colony that became Montréal – in a clearing on the shore of the St. Lawrence River. They were thousands of miles from home, hundreds of miles from the nearest European colony, amid less than friendly natives.

But against all odds, Ville Marie endured. That same year, Jeanne opened a very humble hospital in her own home where she treated both natives and settlers. Two years later she moved the hospital to larger quarters on rue St. Paul.

Portrait of Marguerite de Youville at Montréal's Musée M. d'Youville

34 years of her life led a perfectly conventional existence. Then in 1640, her father died and Jeanne, still single and without marital prospects, was caught up in the religious fervor that was

Maison St.-Gabriel, now the Montréal Heritage Museum, was built in 1668

Until her death in 1673, Jeanne worked tirelessly for the colony's success. She made three gruelling voyages back to France to recruit nurses and teachers for the fledgling city and to raise money for defense and construction. Her efforts earned her the title of Co-founder of Montréal.

The second formidable Frenchwoman in Montréal's history was Marguerite Bourgeoys, Canada's first schoolteacher. She, too, was captivated by the idea of establishing a truly Christian community in the New World and in 1653, left her home in Troyes for Ville Marie. She opened her first school in 1657 and returned twice to France to recruit women to help her. To ensure greater freedom, Marguerite founded the Congrégation de Notre Dame, an uncloistered community that still exists. Not only did they teach the children of colonists and First Nations, they also trained the Filles du Roy (Daughters of the King) – girls of good but poor families sent from France to be the wives and mothers of New France.

The third remarkable female, Marguerite d'Youville (1701–1771), was born in Canada and, in fact, became the country's first native-born saint. A holy life, however, is not always a happy one. Marguerite was orphaned in her youth and married off at 21 to an adulterous whiskey trader who treated her abominably. Widowed at 29, with three young children, she set out to alleviate the misery of others. Marguerite rescued a foundering hospital

A pious pose captures the devotion of Marguerite Bourgeoys

from ruin in which to make a home for the city's down-and-outers. She founded a religious order to help her, called the Sisters of Charity, who became universally known – as they still are today – as the Soeurs Grises (Grey Nuns). Marguerite d'Youville was canonized by Pope John Paul II in 1990.

Hôtel Dieu Hospital

The hospital that Jeanne Mance founded – Hôtel Dieu – is still a major medical facility in Montréal. It's now run by the Québec provincial government, but nuns of the Religieuses Hospitallières Saint-Joseph – the order that Jeanne recruited – still have a residence and a museum next door.

Congrégation de Notre Dame

Marguerite Bourgeoys' Congrégation de Notre Dame still has nearly 1,500 sisters working in seven Canadian provinces, three American states, Japan and Central America. In Montréal, the order runs Villa Maria, a private girls' school, and Marianopolis, a coed pre-university college.

Canada's cookin'

The late Fernand Lachance often admitted that he was doubtful when a customer in his snack bar in rural Québec asked him to dump gravy and cheese curds into his bag of french fries. "That'll just make a heck of a mess," he protested, using the very French-Canadian word for mess – *poutine*. That was in 1957. Now *poutine* is a favorite in hamburger joints and snack bars across Canada. Even big chains like Burger King and McDonald's feature it occasionally. There are several different versions – the Italian one, for example, uses spaghetti sauce and Parmesan – but the original is still best: hot french fries covered in rubbery cheese curds smothered with dark, glue-like gravy.

If that's not enough to make your arteries crackle, you could try another great Québec contribution to popular cuisine – the smoked-meat sandwich. This features a tall stack of smoked, spiced beef brisket squeezed between two pieces of rye bread. The dish, a Montréal icon, originated with Jewish immigrants from Romania who flooded into Montréal in the late 19th and early 20th centuries.

The origins of *poutine* and smoked meat reflect the nature of most Canadian food – a hodgepodge of ethnic imports tempered by local tastes. It began with the French settlers, who lived on a hearty diet of *fèves-au-lard* (baked beans), thick pea soup and *tortière*, a kind of meat pie flavored with cloves and other spices – all of which are still popular.

But much of Canada's most distinctive food is purely indigenous. It was

Imaginatively presented poached salmon with fiddleheads

The First Nations who discovered how to turn the sap of the sugar maple into syrup and today Canada produces more than 70 percent of the world's supply. Traditional springtime sugaring-off celebrations have become a year-round industry, with *cabanes-à-sucres* (sugar shacks) all over eastern Canada offering feasts of ham, beans, pancakes, potatoes and even eggs – all cooked in and flavored with maple syrup.

On the west coast, it was the indigenous Haida and Sechelt people who taught white settlers how to catch the king and coho salmon, and more importantly, how to barbecue them on cedar planks over hot coals. This sweetly succulent dish is still British Columbia's tastiest contribution to Canadian cuisine.

First Nations, too, were the first to harvest fiddleheads in the wetlands of the Atlantic coast. These coiled young leaves of the ostrich fern are delicately delicious steamed and served with melted butter. They partner well with a more robust Atlantic product, the cod tongues and cod cheeks so beloved of Newfoundlanders. Rolled in crumbs and fried or baked with a little onion and salt, they taste a little like a poor man's shellfish.

Prime cuts of succulent beef are never better than when served straight from the barbecue

In Québec, French culture blends with Canada's national traits of friendliness and enthusiasm

jaser avec

.... or "chat with the folks" ....

CANADIAN FRENCH

In the late 1990s, an odd word crept into the lexicon of California's "Valley girls," joining the notorious "omigod" and the ubiquitous "like." The word was "fiche" (pronounced *feesch*), and it meant "scram"or "beat it." Teen girls used it mostly to discourage nerdy males. The word's precise origin remains a mystery, but the best guess of California's pop-etymologists is that it came from French Canada, and was an abbreviation of *Fiche moi la paix,* more literally "Leave me in peace," but roughly translated as "scram"or "beat it."

The word's appearance among the nubile denizens of the San Bernardino Valley is a testament to the vigor of Canadian French. Upper-class Parisians might sniff contemptuously at the broad accents and unbuttoned pronunciation of their Canadian cousins, but the fact is the language is flourishing – and probably would be even without the province of Québec's laws limiting the public use of other languages.

And it is, in some ways, more French than the language you hear in Paris these days. Most Québecers, for example, still get their medication at the *pharmacie,* not *le drugstore,* and go camping on the *fin de semaine* rather than *le weekend.* They might, however, go both places in their *char* rather than their *voiture,* and a romantic male might bring his *blonde* (girlfriend) camping – even if she's a brunette. (A female, incidentally, would bring her *chum.*)

Not all Canadians, of course, speak French the same way – any more than Albertans and Newfoundlanders speak the same brand of English. There's a world of difference between the private-school French spoken in subur-

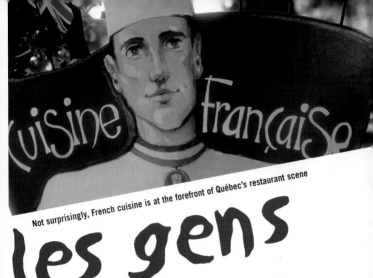

Not surprisingly, French cuisine is at the forefront of Québec's restaurant scene

les gens

ban Outremont, for example, and the consonant-challenged *joual* of less prosperous parts (the dialect gets its name from the way its users pronounce *cheval*, the French word for "horse"). Acadian French, of the Maritime Provinces, is different again.

Generally though, Canadian French tends to be less formal than that spoken in France. Canadian francophones – especially those under 30 – lapse quickly into the familiar *tu* and *toi*, reserving the formal *vous* for things

like job interviews. All of which makes it a pretty friendly language to pick up. A quick glance through your high-school *grammaire*, and you'll be ready to drop into a St. Denis Street bistro to *jaser avec les gens* (chat with the folks) and maybe cough up a few *piastres* (dollars) to buy a round or two. When you leave, be sure to *donner un bec* (a friendly, two-cheek kiss) to your new friends.

The tricolor and Québec provincial flag fly proudly here

Uniquely Canadian expressions

À cet heure (pronounced *asteur*): Now.
Dépanneur: A convenience store (used by all language groups in Québec).
En plâtre: Clumsy (literally translates as "in plaster"), as in *te bien en plâtre* – you are so clumsy. (Acadian)
Niaiseux: An irritatingly stupid person or situation.
Plate, as in (*c'est plate*): Means either boring or disagreeable.
Prends tes jambes: literally, "take your legs," meaning "run like hell." (Acadian)
Tanné: Exasperated, as in *je suis tanné.*

Chuckwagon Races

The Calgary Stampede's most hair-raising events are the chuckwagon races. Four fully-loaded wagons, each pulled by eight horses with a single outrider thunder around the track at a breakneck pace. Spills are frequent; thrills are guaranteed.

Festivals

The chuckwagon races at the Calgary Stampede are among the most exciting events in the country

Let's face it: Just about anyone can organize a festival in the summer when the sun is warm, the sky is blue and everyone's in the mood to dance barefoot in the grass. The real test is to throw an outdoor party in winter when it's cold enough to make your nostrils crackle and your spit freeze before it hits the ground.

Canadians are as good as anyone at the first, with enough festivals, fairs and celebrations to fill just about every day in July and August. But they really excel at the second.

The granddaddy of Canada's cold-weather celebrations is the Carnaval de Québec, which traces its roots to the 19th century when Québec City's devout colonists prepared for Lent with a last loud blowout – literally a "farewell to meat," or "carne vale" in Latin. Lent may have gone out of fashion, but carnival hasn't. Today's 17-day festival might be more family oriented than its Rio counterpart (and revelers are certainly more thoroughly covered) but the fun is still uninhibited, thanks to liberal doses of a concoction called caribou (equal parts grain alcohol and sweet, red wine, with maybe a dash of brandy).

Snow, ice and subzero temperatures add a dimension of endurance to the carnival's

It's not just music at the Montréal Jazz Festival

glittering nighttime parade through the narrow, cobbled streets of Old Québec. The same streets serve as a course for one of North America's most unusual dogsled races, and a gallery for some of the world's most talented ice sculptors. The most unusual event, though, is the "canoe race" across the St. Lawrence River. The craft involved are actually double-ended boats that five-person crews paddle, haul and push through, around and over the ice floes choking the river.

Dozens of cities and towns across the country have similar winter festivals, and one of the most successful is Ottawa's two-week Winterlude in February, a family-focused festival that's largely centered on the "world's largest ice rink" – a 7.8km (4.8-mile) stretch of the frozen Rideau Canal.

Ottawa is at its most colorful, however, in spring, when it celebrates the Tulip Festival, which originated in a little royal gratitude. In the fall of 1945, Princess Juliana of the Netherlands gave Ottawa 100,000 tulip bulbs to show her appreciation for the safe haven she and her family found there during World War II. Ever since, the National Capital Region has gone just a little tulip nuts every May, with tulip-themed fashion shows, boat

parades and fireworks – not to mention the millions of tulips in every imaginable color – more than 300,000 on Parliament Hill alone.

The early-summer obsession in nearby Montréal is jazz, and has been ever since the city staged its first annual International Jazz Festival in 1979. That relatively modest street party has since grown into the world's largest jazz celebration, attracting over the years such stars as Count Basie, Ella Fitzgerald, Wynton Marsalis and Diana Krall. The festival's big galas have ticket prices to match, but true to the original street-party vision, most of the 400 concerts are free, with big outdoor sound stages set up in downtown Montréal.

In early September the festival focus shifts to Toronto, when you can't walk down Bloor Street without bumping into a director, an actor or a screenwriter. The city's full of them for the Toronto International Film

Ice breakers

The boat race across the ice-choked St. Lawrence River during Québec City's winter carnival harks back to the days before large-span bridges when the North-Shore city relied on daring boat-men to keep communication with the South Shore open.

First Nations events keep tribal culture alive

Festival, one of the most important on the continent. More than 300 movies from 60 countries are screened over the ten days of the festival, and it attracts such film-makers as Bille August, Terry Gilliam, Gus Van Sant and John Sayles, not to mention Canadians Atom Egoyan and Denys Arcand, and stars like Kevin Bacon, Orlando Bloom, Sandra Bullock, Matt Dillon, Dustin Hoffman, Bob Hoskins and Sean Penn.

Over on the east coast every October Nova Scotia's scenic Cape Breton Island hosts the Celtic Colours Festival – 10 days of concerts and dances that features musicians from all over the Celtic world, including Brittany, Scotland, Wales and Ireland. But much of the considerable talent on display is local. Many Cape Bretoners are descended from immigrant Scots, and they've not only kept alive the music, they have produced some of the world's best fiddlers.

Music hardly figures in what Calgarians call the "greatest show on Earth." An exaggeration, maybe, but the Calgary Stampede is the world's biggest rodeo and the greatest outdoor show in Canada. For ten days in July it draws cowboys from all over the world hoping for a share of the more than $1 million in prizes by busting broncos, riding bulls and roping calves. The spectacle attracts more than a million visitors each year, and they all seem to have a Stetson and cowboy boots, even if they work as accountants or lawyers the rest of the year.

first nations art

Jean-Louis Newashish, an Atikamekw Indian from the Québec village of Manawan, still makes traditional canoes the old fashioned way, sewing sheets of birchbark to hand-cut cedar frames with cords of spruce roots. He decorates them by hand, too, with little motifs along the gunwales and a carefully etched Indian head, beaver or eagle on the bow.

A 4m (13-foot) canoe – a 400-hour project – costs about $6,000, but it's worth every dime. A Newashish canoe isn't just a superbly maneuverable watercraft; it's a work of art that would

look almost as good hanging in your living room as it would crossing a lake at sunset.

The saga of Canada's relations with its aboriginal peoples – the Inuit of the far north and the dozens of Indian nations farther south – has been pretty dismal, often marked by distrust, prejudice and betrayal. Although Canada is one of the world's most prosperous countries, many of its First Nations people live in remote, squalid reservations where violence and substance-abuse are endemic. But Mr. Newashish's modest endeavor is a hopeful sign of a new pride emerging among Canada's aboriginals as they rediscover the richness of their cultures and find ways to adapt them to the 21st century.

It probably began in the 1950s, when the world discovered the fluid beauty created by Inuit artists out of soapstone and ivory. Their works have almost become a Canadian cliché like maple syrup and hockey fights. But their success with collectors helped transform the economies of many northern communities, and opened the door for other groups.

On the west coast, for example, native artists drew on the mythology of such Pacific nations as the Haida and the Squamish for inspiration. One of the most successful was the late Bill Reid, whose red-and-black prints of such spiritually significant creatures as the raven, the eagle and the orca are almost shockingly vivid. He also carved totems and, like Mr. Newashish far to the east,

Opposite and above: First Nations carvings represent stylized images of everyday life

Left: a Newashish canoe at the Canadian Museum of Civilization in Gatineau

built canoes. Not birchbark, but oceangoing cedar dug-outs decorated with intricately carved Haida designs.

The Museum of Anthropology (➤ 56) in Vancouver has some excellent exhibits, but one of the greatest monuments to the revival of native culture is the First Peoples' Gallery in the Canadian Museum of Civilization in Gatineau, Québec (➤ 98). Its extensive collection of Indian and Inuit arts includes one of Mr. Reid's canoes and the finest assembly of totem poles in the country. Equally impressive is the museum building itself, a huge structure with few straight lines that looks as if it were formed by the forces of nature rather than construction crews. It, too, is the work of an aboriginal artist – Douglas Cardinal, a Blackfoot from the plains of Alberta and one of Canada's leading architects.

Did You Know...?

It's big!
Canada, at nearly 10 million sq km (3.8 million square miles) is the second-largest country in the world – bigger than both the U.S. and China and outsized only by Russia.

C'est énorme
Québec – the largest of Canada's 10 provinces at 1.5 million sq km (579,000 square miles) and the heart of French Canada – is nearly three times the size of France.

Banting and Best
Two Canadians – Frederick Banting and Charles Best – gave diabetics around the world new hope in 1921 when they isolated insulin.

Water, water...
Canada's lakes and rivers contain about 20 percent of the world's fresh water supply. Unfortunately for thirsty cities in the south and the US, 60 percent of it flows north.

Royal Canada
Canada is a monarchy. The official head of state is the reigning monarch of Britain, represented in Canada by a Governor-General appointed by the federal government in Ottawa.

Train lag
Scottish-Canadian railroad engineer Sir Sandford Fleming is responsible for jet lag. In 1878, he devized standard time zones to simplify train scheduling. Previously rail companies had to contend with hundreds of different local times.

Sporting hero?
George Retzlaff, the first producer of C.B.C.'s Hockey Night in Canada, invented that staple of sports broadcasting – the "instant replay" He used a new "hot processor" in 1956 to develop a recording of a goal within 30 seconds.

...it's Superman!
The Man of Steel is half Canadian. Toronto-born Joe Shuster dreamed up the idea of Superman with his high-school pal, Jerry Seigel, of Cleveland, Ohio. Superman's girlfriend in the movies was played by the all-Canadian Margot Kidder.

...it's Superlative!
Man-made attractions include the world's largest Easter egg (in Vegreville, Alberta), the world's largest lobster (in Shediac, New Brunswick) and the world's largest elk (in Oranole, Manitoba).

Winnipeg the Pooh
The real-life bear that inspired A.A. Milne's Winnie the Pooh stories was born in Canada. In fact, his name is short for Winnipeg, the capital of Manitoba.

Finding Your Feet

First Two Hours

Arriving in Canada

There are scheduled international flights to all of the airports listed below, with linking flights to many domestic airports. All the airports listed below offer full transportation services, duty-free shops, currency exchange facilities and bookstores, and most are completely wheelchair accessible. In addition to airport taxes and security charges, some Canadian airports levy an Airport Improvement Fee (usually $10–15 per person) on departing international passengers, and this must be paid directly to the airport.

Vancouver International Airport

- **Vancouver International Airport** is 6.5km (4 miles) south of the city in the suburb of Richmond.
- The **Airporter bus** (www.yvrairporter.com) links the airport with the city's major hotels, the cruise ship terminal and the downtown bus depot/train station. Buses depart from the International and Domestic arrivals level every 20 minutes 9am–9:30pm. One-way fare $13, child $6, family $26. **Public buses** are also available: No. 424 picks up at the domestic terminal, 100 and 98B from the Airport Bus Terminal. Fares depend on destination, and you need the exact amount in cash. There are also **courtesy shuttles** to some hotels.
- Licensed **taxis** line up outside the terminals 24 hours a day, and are metered. The fare to downtown is about $25, assuming no traffic hold-ups. Wheelchair-accessible taxis are also available.
- **Car rental** agencies with desks at the airport include Alamo, Avis, Budget, Hertz, National and Thrifty. Discount, and Enterprise have offices nearby and will pick up.

Calgary International Airport

- The **airport** is 17.5km (10.5 miles) northeast of downtown Calgary, about a half-hour drive.
- Several companies run **shuttle buses** to various destinations. Airport Shuttle Express Ltd (www.airportshuttleexpress.com) operate five- and ten-seat vehicles at about half the cost of a taxi to downtown Calgary, and shuttles to various ski resorts. Their airport check-in counter is on the Arrivals level. Calgary Transit bus 57 serves the airport.
- **Car rental** agencies with desks in the airport include Alamo/National, Avis, Budget, Hertz, Enterprise and Dollar/Thrifty. Discount has locations nearby.

Ottawa: Macdonald-Cartier International Airport

- **Ottawa Airport** is 17.5km (11 miles) from downtown.
- Public transit bus 97 picks up outside the level 1 Arrivals area (post 14). The fare to downtown is $3 (children 6–11 $1.50; under 6 free). Purchase tickets from the Ground Transportation Desk on level 1, at the center door of the Arrivals area There is also the hotel shuttle to various downtown hotel locations, which runs every half hour between 5:35am and 12:05am ($14 one way, $11 each for a party of two, $8 each for a party of three; children 8–14 $8; under 8 free).
- **Taxis** to downtown cost around $30.
- **Car rental** Alamo/National, Avis, Budget, Enterprise and Hertz all have desks in the Arrivals area.

Toronto: Pearson International Airport

- **Pearson International** is 29km (18 miles) northwest of dowtown.
- Several buses serve the airport. The downtown Airport Express ($16.45) and Airport Rocket ($2.75) services pick up at all three terminals and operate daily between around 5am and 2am, every 20 or 30 minutes.
- **Taxis** cost around $45–50, including taxes, to downtown. Toronto taxi drivers aren't all familiar with the entire city, so unless you are headed for a major hotel or landmark building you will probably need to tell them the street address and its nearest major intersection.
- **Car rental** agencies are in the parking garages of terminals 1 (basement level), 2 and 3 (ground level). Companies include Alamo/National, Avis, Budget, Dollar/Thrifty and Hertz. Discount and Enterprise are not located in the airport, but will pick up and drop off there by arrangement.

Montréal: Pierre Elliott Trudeau International Airport

- Montréal's **former Dorval Airport** has undergone a transformation. Most of the work is finished, but the upgrading of the domestic jetty will continue through 2007. Major road improvements around the Dorval Interchange will take place from 2007 to 2009. Finally, at some point in the future, an express rail shuttle to downtown will be established. It is on Montréal island, 22.5km (14 miles) southwest of downtown.
- A **bus** shuttle service, L'Aérobus, links the airport with downtown (and with Mirabel Airport). The one-way fare to downtown is $13 (seniors $11.50; child $9.25); transfer to Mirabel is free for passengers making flight connections within 15 hours.
- A **taxi** to downtown will cost around $35, and around $75 to Mirabel Airport.
- For **car rental**, Alamo, Avis, Budget, Dollar, Enterprise, Hertz, National and Thrifty all have desks in the airport.

Halifax International Airport

- **Halifax International Airport** is about 40km (25 miles) north of downtown, off exit 6 of Highway 102. The drive by car to downtown takes 30–45 minutes, depending on traffic conditions.
- The **AirBus shuttle bus** runs to downtown at regular intervals from about 6am to 1am daily ($16 one way). Services to other Nova Scotia and Prince Edward Island destinations are also available (tel: 902/873-1223 for information).
- **Taxis** wait outside the arrivals building, and the fare to downtown is about $53.
- **Car rental** desks in the airport are operated by Alamo/National, Avis, Budget, Enterprise, Thrifty/Dollar and Hertz.

Tourist Information Offices

Each province and territory has a main tourism office, in addition to numerous information points in the towns and cities.

- **Alberta**: Travel Alberta, Suite 760, 999 8th Street S.W., Calgary, Alberta T2R 1J5, tel: 403/509-2590; www1.travelalberta.com
- **British Columbia**: Tourism British Columbia, Box 9830, Southern Provincial Government, Victoria, British Columbia V8W 9W5, tel: 250/387-1642; www.HelloBC.com
- **Manitoba**: Travel Manitoba, 155 Carlton Street, 7th Floor, Winnipeg R3C 3H8, tel: 204/927-7838; www.travelmanitoba.com
- **New Brunswick**: Department of Tourism and Parks, P.O. Box 6000, Fredericton, New Brunswick E3B 5H1, tel: 506/457-6701; www.TourismNewBrunswick.ca

- **Newfoundland & Labrador**: Department of Tourism, Culture and Recreation, P.O. Box 8700, 2nd Floor, West Block, Confederation Building, Higgins Line, St. John's, Newfoundland, tel: 709/729-2830; www.gov.nl.ca
- **Northwest Territories**: Northwest Territories Tourism, Box 610, Yellowknife, Northwest Territories X1A 2N5, tel: 867/873-5007; www.explorenwt.com
- **Nova Scotia**: Nova Scotia Tourism and Culture, P.O. Box 456, Halifax, Nova Scotia B3J 2R5, tel: 902/425-5781; http://novascotia.com
- **Nunavut**: Nunavut Tourism, Box 1450, Iqaluit, Nunavut X0A 0H0, tel: 867/979-6551; www.nunavutTourism.com
- **Ontario**: Ontario Tourism, 10th Floor, Hearst Block, 900 Bay Street, Toronto, Ontario M7A 2E1, tel: 800/668-2746; www.ontariotravel.net
- **Prince Edward Island**: Tourism PEI, P.O. Box 940, Charlottetown, Prince Edward Island C1A 7M5, tel: 902/368-4444; www.gov.pe.ca
- **Québec**: Tourism Québec, P.O. Box 979, Montréal, Québec H3C 2W3, tel: 800/363-7777; www.bonjourquebec.com
- **Saskatchewan**: Tourism Saskatchewan, 1922 Park Street, Regina, Saskatchewan S4N 7M4, tel: 877/237-2273; www.sasktourism.com
- **Yukon**: Tourism Yukon, P.O. Box 2803, Whitehorse, Yukon Y1A 2C6, tel: 867/667-5034; http://travelyukon.com

Prices

The cost of admission for museums and places of interest mentioned in the text is indicated by the following price categories

Inexpensive – under $4   **Moderate** – $5–$9   **Expensive** – more than $10

Getting Around

By Plane

Canada is a huge country, but it is not difficult to get around if you have the time. There's a network of domestic flights linking large and small towns and cities, plus some of the remote areas of the north. Domestic airlines include:

- **Air Canada Jazz**: a subsidiary of the national airline, offering a range of services to 86 Canadian destinations; www.aircanadajazz.com
- **Air North**: links Vancouver, Calgary, Edmonton, Yukon, Northwest Territories and Alaska; www.flyairnorth.com
- **Canadian North**: access to communities throughout the north from Calgary, Edmonton and Ottawa; www.canadiannorth.com
- **First Air**: flights to destinations in the north from Edmonton, Ottawa and Montréal; www.firstair.ca
- **Westjet**: scheduled flights to domestic and U.S. airports; www.c1dsp.westjet.com

By Train

The national rail company is **VIA Rail** (www.viarail.ca; in the U.K., tel: 0845 644 3553), which operates an efficient, clean and comfortable service on its comprehensive network. The famous transcontinental route offers a scenic journey of a lifetime in beautifully restored trains with observation cars. Comfort (economy) and Sleeper options are available, and you can purchase a **Canrail Pass** allowing 12 days of unlimited Economy travel within a 30-day period. Obtain tickets as far in advance as possible as seats reserved for Canrail Pass holders can be limited on some services. Special offers are frequently available on scheduled services.

Scenic tours include the fabulous **Rocky Mountaineer Railtours** (www.rockymountaineer.com), Whistler Mountaineer (www.whistlermountaineer.com) and **Skeena** route in the west. Great trips to take in eastern Canada include those run by the **Québec North Shore & Labrador Railway** (tel: 418/962-7400), while northern Ontario offers the **Algoma Central Railway** (www.agawacanyontourtrain.com) and **Ontario Northland** (www.northlander.ca), which takes you to the edge of the Arctic. In the north, the **White Pass and Yukon Railway** (www.whitepassrailroad.com) is a spectacular narrow-gauge trip to Skagway, Alaska.

Many of Canada's major cities have a **rapid-transit** light railway system, including Calgary and Vancouver; Toronto's GO (Government of Ontario) Trains provide an excellent service to commuter satellite towns on double-decker trains.

Subway (métro; underground) systems are an important part of getting around in Toronto and Montréal, and both link to their underground shopping areas. Maps can be picked up at any subway station, or from tourist information offices.

By Bus

Long-distance buses are a good budget option for seeing Canada – more comfortable than you might imagine, with air-conditioning and washrooms. **Greyhound Canada** (www.greyhound.ca) links Toronto with cities in western Canada and offers good leg-room, movies, music and snacks. There are many provincial bus companies offering intercity and local routes. Look in the *Yellow Pages*, or ask at tourist information offices.

The **Canada Pass** buys you 7, 10, 15, 21, 30, 45 or 60 days of unlimited travel on certain Greyhound and regional bus company services, plus Via Rail's Ottawa–Montréal and Toronto–Montréal routes. A **Rout-Pass** (www.routpass.com) will give you access to more than 35 intercity bus companies that operate in Ontario and Québec. It covers 7, 14 or 18 consecutive days, and is available mid-May to mid-December.

By Boat

Cruises

A number of companies operate cruises on the Pacific and Atlantic coasts and along the St. Lawrence Seaway, including **Holland America** (www.hollandamerica.com), **Norwegian Cruise Lines** (www.uk.ncl.com), **Princess Cruises** (www.princesscruises.com), and **St. Lawrence River Cruise Lines Inc**. (www.stlawrencecruiselines.com). For lake and river cruises in the Canadian interior, contact the relevant tourist information office for details.

Ferries

There are various ferry services giving access to offshore islands, or for hopping between coastal settlements. Advance booking is recommended for some services, particularly at peak times.

- **Alaska Marine Highway** (www.akferry.org) sail from Bellingham and Prince Rupert along the Inside Passage to Alaska.
- **Aquabus** (www.aquabus.bc.ca) and **Granville Island Ferries** (www.granvilleislandferries.bc.ca) operate passenger ferries around False Creek in downtown Vancouver, including commuter services and sightseeing trips.

- **BC Ferries** (www.bcferries.com) have daily services from Vancouver to Vancouver Island and the Gulf Islands, plus an Inside Passage service (► 178–179) and the scenic Bella Coola–Port Hardy service (► 8).
- **Black Ball Transport Inc** (www.cohoferry.com), **Victoria Clipper** (www.victoriaclipper.com) and **Victoria Express** (www.victoriaexpress.com) all offer services from Victoria, British Columbia to various destinations.
- **Bay and NFL Ferries** (www.nfl-bay.com) run services from Wood Island, Prince Edward Island to Caribou, Nova Scotia, from St. John, New Brunswick to Digby, Nova Scotia and from Bar Harbour and Portland in Maine, USA, to Yarmouth, Nova Scotia.
- **Marine Atlantic** (www.marine-atlantic.ca) provides access to Newfoundland from Cape Breton Island, Nova Scotia.
- **Ferries Services Newfoundland and Labrador** (www.tw.gov.nl.ca) link Newfoundland with Labrador runs a service between St. Barbe, Newfoundland and Blanc Sablon, Québec.
- **Ontario Northland Ferries** (www.bmts.com/~northland/) have services from Tobermory to Montoulin Island and from Kindsville and Leamington to Pelee Island.

By Taxi

Taxis are widely available in all towns and cities and can be picked up at taxi stands or booked by telephone. In Toronto (where you can also hail cabs on the street downtown) not all drivers are familiar with the entire city – you will need to tell them the street address *and* the nearest major intersection.

Car Rental

Car rental is quite expensive in Canada, and there may be restrictions. Some companies will not let you take the vehicle outside the province in which it was rented, and if you want to drop off at a different location, surcharges can be extremely high. Make sure you get an unlimited mileage deal and full insurance coverage.

Driving

Public transportation is best in downtown areas, or for covering long distances in the shortest time, but a car is invaluable everywhere else.

Rules of the road

- **Drive on the right** and overtake on the left, but on multilane highways you can overtake on any side – before changing lanes watch out for vehicles zipping past you on either side.
- Unless there's a sign indicating otherwise, you can **turn right on a red light** (except in Quebec), as long as the road is clear. Always come to a complete stop first.
- At **four-way stops** (indicated by a black-and-white sign) whoever gets to the junction first gets to go first, then the other vehicles take their respective turn.
- At traffic lights, a **flashing green light** lets you turn left across the high-way (sometimes you get a green arrow instead).
- **Road conditions** are generally good – though winter weather can cause potholes and cracked edges – and traffic is light once you get out of the cities. There are some unpaved roads in more remote areas.

Accommodations

The recommended places to stay in this guide have been carefully selected to offer a cross-section of prices and styles, and each has been inspected and approved by the American Automobile Association (AAA). For details of the grading system, see page 40. Further information is available by visiting www.aaa.com. The selections in this book range from city hotels and upscale resorts of the highest international standard to bed-and-breakfasts in historic homes, plus simple motels and housekeeping (self-catering) cottages. Standards of accommodations are generally high and Canadians are renowned for their friendly hospitality. The AAA categorize the types of accommodations in the following way:

Hotels
These vary in size, but all offer a full range of services, including a variety of eating options, stores, conference amenities and recreational activities.

Resorts
Generally in the luxury bracket, resorts are aimed specifically at the vacation market and provide a variety of restaurants and an excellent range of leisure amenities, such as a golf course, or access to winter sports areas.

Motels
Generally low-rise, with convenient parking, motels offer limited services – for instance, many have no restaurant or public areas and no recreational facilities, though this is not always the case. They are usually located close to main highways, but can be quite close to downtown areas.

Bed-and-Breakfasts
A home-away-from-home atmosphere is usually the norm, and most will be owner-operated with friendly, personal service. A Continental or full hot breakfast is included in the room rate. Many bed-and-breakfasts are in interesting historic buildings or cozy family homes.

Country Inns
These are similar in style to bed-and-breakfasts, but are usually larger in scale with spacious public areas, and they will have a dining facility that serves at least breakfast and dinner.

Lodges
Typically a low-rise building, often of rustic architecture and decor and with a restaurant. There are also fishing and hunting lodges, often in remote wilderness locations, that specialize in vacations for enthusiasts and organize the activities.

Ranches
Offering entertainment and recreation with a Western theme, ranches usually provide all-inclusive packages to cover meals and activities such as horseback-riding and barbecues.

Cottages
Usually a group of individual units in a rural location. They will incorporate a living area, cooking facilities and one or more bedrooms, and often have a verandah and/or lawned area with a barbecue.

Condominiums/Apartments

Aimed at the vacation or extended-stay market, these consist primarily of a suite with living room, full kitchen, eating area and one or more bedrooms; studio apartments may combine the sleeping and living area.

Hostels

Most of the major cities have low-cost hostel lodgings, usually in dormitories, but they may have some double and family rooms. They generally have cooking facilities, communal areas where you can get to know other hostelers. Barbecues and tours are sometimes on offer.

University Residences

Some universities rent out their student accommodations during the long summer break. These usually take the form of single or double rooms with private bathrooms and a shared kitchen. They are fairly basic, but comfortable, and offer a budget option in a downtown (or close by) location.

Reservations

Making reservations is advisable, particularly if you have special requirements or are touring Canada's vast empty spaces, but even in cities, you might have difficulty finding what you want at the last minute if there's a convention in town or a big festival taking place. You can often get the best room rates by reserving early. On the other hand, if you just show up somewhere and a room is available, you may well be able to strike a last-minute deal. It's always worth asking if any discounts or special offers are available (and mention the fact if you are a AAA or CAA member).

AAA Diamond Ratings

The listings in this guide have all been inspected and approved by the American Automobile Association and use the following ratings system.

WWWWW The ultimate in luxury and sophistication, these places are first class and the physical attributes are extraordinary in every manner. Often renowned, they offer a world-class and opulent experience. Staff offer meticulous service and exceed all expectations, while maintaining an impeccable standard of excellence. Many personalized services and amenities enhance an unmatched level of comfort.

WWWW Upscale establishments in which accommodations are refined and stylish. There's an enhanced level of quality throughout, and an extensive array of amenities combined with a high degree of hospitality, service and attention to detail. Highly proficient staff demonstrate a profound desire to meet or exceed guest expectations. Many of Canada's prominent, historic hotels are included in this category.

WWW These places appeal to travelers with comprehensive needs, and have a distinguished style, including superior furnishings, amenities and level of comfort provided. Service is typically semi-formal and proficient.

WW More than basic lodgings, these establishments exhibit modest enhancements to the overall style, service and decor. They are usually informal and room rates offer good value.

W Essentially, this category includes the no-frills accommodations that appeal to the budget-minded traveler, meeting the basic needs of comfort, cleanliness and hospitality.

Food and Drink

Canada is one of the most multi-ethnic nations in the world, and this is reflected in the range of cuisines available in most cities. Standards are generally high and portions generous and, particularly to visitors from Europe, prices are very reasonable. Service is invariably friendly and efficient.

Home-grown, top-quality ingredients of all kinds, including organically grown produce, is plentiful: the Atlantic, Pacific and Arctic oceans provide wonderful seafood – notably east-coast lobsters and mussels and Alaskan king crabs; rivers are full of salmon at spawning time and lakes have some unusual freshwater fish. There's prime beef and pork (though lamb is not particularly plentiful here) and game including venison, bison and caribou. The southern climate is perfect for growing fruit and vegetables of every kind – juicy peaches and berries, grapes for Niagara and Okanagan wineries, several succulent varieties of corn (peaches-and-cream is one of the best), the famous Prince Edward Island potato and, of course, maple syrup.

Restaurants
Types of restaurant vary enormously, with top-class establishments matching the best that the rest of the world has to offer. There is every kind of national theme you can imagine, together with traditional Western-style steak houses. Lots of places have sidewalk or terrace seating to make the most of the summer weather, and all the major cities (and Niagara Falls) have revolving restaurants to show off their best views. Some restaurants offer table d'hôte, a set menu with a set price, a less expensive option than the à la carte menu.

Bistros and Cafés
These tend to be informal, with simple but good food at reasonable prices, though some of the chic designer cafés in swanky downtown areas can be more pricey. Generally, though, this category includes lively cosmopolitan eateries full of noise and bustle, cozy cafés with a grandma's parlor atmosphere, and the quintessential 1950s-style diner. Victoria, BC, is also famous for its English-style tearooms.

Pubs and Bars
Food is increasingly on offer in pubs and bars, in the form of down-to-earth standards such as burgers, nachos, pasta, and fish and chips. Some offer more sophisticated fare, and brewpubs are a particularly attractive option, serving ales made on the premises.

Opening Hours
- Generally **lunch** is served between noon and 3pm.
- Sunday **brunch** is very popular and is usually available from 10:30 or 11am until about 3:30pm.
- **Dinner** service begins around 6 or 7pm.
- Big cities have many restaurants that **stay open late** into the night, but in more rural areas and small towns, they usually close at 9pm.
- Outside these general hours, some places open at 6:30am for **breakfast**, some serve food all day, and there's even occasional **24-hour service**.

Reservations
It is always a good idea to reserve a table if the time or the place is important, but some places do not accept reservations – you just have to show up and wait if necessary.

Payment
If you are planning on splitting the restaurant check between members of your party, let the wait staff know in advance of ordering, and they will be happy to issue separate checks. Make sure in advance that your credit or debit card is acceptable if you plan to pay by this method. Remember that taxes are additional to the menu prices.

Tipping
The standard restaurant tip is 15 percent. You will generally get the option of adding it to your credit card payment. Tips are expected throughout the industry, even in pubs and the most inexpensive diners, where wages for wait staff are calculated on the basis that tips will bring it up to an acceptable level. Service is generally of a high standard in Canada, but if it is ever disappointing, you retain the right not to tip.

What to Drink
- **Wine** is expensive in Canada, particularly the ones imported from Europe and the US, but there are some excellent domestic varieties from the wineries of the Niagara region and B.C.'s Okanagan Valley that are well worth trying.
- In addition to the huge **brewing** giants Molson and Labatts, there are a number of microbreweries and brewpubs producing English-style ales. If you're in the Atlantic Provinces, sample the excellent beer from the Alexander Keith Brewery in Halifax.
- When it comes to **liquor**, Canadian Club is the national distillation. And if someone tells you to drink Canada Dry, it's not a challenge – they'll be referring to the ginger ale mixer.

What to Eat
For an introduction to the idiosyncracies of Canadian cuisine, ➤ 22–23.

Shopping

Canada is an incredible place to shop, not just for the huge and compre-hensive range of goods available, but also for the friendly and helpful service, the constant availability of places to rest and get a bite to eat, easy parking (outside downtown areas, at least) and prices that are generally very attractive to visitors from abroad.

Arts and Crafts
Outstanding hand-made items produced by First Nations and Inuit artists and artisans are to be found in stores and galleries throughout the coun-try, including **native-run outlets** on reservations. These will offer a range of wonderful carvings in wood and soapstone, suede and leather clothing and moccasins, jewelry, drums and dreamcatchers (➤ 30–31).

Crafts introduced by the early **pioneers** from Europe include quilts, hooked rugs and household items, and these are available in many small-town specialty stores, as well as some of the living history "villages."

■ **Art galleries**, such as the National Gallery of Canada (➤ 98) and Toronto's Art Gallery of Ontario (➤ 106), usually have a good selection of prints of paintings by First Nations artists and the Group of Seven (Canadian artists whose landscape paintings of Canadian scenes are particularly inspirational). They make excellent souvenirs.

■ **Modern crafts**, including ceramics, glass and jewelry are also widely available, and local tourist offices can tell you where to find workshops and stores producing good-quality items.

Clothing and Fashion

Not surprisingly, there are excellent ranges of **outdoor and winter-sports wear** designed to withstand extreme cold, and these are cheaper in the city malls than in the upscale mountain resorts. Canada has a number of accomplished and imaginative **fashion designers**, too, whose creations are available alongside international labels in the chic city boutiques.

Shopping Malls

The fact that Canada has the two largest malls in the world – **West Edmonton Mall** in Edmonton, Alberta (➤ 82) and **Metrotown** in Burnaby, British Columbia (➤ 70) – give an idea of how important shopping is here. There are malls everywhere, even in quite small communities, and in the major cities they are huge, completely undercover to beat the winter weather, and generally surrounded by large parking lots. Often, malls also include movie theaters as well as the usual restaurants.

In addition to the regular malls, there are outlet malls full of big-name stores selling at discounted prices. You can get up to 70 percent off discontinued lines and surplus stock from designer clothing and sports footwear to household items and electronics.

Markets

Market shopping is very popular, and all the major cities have permanent market locations where producers and wholesalers offer mountains of fresh fruit and vegetables, deli items, clothing, arts and crafts, often accompanied by street entertainers and inviting aromas.

Check out the **Granville Island Public Market** in Vancouver, the **Forks Market** in Winnipeg, Ottawa's **Byward Market**, Toronto's **St. Lawrence Market**, **Maisonneuve**, **Jean-Talon** and **Atwater** markets in Montréal, the **Public Market** in Québec City, and **Boyce's Farmers' Market** in Fredericton, New Brunswick, and Halifax Farmers Market – believed to be the oldest in North America.

Flea markets are popular, too, most of them temporary but regular on a specific site. **Dr. Flea** in Toronto is in a permanent building, every weekend, and includes a farmers' market.

Opening Hours

Stores are usually open Monday to Saturday from 10am to 6pm, with late opening on Thursday and Friday, and on Sunday from noon. However, times vary and big city stores may open well into the evening most days. The malls usually stay open until between 7:30 and 9pm.

Credit Cards

Canada is a plastic society, and credit and debit cards are widely accepted. However, it's always best to check whether your particular card is accepted before you get too far with your purchases. Some retailers use the system whereby you enter your four-digit security PIN into a machine rather than sign a sales docket, so you'll need to memorize your number.

Entertainment

There's a rich cultural life in Canada and the arts in all their forms are strenuously and enthusiastically promoted at all levels, from national opera and ballet companies and provincial orchestras to small-town theaters. Nightlife includes live music venues, jazz and blues clubs, nightclubs and casinos with Las Vegas-style shows.

Toronto

The **entertainment capital** of the country, Toronto has a thriving theater district hosting all the big Broadway-style blockbusters, magnificent state-of-the-art concert halls, intimate theaters and arts centers producing less mainstream works, stadiums for megastar rock concerts, and an internationally famous comedy club. It's also home to some of the best live music venues in the country, cool jazz clubs and the hottest dance clubs.

Montréal

Montréal adds a touch of French *je-ne-sais-quoi* to its nightlife. Many theater productions are in French and you'd need a good grasp of the language to get the best out of the experience. There are English-language productions, too, and some movies are shown in their original language. Montréal is also known for its thriving jazz scene and arts festival.

The Best of the Rest

Vancouver is also very lively, with an excellent theater and music scene, and the provincial capitals of the **Prairies** also have plenty to offer, from their own symphony orchestras to the country music that suits their thriving cowboy culture. The cities of the **Maritimes** are smaller and quieter, perhaps a tad less sophisticated, but are not devoid of good theater, nightclubs and live music, and they have a world-famous heritage of Celtic-style fiddle music and dance. The **North** tends to fall back on its Gold Rush heritage, with vaudeville-style saloon shows and the like, and the most spectacular entertainment here might well be watching the *aurora borealis* while you keep warm with a mug of hot chocolate.

Festivals

Thousands of festivals take place throughout the country every month, celebrating just about everything – the arts, food and drink, national cultures, sports, wildlife, even the winter weather. To find out what's on where contact the relevant tourist information offices.

Spectator Sports

Hockey and **curling** are the winter obsessions, with **baseball**, **Canadian football** and **basketball** taking over in summer. There's healthy rivalry, plenty of vocal support and a good atmosphere among the crowds at the stadiums. There are **racetracks** within easy reach of all the major cities for thoroughbred and harness racing – Toronto's Woodbine track hosts the major classic races. The **Canadian Golf Open** is held at a different course each year.

Tickets

A number of theaters, stadiums and sport venues use **Ticketmaster** to sell tickets for events. Buy online at www.ticketmaster.ca or check them out in the *Yellow Pages*. The price of tickets generally includes national and provincial taxes.

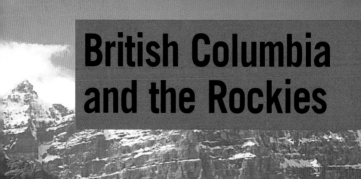

British Columbia
and the Rockies

Getting Your Bearings

At first glance British Columbia seems to have it all, and in-depth exploration only reinforces that first impression. In addition to the beautiful and historic provincial capital of Victoria there's the vibrant city of Vancouver – both cities are consistently on the list of best places in the world to live – plus interesting towns and small artsy enclaves dotted around the interior and islands. There's history here, too, with a strong First Nations culture and reminders of the early pioneers and Gold-Rush days.

Hiking in the mountains of the West is well rewarded

The landscapes in B.C. are spectacular – magnificent mountains, the wilderness areas of the north, rain forests, hot springs, rolling ranchlands and river valleys, vineyards producing first-class wines, and the orchards of the Okanagan, which is one of North America's premier fruit-growing regions. The Pacific coastline, with its forested fjords, wide inlets, islands and the legendary Inside Passage, offers some of the best scuba-diving sites in the world, superb whale-watching, scenic coastal cruises, and unspoiled beaches. This chapter also encompasses the part of the province of Alberta that lies within the Rocky Mountains.

British Columbia is the only province in Canada where the average winter temperatures remain above freezing point, and yet up in the Rockies and Coast Mountains the winter sports are excellent. Whistler, gearing up for the 2010 Winter Olympics, is the most famous ski resort, heading a list of places where you can enjoy downhill and cross-country (Nordic) skiing, snowboarding, dog-sledding and extreme sports. Summer activities include great golf, horseback riding, river-rafting and coastal cruises, wildlife safaris and hiking.

Cultural life is diverse and absorbing, encompassing the full range of arts, entertainment and nightlife. Vancouver and Victoria are the hotspots, with year-round programs that include all kinds of festivals, an opera season, world-class classical performances and a variety of theater productions. There is also a huge range of dance clubs, jazz and blues venues, live rock and comedy clubs. Night or day in B.C. and the Rockies, you could stay for ever and not see everything.

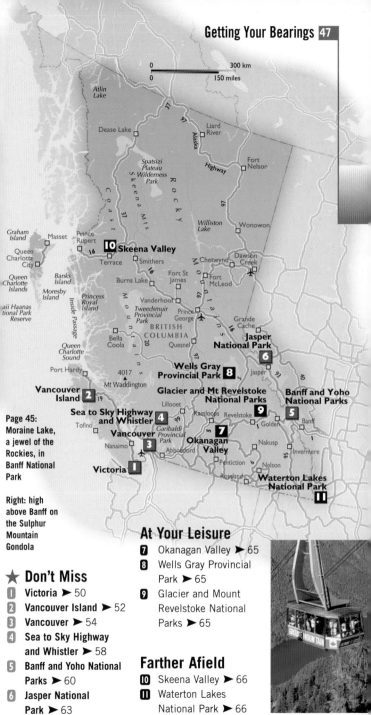

Page 45:
Moraine Lake,
a jewel of the
Rockies, in
Banff National
Park

Right: high
above Banff on
the Sulphur
Mountain
Gondola

Breathtakingly beautiful, this region incorporates vibrant cities, fascinating First Nations heritage and outdoor activities in superlative national parks.

B.C. and the Rockies in Seven Days

Day One

Morning Start at Vancouver Island, with an exploration of **1 Victoria** (➤ 50–51). Stroll along the waterfront walk around the Inner Harbour, then head for the **Royal British Columbia Museum** and Thunderbird Park.
Lunch Visit the Pacific Restaurant and Terrace on Belleville Street (250/380-4458) for creative West Coast cuisine.
Afternoon Take a quick look around the **Maritime Museum**, then head down to the harbor for a sightseeing cruise. Back on land, go for afternoon tea at the Fairmont Empress Hotel (➤ 67), a Victoria institution. Walk it off by doing a bit of browsing in the city's attractive shopping streets.
Evening Catch a show at one of Victoria's excellent theaters and pop into the Sticky Wicket Pub (➤ 51) for a beer.

Day Two

Morning Head out of Victoria to explore the rest of **2 Vancouver Island** (➤ 52–53) via Oak Bay and **Butchart Gardens**, then continue up to Duncan.
Lunch Sample authentic First Nations' cuisine at the Riverwalk Café at the **Quw'utsun Cultural and Conference Centre** (➤ 52) and stay on to tour the exhibits there.
Afternoon Drive up through Nanaimo and Port Alberni and head for Tofino (➤ 53), out on the west coast. Take a stroll on **Long Beach**.
Evening Have a meal and stay overnight at the BestWestern Barclay Hotel at Port Alberni (tel: 250/724-7171 or 1-800/780-7234; $$).

Day Three

Morning Start out early for the drive back down to Nanaimo, and catch the ferry to **3 Vancouver** (➤ 54–57). From the ferry terminal make your way to Granville Island.
Lunch Have lunch at the Dockside Restaurant at the Granville Island Hotel (➤ 67).
Afternoon Spend a leisurely afternoon strolling around Granville Island, browsing its arts and crafts and soaking up the atmosphere. Find a sidewalk café for a break.
Evening Sample some of Vancouver's famous nightlife, and have dinner at the Blue Water Café on Hamilton Street (tel: 604/688-8078; $$$).

Day Four

Morning Still in Vancouver, visit the excellent **Museum of Anthropology**, on the U.B.C. campus, then head over to Chinatown for a stroll around the **Dr. Sun Yat-Sen Classical Chinese Garden**.
Lunch Enjoy an authentic Chinese lunch at one of the many restaurants in Chinatown.
Afternoon Drive the **4 Sea to Sky Highway** (➤ 58–59) up to **Whistler** (➤ 59) and take the Whistler Village Gondola to the top of Whistler Mountain. Relax over a cup of tea on one of the sundecks and enjoy the view.
Evening If the Fairmont Chateau Whistler hotel (tel: 604/938-8000 is beyond your budget, stay elsewhere and just come here for dinner.

Day Five

Morning Drive back to Vancouver and fly to Banff, then rent a car to explore **5 Banff and Yoho National Parks** (➤ 60–62).
Lunch Feast on buffalo steak or wild salmon at the rustic Buffalo Mountain Lodge (tel: 403/410-7417) on Tunnel Mountain Road.
Afternoon Visit the **Cave and Basin National Historic Site**, then take the **Banff Gondola** to the top of Sulphur Mountain for spectacular views and a hike in the mountains.
Evening Have an early evening soak in **Banff Hot Springs**, and enjoy a relaxing evening in the town of Banff.

Day Six

Morning Set out as early as possible on the **Bow Valley Parkway** to **Lake Louise** (➤ 61). After soaking up the view before the tour-bus crowds arrive, pick up some picnic provisions in Lake Louise Village, then take the **Icefields Parkway** north (➤ 180–181).
Lunch There are picnic tables and restrooms at Bow Lake, Herbert Lake, Saskatchewan Crossing and Coleman on the Icefields Parkway.
Afternoon Stop at the Icefields Centre for a pre-booked (tel: 877/423-7433) "Snocoach" trip (expensive) onto the Athabasca Glacier, then continue north to **Jasper**.
Evening Treat yourself to a night at the Fairmont Jasper Park Lodge (tel 780/852-5107; toll-free 800/257-7544; $$$).

Day Seven

Morning Drop in at the interesting Jasper Information Centre in **6 Jasper National Park** (➤ 63–64), then take the Jasper Tramway up **Whistlers Mountain** for a refreshing hike to the summit.
Lunch Eat in the restaurant at the top of Whistlers Mountain.
Afternoon/evening Drive to **Maligne Lake**, stroll the lakeshore and rent a boat to paddle over to Spirit Island. Later find a place with a westerly view and stick around to see the sun set over the mountains.

❶ Victoria

The provincial capital of British Columbia is incredibly pretty, with a wealth of historic buildings, a lovely harborfront and all the main attractions within a few city blocks. Known as "Canada's Garden City," it has colorful floral displays every-where you turn, and though it is a sophisticated city, Victoria is proud to maintain a "village" atmosphere.

More than a touch of British influence lingers on – double-decker buses, red telephone booths, cricket games in Beacon Hill Park, and English-style shopping streets lined with stores selling crafts and souvenirs. Market Square has a great atmosphere, and Fan Tan Alley in Chinatown is Canada's narrowest street, with lots of tiny stores.

Victoria has one of the world's finest natural harbors and was once the regional headquarters of the Hudson's Bay Company and a major port for the British Navy's Pacific Fleet. Now the **Inner Harbour**, overlooked by the imposing, copper-domed Parliament Buildings and the grand Empress Hotel, is the focal point of the city, full of pleasure craft, ferries, sightseeing and whale-watching boats, and flightseeing floatplanes. This is the atmospheric heart of Victoria, bustling with boat crews, day-trippers and entertainers.

Close to the Parliament Buildings is the excellent **Royal British Columbia Museum**, which should not be missed. Highlights include a series of superb natural history dioramas portraying various B.C. environments and the wonderful First Nations galleries, with reconstructions of dwellings, totem poles and Haida carvings. The modern history galleries feature a fascinating old town street exhibit, a cannery and a replica of H.M.S. *Discovery*. The museum also houses the National Geographic IMAX theater. Just behind the museum, **Thunderbird Park** has the best collection of totem poles in the world.

At the **Maritime Museum of British Columbia** you can learn all about explorers such as George Vancouver, James Cook and Sir Francis Drake, whalers and fishermen, merchants and military vessels. Also on display is the *Tilikum*,

---

➕ **202 B1**

Tourism Victoria
✉ 4th Floor, 31 Bastion Square ☎ 250/414-6999, www.tourismvictoria. com; also Visitor Centre at 812 Wharf Street ☎ 250/953-2033

Royal British Columbia Museum
✉ 675 Belleville Street ☎ 250/356-7226 or 888/447-7977; www.royalmuseum.bc.ca ⏲ Daily 9–5, closed Dec 25 and Jan 1
💵 Expensive 🎁 Gift shop

Maritime Museum of British Columbia
✉ 28 Bastion Square ☎ 250/385-4222 ext 102, www.mmbc.bc.ca
⏲ Daily 9:30–4:30 (mid-Jun to mid-Sep to 5). Closed Dec 25
💵 Moderate

an 11.5m (38-foot) native dugout canoe that went round the world at the turn of the 20th century. Across from the museum, Bastion Square is the site of Fort Victoria, the original settlement here.

Oak Bay is one of the most attractive suburbs of the city – and one of the most English. Its stately avenues are lined by large homes with colorful gardens, and you'll see the best architecture along Marine Drive on the rocky coastline. The oak trees that gave the settlement its name are Garry oaks, which are native to the island and have become quite rare.

Opposite: Thunderbird Park has some splendid totums

TAKING A BREAK

Go to the **Fairmont Empress Hotel** (► 67) for afternoon tea or call in at the **Sticky Wicket Pub** on Douglas Street – two Victoria institutions that reflect the British heritage.

Victoria's busy Inner Harbour is the focus of the city

VICTORIA: INSIDE INFO

Top tips If you plan to take a **whale-watching trips** from Victoria, make sure the one you select is a member of the Whale Watch Operators Association, which regulates the industry to ensure the safety of the passengers and the whales.
• There are lots of **sightseeing boats** moored up at the Inner Harbour, but you can't do better than the one operated by the Victoria Harbour Ferry. Quaint vessels, carrying a maximum of 12 passengers, tour the Inner and Outer harbors and continue out to Gorge Park, north of the city, all for $17.

Hidden gem The diminutive **Abkhazi Garden** on Fairfield Road was originally laid out in 1946 by Georgian Prince and Princess Abkhazi, and is a delightful half-hectare (1 acre), with mature trees and flowering shrubs. It was saved from the developers shovel in 1999 by the Land Conservancy of British Columbia, who are still struggling to cover the mortgage repayments.

2 Vancouver Island

Stretching about 500km (300 miles) from tip to tip, Vancouver Island is separated from the mainland by a narrow stretch of water that sets it apart in more ways than one. Though it's home to the provincial capital, there's a particular tranquility and a more laid-back atmosphere here. With its temperate climate, the island has a burgeoning wine industry, year-round golf and a permanent population of orcas offshore.

Windswept Long Beach, in the Pacific Rim National Park, is great for beachcombing

Heading north out of Victoria, the first big attraction is the famous **Butchart Gardens**, which began as a project to pretty-up a worked out quarry and developed into one of Canada's most glorious gardens. Farther north, **Duncan** is famous for its totem poles – more than 80 of them – each of which depicts a First Nations legend or a real family history. There's a strong Cowichan presence in the area, and their superb **Quw'utsun' Cultural and Conference Centre** offers an insight into their history and lifestyle. It includes the world's largest carving house, where in summer you can watch craftsmen in action. The center also organizes three-course salmon barbecues (Jul–Sep, Thu–Sat at noon; $35, child $26), which feature traditional songs and dancing. To the west, Lake Cowichan is at the heart of the island's principal wine region.

A little way north is **Nanaimo**, with a fine natural harbor that's home to a working fishing fleet as well as the many pleasure craft. Main attractions are the tiny, white-painted **Bastion**, built by the Hudson's Bay Company in 1853, and the **Nanaimo District Museum**, which has good displays on local First Nations and the coal-mining industry.

Beyond Nanaimo, at Parksville, Highway 4 heads west to **Port Alberni**, the main center for the **Pacific Rim National Park**. The park protects 400sq km (193 square miles) of some of the most diverse and abundant ecosystems in North America, including virgin temperate rain forest, superb beaches (notably **Long Beach**) and remote islands. It's also on the migration routes of many whale species. Summer sunsets here are as magnificent as the winter storms. Bounded on the west by the Pacific Ocean and on the east by the aptly named Insular Mountains, there remains a tangible sense of being cut off from the world. The park also protects more than 290 native archeological sites. **Tofino**, at the northern extremity, offers various excursions, and there's a boardwalk through the forest to **Hotsprings Cove**, where naturally hot water flows into rock pools where you can bathe overlooking the ocean.

The northern tip of the island is capped by the **Cape Scott Provincial Park**, a forested wilderness that's home to black bears, cougars, wolves and deer. It has a spectacular coastline where sea lions and seals bask on the rocks and offshore islands.

TAKING A BREAK

The restaurant at the **Wickaninnish Inn** (near Tofino, tel: 250/723-3100) has a wonderful location on a rocky headland and great seafood.

✚ 202 B2

Tourism Vancouver Island
✉ 203–335 Wesley Street, Nanaimo
☎ 250/754-3500; www.vancouverisland.travel

Butchart Gardens
✉ 800 Benvenuto Avenue, Brentwood Bay
☎ 250/652-4422 or 1-866/652-4422,
www.butchartgardens.com ◐ Apr daily 9–5;
May 9–6; early Jun 9–7; mid-Jun to Aug
9am–10:30pm; early Sep 9–9; late Sep 9–5;
early Oct 9–4:30; late Oct 9–4; Nov 9–3:30;
early Dec 9–9; Dec 25 1–10; mid-Dec to early
Jan 9am–10pm; mid-Jan to Feb 9–3:30; Mar 9–4
💰 Expensive 🍴 75 🎁 Gift Shop

Quw'utsun' Cultural and Conference Centre
✉ 200 Cowichan Way, Duncan
☎ 250/746-8119 or 1-877/746-8119,
www.quwutsun.ca ✉ May–Sep daily 10–5;
Oct–Apr 10–4 💰 Expensive

Nanaimo District Museum and Bastion
✉ 100 Cameron Road, Nanaimo
☎ 250/753-1821, www.nanimomuseum.bc.ca
◐ Daily 10–5. Closed Sun–Mon in winter
(Bastion summer only) 💰 Inexpensive

Wickaninnish Interpretive Centre
✉ Long Beach ◐ Mid-May to mid-Sep
daily 10:30–6

VANCOUVER ISLAND: INSIDE INFO

Top tips A great way to get from the southern part of the island to points north is via the **ferry** (for vehicles and passengers) that runs from Brentwood Bay to Mill Bay. It's not only a short-cut, it's a wonderfully scenic route.
• To walk the **West Coast Trail** you'll need to obtain a permit from the national park authority and attend an orientation session.

Hidden gem The **North Island Wildlife Recovery Centre** in Errington, near Parksville (tel: 250/248-8534; open Apr–Oct daily 10–4; all year for animal drop-off), cares for sick, injured or orphaned wildlife, and releases as many as possible back into the wild. In addition to its nature museum and any animals that happen to have been brought in, you'll see permanent resident Brian the Eagle. After his beak was damaged in a shooting incident he was provided with a prosthetic version that was devised and fitted by a local dentist.

③ Vancouver

Vancouver is constantly at the top of the "Best Places in the World to Live" list, and with good reason. A glittering downtown sits astride the Fraser River estuary, encircled by the waters of the Burrard Inlet, English Bay and False Creek; to the north is the magnificent backdrop of the snow-capped Coast Mountains, while the foreground includes the distinctive Canada Place and the leafy expanse of Stanley Park. It's also a supremely cosmopolitan city with lots to see and do.

Vancouver ferry rides are as good as sightseeing trips

A good place to start is in the oldest part of town, **Gastown**. It takes its name from "Gassy" Jack Leighton, who opened a bar here in 1859 to serve workers in the local lumber industry, and the community that soon developed was incorporated in 1869 and named Granville. Today, its cobblestoned alley-

VANCOUVER: INSIDE INFO

Top tips The **See Vancouver & Beyond Smartvisit Card** (tel: 604/295-1157 or 1-877/295-1157; UK tel: 0800/731-6276; www.seevancouvercard.com) offers free admission to a long list of popular attractions. A two-day pass costs $99, three days is $129 and five days costs $199 (around half-price for children) and there may be discounts for ordering online.
• Even getting around this lively city is fun, with **Aquabus**, **Seabus** and **ferry services** linking waterfront areas, the **Skytrain** whisking you around on land, largely on elevated sections with wonderful views, and the **Downtown Historic Railway** making short tours on an old interurban tram.

Hidden gem Dwarfed by the surrounding skyscrapers, the tiny **Christ Church Cathedral** (tel: 604/682-3849) is one of very few 19th-century buildings still standing in downtown, and has stained-glass windows by William Morris.

ways and courtyards are lined with restored brick buildings
housing boutiques, antiques stores, art galleries and restaurants that can occupy a pleasant couple of hours wandering.
Look for the famous Steam Clock, the world's first, on the
corner of Water and Cambie streets (performances on the
quarter-hour) and the statue of Gassy Jack on Maple Tree
Square. The shopping and entertainment heart of the city is
the area around Robson Street and Granville Street, a round-
the-clock hive of activity and great for people-watching.
Yaletown is another shoppers' heaven, with high-end fashions,
galleries and an eclectic selection of independent stores.

At Cambie Street, you can pick up the Silk Road walking
route (identified with colored banners), which leads to the
Millennium Gate entrance to **Chinatown** and beyond, incorporating all of the attractions in this exotic neighborhood.
After San Francisco, Vancouver has the largest Chinese
community in North America, and is full of stores selling all
kinds of Oriental goods. Go to the **Chinese Cultural Centre**
to discover why Vancouver has such a large Chinese population and how they have contributed to city and national
culture. They lead guided walking tours through Chinatown
in summer. There's a wonderful night market, too, in summer.
The restaurants offer superb authentic cuisine and attractions

Stanley Park is a great place for recreation within the city

A reminder, in Stanley Park, of B.C.'s strong First Nations heritage

include the beautiful **Dr. Sun Yat-Sen Classical Chinese Garden**. Replicating a 14th-century Ming scholar's garden, it reflects the subtle balance between yin and yang, with gardens, courtyards, pavilions, bridges and covered galleries. It was constructed by Chinese workers, and no nails, screws or power tools were used.

Vancouver has a number of fine museums, but if you have time for only one of them, make sure it's the **Museum of Anthropology** at the University of British Columbia. Its vast, 15m (49-foot) high entrance hall contains towering totems and massive sculptures from West Coast First Nations tribes. Leading on from here are galleries of ethnographic materials from many parts of the world, including some 6,000 objects relating to the local First Nations. The highlight of the entire collection is the enormous *The Raven and the First Men*, by Bill Reid (► 31), displayed in the Rotunda. Real museum buffs can also visit the **Vancouver Museum**, **Telus World of Science**, and a clutch of specialist museums covering subjects from minerals to maritime matters to model trains – and there's the **BC Sports Hall of Fame**, too.

It is absolutely obligatory to spend some time on **Granville Island**, with its atmospheric narrow streets, high-quality artists' and artisans' workshops and galleries, and street entertainers. This is also home to some of the city's hottest restaurants and nightspots, innovative theater companies and comedy clubs. The **Public Market** has a wonderful array of fresh foods, crafts, flowers and coffee shops, and there are some unusual and quirky items in the island's stores.

Bringing the countryside right into the city, **Stanley Park** is a huge green oasis jutting out into the Burrard Inlet, 400ha (1,000 acres) that incorporates unspoiled natural woodland, parkland, beaches, playgrounds and all kinds of recreational facilities. It's a haven for wildlife as well as Vancouverites. In addition to the tennis courts, lawn bowling and swimming pools, you can cycle or rollerblade around the Seawall that encircles the park. For kids there's a farmyard, miniature railway, waterpark and swimming pool, as well as the superb **Vancouver Aquarium Marine Science Centre**. It's the largest in Canada, and among the 60,000-plus creatures here, you can get up close to beluga whales, sharks, sea lions, sea otters and dolphins.

The **North Shore** has some of the best outdoor attractions, including 1,250m (4,100-foot) **Grouse Mountain**, where the Skyride gondola will whisk you up to the top for a panoramic vista. There's a First Nations feast house and cultural center up here, and the **Refuge for Endangered Wildlife**, where you can see orphaned grizzly bears, cared for until they can be returned to the wild. All of this is within a few minutes of downtown, as is the **Capilano Regional Park**, which protects an area of first-growth temperate rain forest with some huge Douglas firs. Those with a head for heights can cross the very strong, but disconcertingly pliable **Capilano Suspension Bridge**, spanning the gorge high above the Capilano River.

The splendid ship's figurehead of the *Empress of Japan* can be found in Stanley Park

In contrast to the sights, it's worth while just soaking up the atmosphere of the various neighborhoods – upscale Yaletown, with its designer stores, hip pubs and galleries; cosmopolitan Kitsilano, full of trendy cafés and clothes; and Commercial Drive, Vancouver's "Little Italy."

TAKING A BREAK

The **Granville Island Coffee House** (tel: 604/682-7865; $), behind the Arts Club Theatre, has good snacks and light lunches, plus 30 minutes' free internet/email access for customers.

🞤 202 C2

Vancouver Tourist Information Centre
✉ Waterfront Centre, Plaza Level, 200 Burrard Street ☎ 604/683-2000, www.tourismvancouver.com

Dr. Sun Yat-Sen Classical Chinese Garden
✉ 578 Carrall Street ☎ 604/662-3207, www.vancouverchinesegarden.com 🕐 May to mid-Jun and Sep daily 10–6; mid-Jun to Aug 9:30–7; Oct–Apr 10–4:30. Closed Mon Dec–May, Dec 25 and Jan 1 💷 Moderate ❓ Gift shop

Museum of Anthropology
✉ 6393 Marine Drive NW ☎ 604/822-5087 🕐 Mid-May to early Sep daily 10–5 (also 5–9pm Tue); early Sep to mid-May Tue 11–9, Wed–Sun 11–5. Closed Dec 25 💷 Moderate ❓ Gift shop

Telus World of Science
✉ 1455 Québec Street ☎ 604/443-7440, www.scienceworld.ca 🕐 Daily 10–6 💷 Expensive

Vancouver Museum
✉ 1100 Chestnut Street, Vannier Park ☎ 604/736-4431, www.vanmuseum.bc.ca 🕐 Daily 10–5 (also 5–9 Thu) 💷 Expensive

Vancouver Aquarium
✉ 845 Avison Way ☎ 604/659-3474, www.vanaqua.org 🕐 Jul–Aug daily 9:30–7; Sep–Jun 10–5:30 💷 Expensive

Grouse Mountain
✉ 6400 Nancy Greene Way, North Vancouver ☎ 604/980-9311, www.grousemountain.com 🕐 Daily 9am–10pm 💷 Expensive

4 Sea to Sky Highway and Whistler

There's romance in the name of the Sea to Sky Highway, but it's far surpassed by the scenery. Craggy mountains, cloaked in rain forest and cut through with foaming white waterfalls, tower above the blue water of Howe Sound. Inland are lake-studded valleys, alpine meadows, extinct volcanoes and glaciers. And it's all within a two-hour drive from Vancouver.

An atmospheric mist rises over beautiful Howe Sound

The starting point of the Sea to Sky Highway, more prosaically Highway 99, is at the pretty little town of **Horseshoe Bay**, on the tip of West Vancouver. Its painted clapboard houses cluster on the steep hillside above a bay dotted with sailboats from the marina. The harbor is also a terminal for ferries

SEA TO SKY HIGHWAY AND WHISTLER: INSIDE INFO

Top tips Bring something **warm to wear** if you're going underground at the BC Museum of Mining. The temperature down there is 12°C (54°F) year-round.
• If you want to see **bald eagles** in large numbers, visit between November and March, when they arrive in their thousands to feast on salmon.

Hidden gem One-Mile Lake in Pemberton is a wonderfully peaceful haven to get away from the bustle of Whistler. It has a boardwalk across its northern marshes and is great for spotting birds, particularly during the migrations.

heading north or across to Vancouver Island. From here, the highway heads north along Howe Sound to the seaside and artisan town of Lions Bay (the "lions" are twin mountain peaks above the town), with a sand beach, boating and hiking trails into the mountains.

Beyond here, you soon reach **Britannia Beach** and the **BC Museum of Mining**. A working mine until 1974, and at one time the British Commonwealth's largest copper producer, it is now a National Historic Site offering underground tours, mining demonstrations, gold panning and several interesting exhibits.

At about the midway point you reach **Squamish**, at the head of Howe Sound, surrounded by spectacular mountain scenery, renowned as one of the world's premier mountain-biking locations. It's also home to the **West Coast Railway Heritage Park**, with a fine collection of rolling stock, tracks, buildings and equipment, and evolving streets of historic buildings. There are eight provincial parks nearby, and the area around Brackendale, to the north, has the largest concentrations of wintering bald eagles in the world, which come to feed on the plentiful salmon. Leaving the

> **Whistler is among the finest winter sports resorts in the world**

coast now, the route heads northeast through the Garibaldi Provincial Park to **Whistler**, an upscale, year-round resort and one of the best winter sports destinations in the world, with a huge range of summer activities too. Man-made and traffic free, the "village" is full of luxury hotels, restaurants, designer boutiques and craft galleries, but prices here are not as high as you might expect and, in true Canadian style, it is friendly, relaxed and welcoming.

TAKING A BREAK

A good place to break the journey is at the **Howe Sound Inn and Brewing Company** (tel: 604/892-2603 or 800/919-2537; $$) at 37801 Cleveland Avenue, Squamish.

Highway Improvements

A major improvement scheme is being carried out on the Sea to Sky Highway, with completion due in 2009, in time for the 2010 Winter Olympics. In the interim, be prepared to encounter construction along the way. For up-to-date information call 1-877/4SAFE99 or visit www.seatoskyimprovements.ca.

✚ 202 C2

Tourism Whistler
✉ 4010 Whistler Way, Whister ☎ 604/938-2769 or 877/991-9988; www.mywhistler.com or www.tourismwhistler.com ◷ Daily 9–5

BC Museum of Mining
✉ PO Box 188, Britannia Beach

☎ 1-800/896-4044 ext.227; www.bcmuseumofmining.org ◷ Early May to mid-Oct daily 9–4:30; mid-Oct to early May Mon–Fri 9–4:30
💲 Summer: expensive; winter: moderate (prices include gold panning)

West Coast Railway Heritage Park
✉ Squamish ☎ 604/898-9336; www.wcra.org
◷ Daily 10–4 💲 Expensive

5 Banff and Yoho National Parks

Banff National Park was the first of Canada's 40 national parks to be established (1885), and enjoys enduring popularity with its spectacular and accessible mountain scenery. Neighboring Yoho (Cree for "awesome") lives up to its name.

Banff town makes a good base for exploring both parks, with a good selection of places to stay, restaurants, upscale shopping and some interesting places to visit. It is located on the Bow River and almost encircled by mountain peaks.

This is where the whole national park concept took shape, when railroad engineers discovered hot springs southeast of the town and started a tourist boom. Visitors can no longer soak in those waters, now the **Cave and Basin National Historic Site**, but you can go into the cave, see the pool and smell the sulfur. An exhibition tells the history of the spring, sacred to the Stoney First Nations, and local ecology. You *can* soak in the **Banff Upper Hot Springs** close by, where the water temperature averages 38ºC (100ºF). There's a modern spa here, with

✚ 203 E2

Banff and Lake Louise Tourism
✉ 224 Banff Avenue, Banff ☎ 403/762-8421; www.banfflakelouise.com, www.pc.gc.ca

Yoho Visitor Centre
✉ Field ☎ 250/343-6783 ⏰ May–late Jun daily 9–5; late Jun–early Sep 9–7 (late Sep to 5); early Sep–Apr 9–4 🎫 Day pass: moderate

Cave and Basin National Historic Site
✉ Cave Avenue, Banff ☎ 403/762-1566, www.pc.gc.ca ⏰ Mid-May to Sep daily 9–6; Oct to mid-May Mon–Fri 11–4, Sat–Sun 9:30–5 🎫 Inexpensive

Banff Upper Hot Springs
✉ Mountain Avenue, Banff ☎ 403/726-1515 or 1-800/767-1611; www.pc.gc.ca ⏰ Mid-May to mid-Sep daily 9am–11pm; mid-Sep to mid-May Sun–Thu 10–10, Fri–Sat 10am–11pm 🎫 Moderate

Banff Gondola
✉ Mountain Avenue, Banff ☎ 403/762-2523; www.banffgondola.com ⏰ Apr–May daily 8:30–6; Jun–Aug 7:30am–9pm; Sep to mid-Oct 8:30–6:30; mid-Oct–Nov 8:30–4:30; Dec–Jan; 10–5; Feb–Mar 10–4. Closed Dec 25 🎫 Expensive

A few facts
Banff National Park (6,641sq km/2,565 square miles), is now part of the UNESCO Canadian Rockies World Heritage Site, as is Yoho, smaller but still perfectly formed at 1,310sq km (505 square miles).

many amenities, but a mid-winter dip in the big outdoor pool when the snow is falling is still the best experience. Next to the Hot Springs, the glass-enclosed **Banff Gondola** climbs Sulphur Mountain for views that can extend as far as 145km (90 miles). At the top there are restaurants, viewing platforms and walking trails.

Head out of town on the scenic **Bow Valley Parkway** to **Lake Louise**, one of the most beautiful spots in the Rockies. The lake, set in a bowl and backed by snow-capped mountains, was discovered in the late 19th century; in 1890 work began on the luxury **Château Lake Louise Hotel**, and visitors have been flocking here ever since. The amazing color of the water, caused by microscopic particles reflecting only the blue-green element of the spectrum, looks even better from above, and many trails head up into the mountains for superb views (the Lake Louise Gondola is an easy alternative).

Going north along the **Icefields Parkway** (➤ 180–181) you'll see some of the most stunning scenery in the Rockies, with a series of views of vertiginous peaks, dazzling blue lakes and sparkling waterfalls – and, of course, glaciers.

Opposite: Banff shopping mall is prettily illuminated

Bottom: visitors throng the promenade at Lake Louise Inset: solitude above Lake O'Hara in Yoho National Park

From Lake Louise, cross the border into British Columbia to **Yoho National Park**, which has a great deal for the casual drive-through visitor, but can also offer more seclusion than Banff National Park for serious outdoor types. It has 400km (248 miles) of hiking trails, many of them day-long, and the most spectacular is the 26km (16-mile) round trip to **Lake O'Hara**, a jewel surrounded by alpine meadows. Other popular attractions are pretty **Emerald Lake** and the **Wapta** and **Takakkaw falls**, the latter with a freefall of 254m (833 feet).

Renting a canoe at Lake Louise is one way to escape the crowds

TAKING A BREAK

The **Château Lake Louise Hotel** (tel: 403/522-3511) is the obvious choice, or hike up to the famous **Teahouse** (call Château Lake Louise Hotel for information) at Lake Agnes.

BANFF AND YOHO NATIONAL PARKS: INSIDE INFO

Top tips If you don't want to hike to **Lake O'Hara**, there's also a bus shuttle from the Visitor Centre. However, numbers are strictly limited to preserve the delicate ecology, and you need to book your seat as much as three months in advance (tel: 250/343-6433).

• **Never venture out on to glaciers on your own**. There are areas of thin ice and holes covered by a thin layer of snow that are quite literally death traps – if the fall doesn't kill you, the cold will. Make sure you take one of the excellent tours from the Icefields Centre.

• If you see **grizzly or black bears or any other wildlife** on the highway, stop at a safe distance (the national parks authority recommend 30m/100 feet from elk and 100m/330ft from bears) and view them from *inside* your vehicle. Keep windows closed and never throw out food for the animals. Unless the wildlife is blocking your way, you should not park on the side of the highway – only in designated parking areas.

• To see the **waterfalls at their best**, visit between late June and the end of July, when the meltwater is at its peak and rainfall adds to the volume in the rivers

Hidden gem It's worth taking the steep 1.6km (1-mile) trail from the **Hoodoo Creek Campground** in the western section of the park to take a look at the **hoodoos**, glacial debris that has been carved by the weather into strangely shaped pillars.

6 Jasper National Park

Away from the Icefields Parkway, this park isn't as crowded as Banff and even short hiking trails offer a real sense of solitude and a glimpse of exciting wildlife, following in the footsteps of bison herds, First Nations and the early explorers.

Jasper is the most northerly park in the UNESCO Canadian Rockies World Heritage Site, 10,878sq km (4,200 square miles) of magnificent scenery. Its main town is **Jasper**, with the gritty character of a working town, one of the earliest places settled by Europeans. Prosperity was assured by the arrival of the railroad in 1908 and the town still benefits from being on two of Via Rail's famous scenic routes – the **Rocky Mountaineer**, which crosses the mountains en route from Vancouver to Edmonton, and the **Skeena**, linking Edmonton with Prince Rupert up on the far northwestern coast.

South from Jasper after 5km (3 miles) is the **Jasper Tramway**, the longest and highest tramway in Canada,

Maligne Lake presents the quintessential face of the Canadian Rockies

ascending to 2,277m (7,472 feet) on Whistlers Mountain. There's another viewpoint on **Mount Edith Cavell**.

On Highway 16 toward Edmonton, take a right turn on to Maligne Lake Road. Stop for a 3.5km (2-mile) hike through **Maligne Canyon**, then follow the river to **Maligne Lake**, the largest glacial lake in North America. Toward the far end, little **Spirit Island** is an icon of the Rockies, and of Canada.

TAKING A BREAK

Try the fusion cuisine and microbrews at the **Jasper Brewing Company** (tel: 780/852-4111; $–$$) in Jasper.

Some forms of
transportation
have changed
little in the
Rockies

➕ 203 D3

Jasper National Park Information Centre
✉ 500 Connaught Drive ☎ 780/852-6176, www.pc.gc.ca ⏰ Mid-June to Aug daily 8:30–7; Oct to mid-Jun 9–6; Sep 9–5

JASPER NATIONAL PARK: INSIDE INFO

Top tips For any hikes in the national park, you should carry at least a liter (nearly 2 pints) of **drinking water** – more for day-long trips – and never scoop it up from the park's waterways, no matter how sparkling and clear they appear. Surface water is often contaminated with Giardia, an intestinal parasite.

• It's tempting to **get up close to the foot of the glaciers**, but beware – chunks of ice as big as a house sometimes break off and come crashing down. Keep to designated trails, or employ a local guide.

• The park still has populations of **creatures that once roamed free** and undisturbed all over the continent – coyotes, elk, cougars, wolves, wolverines and bears to name just a few – but the balance is delicate, even in this protected environment. The woodland caribou is in decline here, so if you see caribou, or signs that they are in the area, take particular care not to disturb them. Consult the park's website for advice about bear encounters.

At Your Leisure

7 Okanagan Valley

This fertile region offers a striking contrast to the majestic Rockies. It's an area of vast rolling grasslands, rivers that offer some of the best rafting in the country, lakes for sailing, orchards, and more than 40 wineries. Many offer tours and tastings.

Kelowna, on the eastern shore of Okanagan Lake, is a vibrant city, with a full calendar of events, and plenty of activities. At the southern end of the valley is the remarkable **Nk'Mip Desert**, 20ha (50 acres) of arid sage grass and ponderosa pine. In the superb $9 million **Cultural Centre**, which opened in 2006, the ancient culture of the Okanagan Nation is explored through hands-on exhibits and film shows, and desert creatures can be seen in an indoor habitat.

✚ 203 D2

Thompson Okanagan Tourism
✉ 2280-D Leckie Road, Kelowna
☎ 250/860-5999 or 800/567-2275;
www.totabc.com

Nk'Mip Desert Cultural Centre
✉ 1000 Rancher Creek Road, Osoyoos
☎ 250/495-7901 or 1-888 495-8555;
www.nkmipdesert.com ⏰ May–early
Oct daily 9:30–4:30; rest of the year
9:30–4 💲 Moderate

8 Wells Gray Provincial Park

In the foothills of the Cariboo and Columbia mountains, Wells Gray is the best of the region's provincial parks with volcanic landscapes, colorful wild flowers, rain forests, lakes and waterfalls. **Helmcken Falls** is the best – more than twice the height of Niagara, at 137m (450 feet). Wildlife includes black and grizzly bears and a large herd of moose.

Visitor Information Centre
✚ 203 D3 ✉ 425 East Yellowhead
Highway, Clearwater ☎ 250/674-2646;
www.wellsgray.ca

9 Glacier and Mount Revelstoke National Parks

On the British Columbia side of the Rockies, these parks protect widely differing landscapes in the Columbia and Selkirk mountains. They are not as accessible as some other parks, particularly Glacier, since its main role is to protect its 400 remote glaciers. Revelstoke is an area of meadowland with high trails that are swathed in wild flowers in summer.

Lake Osoyoos, in the lush Okanagan Valley

✚ 203 D2

Glacier Park H.Q.
✉ Rogers Pass Discovery Centre
☎ 250/837-7500; www.pc.gc.ca/np-pn/
bc/glacier ⏰ Apr–Oct daily 9–5 (mid-
Jun to Aug 8–7); Dec–Mar 7–5. Closed
Nov 💲 Moderate

Mount Revelstoke Park H.Q.
✚ 203 D2 ✉ 301-B 3rd Street West,
Revelstoke ☎ 250/837-7500;
www.pc.gc.ca/revelstoke

Farther Afield

🔟 Skeena Valley

In B.C.'s remote northwest, the Skeena River flows from its source near the Continental Divide to empty into the Pacific at Prince Rupert. It's scenic, but the land route to reach it is not especially interesting and it's better to come by sea (see Inside Passage Cruise, ➤ 178–179). **Prince Rupert** has a busy deep-water harbor serving commercial and passenger vessels. The **Museum of Northern British Columbia** covers the heritage of the Tsimshian First Nations.

Waterton Lakes National Park is home to a herd of buffalo

The valley includes waterfalls, tiny islands and forested slopes backed by the snow-capped Coast Mountains. Highlights include **Terrace**, a logging center with beautiful forests, and New Hazelton's **'Ksan Historical Village** representing the lifestyle and heritage of the Gitxsan people.

➕ 202 B4

Prince Rupert Visitor Centre

✉ 215 Cow Bay Road, Prince Rupert

☎ 250/624 5637 or 800/667-1994; www.tourismprincerupert.com

Museum of Northern B.C.

✉ 100 First Avenue West, Prince Rupert ☎ 250/624-3207; www.museumofnorthernbc.com

🕐 Mon–Sat 9–5, (Jun–Aug to 8pm also Jun–Aug Sun 9–5) 🎟 Moderate

'Ksan Historical Village

✉ Box 326, Hazelton ☎ 250/842-5544 or 877/842-5518; www.ksan.org

🕐 Apr–Sep daily 9–5; Oct–Mar Mon–Fri 9:30–4:30 (museum and shop only) 🎟 Inexpensive ❓ Guided tours (expensive)

🔟 Waterton Lakes National Park

Four ecosystems – mountains, lakes, prairies and alpine meadows – are preserved in this 325sq km (125 square mile) national park, up against the US border, adjacent to Montana's Glacier National Park. Together they form the **Waterton-Glacier International Peace Park**, inaugurated in 1932. Rugged mountain peaks rise dramatically from the flat land and the vegetation of the scree slopes attracts foraging bears.

➕ 203 E1

Waterton Lakes National Park

☎ 403/859-2224; www.parkscanada.pch.gc.ca 🎟 Moderate

For Kids

Kids love creatures, whether it's the creepy-crawlies at **Victoria Bug Zoo** (✉ 631 Courtney Street ☎ 250/384-2847, www.bugzoo.bc.ca 🕐 Daily 🎟 Moderate), the cute domestic animals at the **Children's Farmyard and Miniature Railway** (☎ 604/257-8531 🎟 Moderate) in Stanley Park, Vancouver, or the white beluga whales that feature in an exciting sleepover beside their tank at the **Vancouver Aquarium** (☎ 604/659-3574 for information).

Where to... Stay

Prices

High season room only rates, based on two sharing a double room, excluding taxes

$ under $160 $$ $160–$300 $$$ more than $300

VICTORIA

🥄🥄🥄 Abigail's $–$$$

This is a Tudor-style hotel with English gardens and a lavish spa, close to the Inner Harbour. The 23 bedrooms are furnished with antiques, including some four-poster beds, and most have wood-burning fireplaces. All have private bathrooms, some with Jacuzzi, and the breakfasts are outstanding.

➕ 202 B1 ✉ 906 McClure Street
☎ 250/388-5363, 1-866/347-5054;
www.abigailshotel.com

🥄🥄🥄 Fairmont Empress $$$

A historic icon of the city, located right on the Inner Harbour, the Empress is undoubtedly the best place to stay in the city, the choice of visiting royalty, dignitaries and celebrities. It's pure luxury throughout, with gleaming wood floors and traditional-style furnishings. It has a superb indoor pool and luxury spa, and there are several fine restaurants. Elegant afternoon teas are a famous institution here.

➕ 202 B1 ✉ 721 Government Street
☎ 250/348-8111, 1-800/257-7544;
www.fairmont.com

🥄 An Ocean View Bed and Breakfast $–$$

High on a rocky outcrop, with stunning views of the sea and mountains, this cozy little place is just seven blocks from downtown. It's beautifully furnished and the quirky decor features hand-painted murals. Rooms have private bathrooms, and breakfast is included.

➕ 202 B1 ✉ 715 Suffolk Street
☎ 250/386-7330 or 1-800/342-9986;
www.anoceanview.com

VANCOUVER

🥄🥄🥄 Granville Island Hotel $–$$

This is a great place for soaking up the atmosphere of vibrant Granville Island, and it has wonderful views across the water to the city and mountains. Luxurious penthouse suites have the best views, but all rooms have big windows for good reason. The Dockside Restaurant has an open kitchen, the pub serves beer brewed on the premises, and there's a superb waterside patio. There's a fee for parking ($6 a day).

➕ 202 C2 ✉ 1253 Johnston Street
☎ 604/683-7373, 1-800/663-1840;
www.granvilleislandhotel.com

🥄 Grouse Inn $

This low-rise inn has a central courtyard with parking, gardens and a swimming pool and it's conveniently located for North Shore attractions. It's one of the best in its category in Vancouver, and offers a range of rooms up to two-bedroom suites, some with kitchens. Continental breakfast is included in the price; the restaurant also serves lunch.

➕ 202 C2 ✉ 1633 Capilano Road, North Vancouver ☎ 604/988-7101, 1-800/797-7888; www.grouseinn.com

🥄🥄🥄🥄 Pan Pacific $$$

The ultimate luxury place to stay in Vancouver, right on the harbor, with spectacular views across the water to the mountains. More than 500 rooms and suites, have stylish modern furnishings, cable TV, high-speed internet connection, control-lable air-conditioning and marble bathrooms.

➕ 202 C2 ✉ 300–999 Canada Place
☎ 604/662-8111, 1-800/663-1515;
http://vancouver.panpacific.com

Where to...
Be Entertained

VICTORIA

The provincial capital has some fine theaters, including the **Royal** (805 Broughton Street, tel: 250/386-6121 or 888/717-6121; www.rmts.bc.ca); the **MacPherson** (contact information is the same as for the Royal) and the **Belfry** (1291 Gladstone Avenue, tel: 250/385-6815; www.belfry.bc.ca).

OKANAGAN VALLEY

Among the specialties to look for here are wines from the Okanagan wineries. One that is particularly interesting to visit is **Summerhill Estate Winery** (4870 Chute Lake Road, Kelowna, tel: 250/764-8000 or 800/667-3538; www.summerhill.bc.ca), which matures its wines in a huge pyramid. You can buy unique jewelry from **Okanagan Opal** (7879 Highway 97, Vernon, tel: 250/542-1103; www.opalscanada.com), or even visit the mine and dig for your own opal. This is also a fruit-growing area, so look for stands and cabins selling fruit at the roadside.

BANFF AND JASPER

Of these two mountain communities, Banff is the most tourist-oriented and so the prices are higher here, but quality and choice are excellent. **Banff Avenue** is the main street, lined with stores selling all arts, crafts and clothing. Jasper, a working town populated by mountain people, includes the **Totem Ski Shop** (408 Connaught Drive, tel: 780/852-3078), a good place to get kitted out for mountain sports.

until October 2008; the **Orpheum** (Smithe Street, tel: 604/665-3050); **BC Place Stadium** (777 Pacific Boulevard, tel: 604/ 669-2300; www.bcplacestadium.com); and **General Motors Place** (800 Griffiths Way, tel: 604/899-7400). On a more intimate level, there's theater at the **Granville Island Stage** (1585 Johnston Street, tel: 604/687-1644), and for live music the **Backstage Lounge** (1585 Johnston Street, tel: 604/687-1354) and **Richards on Richards** (1036 Richards Street, tel: 604/687-6794), while Jazz fans should head for **The Cellar** (3611 West Broadway, tel: 604/738-1959). The best gay clubs are **Odyssey** (1251 Howe Street, tel: 604/689-5256) and the long-established **Dufferin** (900 Seymour Street, tel: 604/683-4251).

VANCOUVER

This is where you'll find the biggest venues and the widest choice of entertainment, from stadium rock concerts to intimate jazz clubs. Major venues include the **Queen Elizabeth Theatre Complex** (600 Hamilton Street, tel: 604/665-3050) which will be closed for alterations

with its secondhand bookstores; for new books, **Duthie Books** (2239 West 4th Avenue, tel: 604/732-5344; www.duthiebooks.com; open daily) is an independent bookstore with an excellent range and a fast ordering service. The list of shopping malls is headed by **Metropolis at Metrotown** (604-4720 Kingsway, tel: 604/438-4715; http://metropolis.shopping.ca) in the suburb of **Burnaby**; others include the world's second-largest mall in the sparkling **Pacific Centre** (700 West Georgia Street, tel: 604/688-7236; www.pacificentre.com) and **Lonsdale Quay** (Lonsdale Avenue, North Vancouver, tel: 604/985-6261; www.lonsdalequay.com), in a spectacular harborfront setting, with an indoor market area.

EARTH

Kodak

CAL
STA

Getting Your Bearings

Don't let anyone tell you – and many will try –
that the Prairies are just flat and boring. Sure,
there are vast and featureless wheatfields and
cattle ranges, but there are real gems to be
found in among them. Several features punc-
ture the sky, notably the lovely Cypress
Hills – the highest land between
The Rockies and Labrador –
and the five major cities:
Calgary, Edmonton, Winnipeg,
Regina and Saskatoon.

**The Horseshoe Canyon viewpoint
in Cypress Hills Provincial Park**

Horseshoe Canyon

Map labels: Meander River, Wood Buffalo National Park, Fort Smith, Fort Vermilion, Lake Athabasca, Manning, Peace River, Fairview, ALBERTA, Fort McMurray, Grande Prairie, Valleyview, Slave Lake, Athabasca, La Loche, Swan Hills, Athabasca, Grande Cache, Whitecourt, Westlock, Lac la Biche, Meadow Lake, Hinton, **3 Edmonton**, Vegreville, Lloydminster, Drayton Valley, Camrose, Rocky Mountain House, Ponoka, Red Deer, Provost, Battleford, Wilkie, Canmore, Drumheller, Rosetown, **Calgary 1**, High River, **2 Badlands and Dinosaur Provincial Park**, Claresholm, Brooks, Swift Current, Lethbridge, Medicine Hat, Pincher Creek, **Cypress Hills Interprovincial Park 5**

You can see these cities a long time
before you reach them, their sparkling
high-rise office blocks standing proud
amid the surrounding plains, and the
anticipation this creates is well rewarded.
Each is a modern, vibrant city with world-
class entertainment and festivals, historic
attractions, fine museums and good shopping –
Edmonton has the largest shopping mall in the
world. Their top restaurants feature international cuisines and
employ innovative chefs to shake off the steak-and-ribs image that
continues to stick like barbecue sauce on small-town menus.

The landscapes are cut through with great rivers and dotted with sparkling
lakes, which makes this a great destination for fishing, canoeing and white-
water rafting. There are huge forests, gently sloping wooded hillsides, and
meadows full of wild flowers, with some terrific hiking and cycling trails. In
stark contrast, there is the dusty moonscape of the Badlands of Alberta, the
Great Sand Hills of Saskatchewan, and the Arctic tundra of the far north.

The Prairies have an interesting cultural mix, too, including a very strong
First Nations heritage, a French-speaking community in Winnipeg, and immigrants from all over the globe who are keeping their colorful traditions alive.

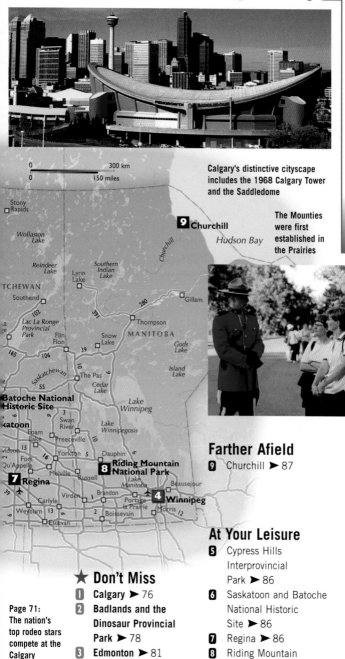

Calgary's distinctive cityscape includes the 1968 Calgary Tower and the Saddledome

The Mounties were first established in the Prairies

0   300 km
0   150 miles

Stony Rapids

Wollaston Lake

Reindeer Lake

Southern Indian Lake

Lynn Lake

9 Churchill

Hudson Bay

TCHEWAN

Southend

102

Lac La Ronge Provincial Park

Flin Flon

Gillam

280

391

Thompson

Snow Lake

MANITOBA

Gods Lake

165

106

39

Saskatchewan

The Pas

Cedar Lake

Island Lake

Batoche National Historic Site

katoon

Foam Lake

Swan River

Preeceville

Lake Winnipeg

55

Lake Winnipegosis

165

vidson

15

Fort Qu'Appelle

16

Yorkton

Dauphin

5

8 Riding Mountain National Park

Farther Afield

Qu'Appelle

Melville

Russell

Lake Manitoba

9 Churchill ➤ 87

7 Regina

39

Carlyle

Virden

1

Brandon

Portage la Prairie

2

Beausejour

4 Winnipeg

Weyburn

13

Boissevain

Morris

12

Estevan

At Your Leisure

5 Cypress Hills Interprovincial Park ➤ 86

6 Saskatoon and Batoche National Historic Site ➤ 86

7 Regina ➤ 86

8 Riding Mountain National Park ➤ 87

★ Don't Miss

1 Calgary ➤ 76

2 Badlands and the Dinosaur Provincial Park ➤ 78

3 Edmonton ➤ 81

4 Winnipeg ➤ 83

Page 71:
The nation's top rodeo stars compete at the Calgary Stampede

Explore the history in the Prairies, from the world's best Dinosaur graveyard to reminders of pioneer days, and enjoy some unique modern cities too.

The Prairies in Five Days

Day One

Morning In ❶**Calgary** (➤ 76–77), rain or shine, head straight for the **Glenbow Museum** (below) to see the amazing First Nations galleries. Afterward wander down to the river for a stroll around Eau Claire Market.

Lunch There are plenty of options in the market area for lunch

Afternoon Choose between the **Heritage Park Historic Village** and **Calgary Zoo**, depending on your personal preference.

Evening Watch the sun go down from the top of the **Calgary Tower**, then take in some Western-style food and entertainment.

Day Two

Morning Drive out to Drumheller (right) and spend the rest of the morning at the **Royal Tyrrell Museum** (➤ 80).

Lunch at the museum restaurant; if it's nice out sit on the terrace overlooking the ❷**Badlands** (➤ 78–80).

Afternoon Set out to drive the 48km (29-mile) Dinosaur Trail and visit the Royal Tyrrell Museum's Field Station in the ❷**Dinosaur Provincial Park** (➤ 78–80)

Evening Drive up to ❸**Edmonton** (➤ 81–82) and spend the night there.

Day Three

Morning Take the Historic Streetcar down to the **Old Strathcona District** and explore its historic streets.

Lunch Strathcona has lots of good pubs and restaurants for lunch

Afternoon Head out to **West Edmonton Mall** (right) for a retail experience and maybe some thrill rides at Galaxyland.

Evening Stay at the mall for dinner and a movie.

Day Four

Morning Explore the **River Valley Parks** and the Muttart Conservatory (left).

Lunch Picnic in the park.

Afternoon Spend the afternoon at **Fort Edmonton Park**.

Evening Get an evening flight over to 4 **Winnipeg** (➤ 83–85).

Day Five

Morning Go down to **The Forks** and explore the National Historic Site and the Market (or the Children's Museum if you have youngsters with you). Take the Splash Dash Water Bus tour.

Lunch Have lunch in one of the Forks Market restaurants.

Afternoon Take the Riverwalk along to the **Manitoba Legislature** (right), then catch the free shuttle bus up to the Exchange District to view the fine architecture and visit the **Manitoba Museum**.

Evening Head for the **French Quarter**, sample some French cuisine and maybe chill at a jazz club.

❶ Calgary

With the snow-capped peaks of the Rocky Mountains on the western horizon, and vast swaths of prairie stretching away to the east, Calgary, on the banks of the Bow River, draws its character from both sides. It has the grit of a hardy mountain community and just a touch of prairie cowboy culture; it has the buzz of a modern city tempered by a well-defined sense of its own history. This is a city of gleaming high-rise towers that bear witness to its economic prosperity, resulting largely from the discovery of oil in Alberta. Though Edmonton is the provincial capital, this is Alberta's commercial hub.

Even though much of the long-range view is now blocked by taller buildings, it's worth going up the 190m (623-foot) **Calgary Tower**, a city icon built in 1968 and now with a glass floor experience. On the ground, it's easy to get around this compact, flat city and its light-rail system is free downtown.

Sooner or later, you'll wind up by the river, where **Eau Claire Market** is a bustling area of fresh produce stands, specialty stores and entertainment venues. On an artificial island in the river, **Prince's Island** is a wonderful oasis of formal gardens, lawns and woodland that's home to raccoons, coyotes and other wild urban creatures.

In the heart of downtown, the **Glenbow Museum** is one of the most important museums in North America, with renowned First Nations exhibits, tracing the history and culture of those who lived here before the Europeans arrived. The other 19 galleries cover pioneers, the Métis uprising, military history, world ethnography and more.

There's living history at the **Heritage Park Historic Village**, south of the city, with more than 150 buildings re-creating life here in the early 20th century. On the eastern side of the city is the superb 32ha (79-acre) **Calgary Zoo**, with an excellent record for wildlife conservation.

Opposite: Eau Claire Market is a colorful part of the city

The Calgary Stampede recalls the land-grabs of pioneer days

Calgary Stampede
Many people visit Calgary for one reason alone, and that is to attend the Calgary Stampede (tel: 403/261-0101 or 800/661-1260; www.calgarystampede.com) in July. The world-famous event recalls the days when land was up for grabs to the first settler to stake a claim. The Stampede is a week of rodeo events, Western entertainment and wagon races, with a frontier town, Indian Village and gambling hall on the Stampede Grounds, and a great party atmosphere throughout the city.

TAKING A BREAK

Try the "cowboy cuisine" at **Buzzards** on 10 Avenue (tel: 403/264-6959; $–$$) or **The Ranchman** on McLeod Trail South (tel: 403/253-1100; $–$$); the latter has rodeo memorabilia and entertainment to add to the atmosphere.

✚ 203 E2

Tourism Calgary
✉ 200, 238–11 Avenue SE ☎ 403/263-8510 or 800/661-1678; www.tourismcalgary.com

Calgary Tower
✉ 101 9th Avenue; 403/266-7171; www.calgarytower.com ⏰ Mid-May to Sep daily 7:30am–11pm; Oct to mid-May 9am–11pm 💰 Moderate

Eau Claire Market
✉ 202, 200 Barclay Parade SW ☎ 403/264-6450; www.eauclairemarket.com ⏰ Mon–Sat 10–6 (to 8 Thu and Fri), Sun and holidays 11–5

Glenbow Museum
✉ 130 9th Avenue SE ☎ 403/268-4100; www.glenbow.org ⏰ Daily 9–5 (also 5–9pm Thu) 💰 Expensive

Heritage Park Historic Village
✉ 1900 Heritage Drive SW ☎ 403/268-8500; www.heritagepark.ab.ca ⏰ Late May–early Sep daily 9–5; mid-Sep to mid-Oct weekends only 💰 Expensive 🚈 LRT Heritage, then park shuttle

Calgary Zoo
✉ 1300 Zoo Road NE ☎ 403/232-9300; www.calgaryzoo.org ⏰ Daily 9–6 (last admission 5) 💰 Expensive

CALGARY: INSIDE INFO

Top tips Make reservations a long way in advance if you're visiting during or for the **Calgary Stampede**. The city fills up very quickly.

• If you are visiting Calgary as a prelude to a vacation in the Rockies, buy your **mountain clothing and footwear** here – it's much less expensive than in Banff.

• Calgary has more than 300km (180 miles) of **pathways** linking major downtown sights and outlying areas, and you can rent bicycles and rollerblades to explore them. Maps are available from the tourist offices and bicycle shops.

2 Badlands and the Dinosaur Provincial Park

Amid the lush prairies, the Badlands are a startling, desolate area almost devoid of vegetation, where the bedrock has been eroded into strange shapes and the land is cut through by deep, twisting canyons. Small wonder that it was considered "bad" by just about everyone from the First Nations to the early settlers. Everyone, that is, except for paleontologists.

In 1883 J. B. Tyrrell stumbled quite by chance across some dinosaur bones here and subsequent excavations, particularly in Dead Lodge Canyon, revealed this to be one of the richest sources of dinosaur fossils in the world. More than 300 complete skeletons have been uncovered here, and the land is still giving up its hoard of treasures.

In 1955 the 73sq km (28 square mile) **Dinosaur Provincial Park** was created to protect the area from the attentions of unauthorized fossil hunters and in 1980 it was declared a UNESCO World Heritage Site. The **Field Station**, an outpost of the Royal Tyrrell Museum (► 80) within the park, is the summer base for paleontologists, and though it is impractical for visitors to be present at the actual excavation site, you can view their meticulous work on new finds in their laboratory. The station has an information point and bookstore, good interpretive displays and a program of summer lectures. The bus tours of the Badlands are highly recommended, offering an excellent view of the landscape, together with explanations of the geological formations.

Opposite: the Royal Tyrrell Museum has superb displays of dinosaur skeletons from the Badlands

---

✚ 203 F2

Drumheller Regional Chamber of Development and Tourism
✉ 60 First Avenue West, Drumheller
☎ 403/823-8100, 1-866/823-8100;
www.traveldrumheller.com

Field Station Visitor Centre
☎ 403/378-4342 ⏰ Late May–early Sep daily 8:30am–9pm; early Sep–early Oct 9–4.30. Winter hours vary, so call ahead ❓ Shop 🍴 Café May–Oct 💲 Inexpensive (May–Oct); free in winter

Atlas Coal Mine National Historic Site
✉ East Coulee ☎ 403/822-2220; www.atlas-coalmine.ab.ca ⏰ May–Jun daily 9:30–5:30; Jul–Aug 9:30–8:30; Sep–Oct 10–5 💲 Moderate

Royal Tyrrell Museum
✉ Highway 838, Midland Provincial Park, Drumheller ☎ 403/823-7707, precede number with 310-0000 for toll-free (in Alberta only) or 1-888/440-4240 (toll-free throughout North America); www.tyrrellmuseum.com ⏰ Late May to early Sep daily 9–9; early Sep to late May Tue–Sun 10–5 💲 Expensive

Centrosaurus

Centrosaurus was a powerful ceratopsian, with a single long horn on its snout. It may have lived in herds for protection, since Centrosaurus probably died in large herds. Dinosaurs very often met such tragedy, the remains of those that perished into their waters.

Aside from the bus tours, the easiest way to see the park is on the 48km (30-mile) **Dinosaur Trail**, a circular route from Drumheller that passes a number of attractions, including the the **Atlas Coal Mine National Historic Site**, a relic of the mining history of the area, and **Horsethief Canyon**, where 19th-century rustlers hid stolen horses. The canyon offers spectacular views, and paths lead to petrified oyster beds, from the days when these rocks were beneath the ocean. The shorter **Hoodoo Trail** along Highway 10 explores the otherworldly rock stacks known as hoodoos, with their multicolored strata and mushroom-shaped caps.

No tour of the Badlands is complete without a visit to the **Royal Tyrrell Museum** at Drumheller. This superlative institution, in a sleek modern building, contains the best dinosaur and fossil collection in the world, with almost 40 complete skeletons. Other displays include re-creations of the marine world that once covered Alberta and B.C., a Burgess Shale exhibit, with models of some of the weirdest creatures you could imagine, and a Cretaceous Garden.

Hoodoos add an otherworldly appearance to the Badlands

TAKING A BREAK

There's a large cafeteria at the **Royal Tyrrell Museum**, with a terrace overlooking the Badlands.

BADLANDS AND DINOSAUR PROVINCIAL PARK: INSIDE INFO

Top tips You'll need sturdy **footwear** for walking the park's rough terrain.
• If you don't have a **tour reservation**, tickets are issued on a first come, first served basis at the Field Station at 8:30 each morning. Tours are always oversubscribed at peak times, and a reservation limit of one tour per day and four tickets per credit card booking is imposed. However, it's always worth checking at the Field Station to see if there are any spare places available.
• It's against the law to **remove fossils** from the park.
• Don't visit the Badlands at all if the **weather** is, or has recently been wet – the heavy clay turns into a quagmire underfoot.

3 Edmonton

Seen from a distance, the high-rise buildings of downtown Edmonton emerge from a sea of green formed by the largest series of urban parks in North America. Close up you will discover century-old buildings and historic neighborhoods, excellent museums and a lively cultural scene. In addition, the provincial capital of Alberta is most famous for two things – shopping and festivals.

Begin your exploration of Edmonton with a ride on the **Historic Streetcar**, dating from 1920, which travels south from the 1912 Alberta Legislature building across the North Saskatchewan River to the **Old Strathcona District**. Originally a First Nations settlement, Strathcona became home to European settlers in the late 19th century and flourished during the Klondike Gold Rush. In 1912, it was incor-

West Edmonton Mall offers many diversions besides shopping

porated into the city of Edmonton, but has retained its historic atmosphere, and has lots of antiques shops, specialty stores, a farmers' market, and good pubs and restaurants.

Edmonton's history is portrayed at **Fort Edmonton Park**, the largest living history park in Canada, with original and reconstructed buildings on streets that represent four different eras of the city's history from a First Nations camp to the 1920s. In addition to buildings populated by costumed interpreters, there are steam train, streetcar and carriage rides.

Down on the river are the lush River Valley Parks, extending for 28km (17 miles) along both banks. Here, the four dramatic glass pyramids of the **Muttart Conservatory** replicate four different ecological environments, with spectacular displays of the relevant plants.

Sooner or later all visitors to Edmonton wind up at **West Edmonton Mall**, 9km (5.5 miles) west of downtown. Not only is this the world's biggest shopping mall, with more than 800 stores it includes a number of superlative leisure facilities and attractions, including the world's largest indoor amusement park; the huge World Waterpark, with thrill rides, waterslides and wave pool; the Deep Sea Derby, an indoor lake with bumper boats; and Sea Lions' Rock and Sea Life Caverns. There's also an NHL-size skating rink and countless other activities and entertainments.

One of the glasshouses of the climate-controlled Muttart Conservatory

TAKING A BREAK

Stop in at the Crêperie (tel: 780/4420-6656) at 103 Street for great French cuisine in a cozy atmosphere.

➕ 203 F3

Edmonton Tourism
✉ 9990 Jasper Avenue ☎ 780/401-7696 or 800/463-4667 www.edmonton.com; also at:
✉ 2404 Gateway Boulevard, at entrance to the city, north of Edmonton Airport
☎ 780/496-8400

Historic Streetcar
✉ PO Box 45040, Lansdowne PO
☎ 780/496-1464; www.edmonton-radial-railway.ab.ca 🕐 Victoria Day weekend–Labour Day weekend daily 11–4, (11–10 during the Edmonton Fringe Festival, usually mid-Aug); Labour Day weekend–Thanksgiving Fri–Sun and holidays 10–4 💲 Inexpensive

Fort Edmonton Park
✉ Fox Drive and Whitemud Drive
☎ 780/496-8777; www.ft.edmontonpark.com
🕐 Late May–late Jun Mon–Fri 10–4, Sat–Sun and holidays 10–6; late Jun–Aug daily 10–6; Sep Sun 10–6 💲 Moderate

Muttart Conservatory
✉ 9626-96A Street ☎ 780/496-8755;
www.edmonton.ca/muttart 🕐 Mon–Fri 9–5:30, Sat, Sun 11–5:30 💲 Moderate

West Edmonton Mall
✉ 2472, 8882-170 Street ☎ 780/444-5200 or 800/661-8890; www.westedmonton.com 🕐 Stores: Mon–Sat 10–9, Sun 11–6. Hours vary for other attractions

---

EDMONTON: INSIDE INFO

Top tips West Edmonton Mall has the **largest parking lot** in the world, with 20,000 spaces. Make a note of your lot and entrance number as you enter the mall so you can find your car at the end of the day.
• If you are planning to use the **LRT system** to get around, the $6.75 day pass is excellent value. It can be purchased from vending machines in stations.

In more depth If you would like to **discover more about Edmonton's history**, guided tours for small groups (up to seven people) organized by Peter's Edmonton Tours (tel: 780/469-2641) provide a personal approach. Alternatively, you can take the creepy after-dark Edmonton Ghost Tour around Old Strathcona and hear stories of unearthly events (available Jun–Aug and Oct; tel: 780/469-3187; www.edmontonghosttours.com).

4 Winnipeg

At the geographic center of Canada, Winnipeg, on the Red and Assiniboine rivers, has a cosmopolitan atmosphere and a great cultural mix. It is home to the largest French Canadian community west of Québec, has some splendid architecture, including a fine cathedral, and is economically prosperous, culturally stimulating, historically fascinating and very attractive.

The dignified Manitoba Legislature is topped by the "Golden Boy"

Where the Red and Assiniboine rivers meet you will find **The Forks National Historic Site**, a historic First Nations meeting place where people still congregate. The 5ha (13-acre) park includes a preserved Aboriginal settlement that's thousands of years old and has many displays charting historical events. It is also home to the **Forks Market**, housing specialty food stores, craft shops and restaurants. Open-air concerts and street theater take place on the Market Plaza and Festival Park. The Manitoba Children's Museum and the Manitoba Theatre for Young People are also here. The Forks is also to be the site of the Canadian Museum for Human Rights, and its stunning building work is under way.

From The Forks, you can get a tour boat, or take a stroll along the Riverwalk. This leads to the **Manitoba Legislature Building**, topped by the city's much-loved icon, the "Golden Boy" statue. Head north up Memorial Boulevard from here and you'll reach the **Winnipeg Art Gallery**, an artistic life-force. The Gallery promotes art in all its forms, and has a lively program of international exhibitions to complement its extensive permanent collection. It contains the largest public collection of Inuit art in the world and has more than 22,500 items in its possession, from a 5th-century Roman bust to 20th-century video art.

The **Exchange District** is a National Historic Site, the early 20th-century heart of the city and its modern commercial hub, where magnificent terra-cotta architecture blends with modern office towers. Here you will find the main theaters and concert halls and the excellent **Manitoba Museum**. Its galleries provide a fascinating walk-through experience of the province's history, from the southern prairies to the frozen north. A star attraction is the replica of the 17th-century ketch, *Nonsuch*, which opened up the trading route to Hudson's Bay. There's also a science gallery with more than 100 interactive exhibits and a planetarium show. Winnipeg's multicultural heritage is also in evidence in the Exchange District, in the Ukrainian Cultural Centre, the Scots Memorial and the Dynasty Building at the heart of the Chinese community.

The Museum of Manitoba has some good dioramas, here featuring a York boat

Opposite: This mural in the Exchange District is part of an anti-graffiti campaign that has brightened the city streets with art works

Across the Red River from The Forks, the **French Quarter** comes complete with French street names, Parisian-style cafés and jazz clubs. At its heart is **St.-Boniface Cathedral**, built in 1968 to replace the original Gothic structure, of which traces remain. Its cemetery contains the graves of many important Francophone citizens, including Louis Riel (1844–85), seen by Manitobans as the founder of the province. The **St.-Boniface Museum** close by tells the story of the rise of the Métis (people of mixed French and First Nations blood).

TAKING A BREAK

Head up to the **Brio Restaurant** (tel: 204/948-0085; $) at the Winnipeg Art Gallery; in summer the rooftop sculpture garden is open for a panoramic view over the city. Or choose from the eclectic range of eateries at the **Forks Market**.

✠ 205 E1

Tourism Winnipeg
✉ 259 Portage Avenue ☎ 204/943-1970
or 1-800-665-0204 (toll-free in North
America; www.destinationwinnipeg.ca
🕐 Mon–Fri 8:30–4:30

Winnipeg Art Gallery
✉ 300 Memorial Boulevard ☎ 204/786-
6641; www.wag.mb.ca 🕐 Tue–Sun 11–5
(also Wed 5–9pm) 💷 Moderate

Manitoba Museum
✉ 190 Rupert Avenue ☎ 204/956-2830;
www.manitobamuseum.ca 🕐 Late
May–early Sep daily 10–5; early Sep to
late May Tue–Fri 10–4, Sat–Sun and
holidays 11–5 💷 Moderate; extra charge
for Science Gallery and Planetarium:
both moderate

St.-Boniface Cathedral
✉ 190 Avenue de la Cathédral ☎ 204/233-
7304 🕐 Late Mar to mid-May Mon–Fri 9–5,
Sun noon–4; mid-May to Sep Mon–Fri 9–5
💷 Free

St.-Boniface Museum
✉ 494 Avenue Tache ☎ 204/237-4500;
www.franco-manitobain.org 🕐 Late Mar to
mid-May Mon–Fri 9–5, Sun noon–4; mid-May
to Sep Mon–Fri 9–5, Sat 10–4, Sun and holidays 10–8; Oct to mid-Nov Mon–Fri 9–5, Sun
noon–4; mid-Nov to mid-Mar Mon–Fri 9–5
💷 Inexpensive

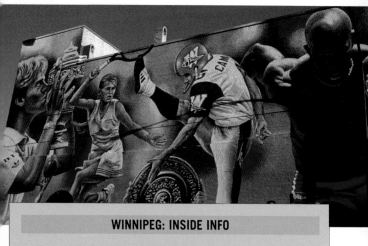

WINNIPEG: INSIDE INFO

Top tips Winnipeg's **Downtown Watch ambassadors,** in red and black uniforms,
are there to offer assistance to visitors; just stop one of them on the street.
• Downtown Spirit is a **free shuttle bus** that operates three routes and links all
major attractions except the French Quarter. Nos. 1 and 2 run Mon–Fri
11–3.30, Sat 11–5.30, Sun noon–5.30; No. 3 runs Mon–Fri 7–7, Sat 11–7.

Hidden gem As you walk around Winnipeg, look for the **100 or so murals**
created as part of an anti-graffiti, clean city campaign.

In more depth To learn more about the history of the French community, you
could attend the unusual **Theatre in the Cemetery,** (Jul–Aug Wed–Fri 2, 4 and
7pm. Call 204/233-8343 or 866/808-8338.

At Your Leisure

Old-style harvest re-created in Saskatoon

5 Cypress Hills Interprovincial Park

Rising some 600m (1,970 feet) from the surrounding prairie, the Cypress Hills form the highest landmass between the Rockies and Labrador. Canada's only interprovincial park, spanning the Alberta-Saskatchewan boundary, it covers 18,400ha (45,450 acres) of lush forests, open grassland and an alpine environment that is home to rare wild flowers. A herd of elk is being reestablished here. The **Fort Walsh National Historic Site**, the restored birthplace of the Royal Canadian Mounted Police, founded during the 19th century to stamp out whiskey smuggling, is populated with costumed guides. The still unpaved **Gap Road**, much as it was when the original Mounties use it, is one of the park's main attractions.

Tourist information
🛏 203 F1 ✉ Elkwater, Alberta
☎ 403/893-3833; Loch Leven, Saskatchewan; 306/662-5411; www.cypresshills.com

Fort Walsh National Historic Site
✉ Maple Creek, Saskatchewan
☎ 306/662-3590; www.cypresshills.com or www.pc.gc.ca 🕐 Mid-May to Sep daily 9:30–5:30 (tel: 306/622-2645 for winter schedule) 💰 Moderate

6 Saskatoon and Batoche National Historic Site

Saskatoon, amid the vast prairies, is a small, friendly city with a low-key atmosphere and a lively arts scene. Its riverbanks are lined by pleasant gardens and woodland populated in summer by pelicans. The **Wanuskewin Heritage Park**, 5km (3 miles) north, depicts the lives of Northern Plains tribes.

A little way north is the **Batoche National Historic Site**, a preserved village with costumed guides that was central to the Métis rebellion of 1885. The Métis, a mixed French and First Nations population, were quelled with much loss of life.

Tourism Saskatoon
🛏 204 B2 ✉ 6-305 Idylwyld Drive N, Saskatoon ☎ 306/242-1206 or 1-800/567-2444; www.tourismsaskatoon.com

Wanuskewin Heritage Park
🛏 204 B2 ✉ RR4 ☎ 306/931-6767 or 1-877/547-6546; www.wanuskewin. com 🕐 Daily 9–9 (closes at 5 fall and winter) 💰 Moderate

Batoche National Historic Site
🛏 204 C1 ✉ 25km (15 miles) east of Rosthern, Saskatchewan ☎ 306/423-6227; www.pc.gc.ca 🕐 Early May–Sep daily 9–5 💰 Moderate

7 Regina

Saskatchewan's capital city looms large on the horizon, its skyscrapers jutting up out of the flat land. It's main claim to fame is as the one-time headquarters of the Mounties, and though their HQ moved to Ottawa in 1920, the **RCMP Training Academy** remained here. A prestigious multi-million dollar Heritage Centre, illustrating the history and role of the RCMP, opened here in 2007. Most of the other main attractions are within

the **Wascana Centre**, one of Canada's largest urban parks.
⊞ 204 C1

Tourism Regina
✉ Highway 1, eastern entrance
☎ 306/789-5099 or 1-800-661-5099 ⏰ Victoria Day to Labour Day Mon–Fri 8–7, Sat–Sun and holidays 10–6; Labour Day to Victoria Day Mon–Fri 8:30–4:30

🎱 Riding Mountain National Park

This is an area of rolling hills rather than spectacular peaks, with huge meadows of fescue grassland merging into forest, supporting a wide range of animals and 733 species of plants. It contains some of the best hiking trails in the province, and Clear Lake is the focus of summer watersports.

Visitor Centre
⊞ 205 D1 ✉ Wasagaming
☎ 204/848-7275; www.pc.gc.ca
⏰ Jul–Aug daily 9:30–8; Sep–Jun 9:30–5:30 💵 Day pass: moderate

The RCMP Musical Ride, based in Ottawa, is often performed in Regina too, and at other events across Canada

Farther Afield

🎱 Churchill

The little town of Churchill, in the far north of Manitoba, has a population of just 3,000 and is surrounded by tundra, and if it were not for one thing, no tourist would ever make the long journey here. The thing that draws visitors is the chance to see polar bears in the only place where they exist side by side with humans. The bears congregate here in summer, but the best time to see them is in October and November when the ice starts to form on Hudson's Bay, giving them access to water and food. "Tundra buggy" tours offer safe, close-up views.

In addition to the polar bears, there are beluga whales and seals and great herds of caribou that migrate through the region twice a year. The **Wapusk National Park** to the southeast, protects important polar bear denning areas and waterfowl migration environments and the mighty **Prince of Wales Fort** can be visited too.
⊞ 205 E4

Parks Canada Visitor Reception Centre
✉ PO Box 127, Churchill ☎ 204/675-8863; www.pc.gc.ca ⏰ Mon–Fri 8:30–4:30 (Oct–Nov also 4:30–8:30)

For Kids

• **Day camps** are a great way to get kids involved and meeting other kids. The Royal Tyrrell Museum organizes special programs for children, including hiking into the Badlands to investigating real dinosaur remains, sleepovers in the Dinosaur Hall, and day camps (tel: 403/823-7707; www.tyrrellmuseum.com).
• Near Calgary, Calaway Park is western Canada's largest **amusement park**, with thrill rides, gentle fun for youngsters and live shows (tel: 403/240-3822; www.calawaypark. com)
• **Water parks** are always popular. Winnipeg's Fun Mountain has waterslides, pools, a hot tub, bumper boats, mini-golf and picnic areas (tel: 204/255-3910; www.funmountain.ca), while at Carlyle in Saskatchewan Kenosee Superslide includes a terrifying eight-story "free-fall" among its 10 water slides (tel: 306/577-2343; www.kenoseesuperlides.com).

Where to... Stay

Prices

High season room only rates, based on two sharing a double room, excluding taxes

$ under $160   **$$** $160-$300   **$$$** more than $300

CALGARY

▼▼▼ Calgary Westways $-$$

A historic home with cozy accommodations and a Victorian theme, plus modern amenities like free internet access and private bathrooms with jetted tubs.

🕂 203 E2 ⊠ 216 25th Avenue S.W. ☎ 403/229-1758, 866/846-7038; www.westways.ab.ca

▼▼▼ Hotel Arts $-$$

Calgary's newest boutique hotel – chic, stylish and very luxurious. Rooms are in restful coffee and chocolate tones with warm lighting, luxury fabrics, goose-down duvets and contemporary furniture (choose a top-floor Jacuzzi Suite for total indulgence). Food is a highlight too, with a top-class restaurant and Raw Bar. Weekend rates are particularly reasonable (outside of Stampede time).

🕂 203 E2 ⊠ 119 12th Avenue S.W. ☎ 403/266-4611 or 1-800/661-9378; www.hotelarts.ca

DRUMHELLER

▼▼ Taste the Past Bed and Breakfast $

Dennis and Denise Simon offer cozy bed and breakfast in this delightful heritage home in downtown Drumheller. Antique furniture and bright, cheerful en-suite rooms set the scene, and breakfast is included.

🕂 203 F2 ⊠ 281 2nd Street ☎ 403/823-5889

EDMONTON

▼▼▼ Fantasyland $$-$$$

This West Ed Mall hotel offers a unique combination of luxury and fun. Though most of its 355 rooms are standard hotel style, there are 120 unrestrained theme rooms depicting Ancient Rome, the African Jungle, Polynesia, the Wild West and more. Comfort is not compromised, even when your bed is in a stagecoach, a simulated igloo or a pick-up truck.

🕂 203 F1 ⊠ 17700 87th Avenue ☎ 780/444-3000, 800/737-3783; www.fantasylandhotel.com

▼▼▼ Union Bank Inn $$

A 1911 bank building imaginatively converted into a chic boutique hotel. Stylish rooms have goose-down comforters and some bathrooms have jet tubs. Extras include Reece bathrobes, and complimentary cheese and wine. The restaurant serves renowned regional cuisine.

🕂 203 F1 ⊠ 10053 Jasper Avenue ☎ 780/423-3600, 888/423-3601; www.unionbankinn.com

WINNIPEG

▼▼ Place Louis Riel $

Winnipeg's only all-suite hotel offers spacious accommodations, each unit with sitting area, separate, kitchen, bathroom, cable TV, internet access, video games and voice mail. There are one- and two-bedroom options too, plus penthouse "Cloud Nine" suites. Works by First Nations artists adorn the walls. There's a restaurant, store and gym. There is a small charge for parking.

🕂 205 E1 ⊠ 190 Smith Street ☎ 204/947-6961, 800/665-0569; fax: 204/947-3029; www.placelouisriel.com

Where to...
Eat and Drink

Prices

Based on the cost of a three-course dinner, excluding drinks and service

$ under $30   **$$** $30–$50   **$$$** more than $50

CHURCHILL

🍷 Polar Inn & Suites $–$$

On the main street, the Polar Inn is a comfortable, convenient base for polar bear and tundra experiences. Spacious rooms and suites have climate control, cable TV, hair dryers and complimentary tea and coffee, and units with kitchens are also available. There's a gift shop with cold-weather clothing and souvenirs.

🛏 205 E4 🖂 153 Kelsey Boulevard
☎ 204/675-8878, 877/765-2733;
www.polarinn.com

SASKATOON

🍷 Country Inn & Suites $

Nonsmoking hotel whose rooms and suites are decorated in cozy country style and each with cable TV and excellent facilities. It's just 5km (3 miles) from downtown.

🛏 204 B2 🖂 617 Cynthia Street
☎ 306/934-3900, 1-888/201-1746;
www.countryinns.com

CALGARY

🍷🍷🍷 La Dolce Vita $$

In typical Italian style, this restaurant caters to the whole family. Upstairs is an informal place where you can take the children, while the downstairs restaurant provides a more formal setting for a romantic dinner for two. The decor is chic and continental, with Italian paintings, and the menu features fresh pasta, veal and seafood prepared to traditional Italian recipes.

🛏 203 E2 🖂 916 1st Avenue Northeast; ☎ 403/263-3445
🕐 Mon–Fri 11:30–2, 5:30–10.30, Sat 5:30–11. Closed Sun

🍷🍷 Brewsters Brewing Company $–$$

With 11 locations in Alberta and Saskatchewan, this is Canada's largest brewpub chain, but every site has its own onsite brewery turning out up to 12 hand-crafted ales. This one is a huge brick building with tables out on the sidewalk in summer. There's a long menu of pub favorites, including "hand-crafted" burgers, thin-crust pizza, steaks and more exotic choices, such as Thai green curry.

🛏 203 E2 🖂 834 11th Avenue S.W.
☎ 403/265-2739;
www.brewsterbrewingco.com
🕐 Daily 11am–midnight

🍷 Nellie's Kitchen $

Fabulous home-cooked breakfasts, available throughout the day, are a highlight of this busting diner, which is particularly popular on weekends. The selections include omelets, french toast and pancakes and there are good lunch options on the menu, too. It's worth a detour just to sample their delicious home-made banana bread.

🛏 203 E2 🖂 738B 17th Avenue S.W.
☎ 403/244-4616 🕐 Daily 7:30am–3:30pm (from 8am Sat–Sun)

EDMONTON

🍷🍷 Da-De-O New Orleans Diner & Bar $

On trendy Whyte Avenue, sample an authentic taste of the South. Retro decor includes booths with jukeboxes and the food is pure Cajun, including hearty jambalaya.

🛏 203 F3 🖂 10548A Whyte Avenue
☎ 780/433-0930; www.dadeo.ca
🕐 Mon–Tue and Thu–Sat 11:30–11 (midnight Fri and Sat) Sun noon–10

La Ronde $$–$$$

Perched on the top floor of the Château Lacombe hotel, this is Alberta's first revolving restaurant, with a spectacular view over the city and a menu of creative regional Canadian dishes. You might start with bison consommé with hempseed dumplings or maple-smoked Atlantic salmon, followed by organic rabbit ragout or roasted wild boar bacon ragout or roasted Arctic char with a lemon caper butter sauce. All of the ingredients used in the restaurant are sourced locally from family farms.

⊞ 203 F3 ⊠ 10111 Bellamy Hill
☎ 780/428-6611, 800/661-8801;
www.chateaulacombe.com ◷ Daily
5:30–10:30, Sun also 10:30am–2pm

The Creperie $

You get an idea of what to expect here from the name, but you may not be prepared for the interesting combinations of crêpe fillings, such as chicken, shrimp and fruit cocktail in a curry cream sauce. There are dishes other than crêpes on the menu, including seafood, filet mignon and chicken à la Florentina. It's worth holding back a little to save room for the heavenly chocolate fondue dessert.

⊞ 203 F3 ⊠ 10220 103rd Street
☎ tel: 780/420-6656;
www.thecreperie.com ◷ Tue–Thu
11:30–10, Fri–Sat 5–10, Sun 5–9

Amici $–$$

This classy, low-lit modern restaurant is a special occasion place, with comfortable upholstered chairs and crisp white linen. Tuscan specialties feature on the daily-changing menu (favorites such as roast quail, linguini with salmon and breast of duck), alongside more exotic choices such as wild boar and bison.

⊞ 205 E1 ⊠ 326 Broadway Avenue
☎ 204/943-4997;
www.amiciwpg.com ◷ Mon–Fri
11:30–2, 5–10, Sat 5–10. Closed Sun

Maxime $

An elegant and very popular restaurant, Maxime is likely to have a mix of couples and families dining on its wide variety of international dishes, which range from sandwiches to succulent steaks. Soft background music adds to the pleasant atmosphere.

⊞ 205 E1 ⊠ 1131 St Mary's Road
☎ 204/257-1521 ◷ Mon–Sat
11am–midnight, Sun 10:30–10

2nd Ave Grill $$

Aimed at an adult clientele, this downtown restaurant attracts the power-lunch crowd during the day and sophisticated couples late at night. That said, the menu has a great range of dishes, from the house specialty soup (wild mushroom and chicken) through interesting salads, sandwiches that come with greens, soup or fries, pasta dishes and stir-fries. Entrées (available after 5pm) might include orange-pistachio crusted salmon, bison tenderloin, sesame seared ahi (tuna), and various steaks. Appetizers are two-for-one after 4pm on Tuesdays.

⊞ 204 B2 ⊠ 10–123 2nd Avenue S.
☎ 306/244-9889;
www.2ndavegrill.com ◷ Mon–Sat
11–11, Sun 5–9

Mediterranean Bistro $$

Big and boisterous, this upscale bistro on the eastern edge of town (just off the TransCanada Highway) has a cool interior in shades of blue, gray and terra-cotta and a long menu of classic European favorites – calamari, bouillabaisse, tiger prawn linguini, beef tenderloin – with some exotic touches in the use of wasabi, chipotle and chili flavorings.

⊞ 204 C1 ⊠ 2589 Quance Street
East ☎ 306/757-1666;
www.medbistro.ca ◷ Mon–Sat 11–3,
5–11, Sun 5–11

Where to... Shop

Though there are vast areas of this region that have little in them bar cattle ranges and wheat fields, the cities offer great shopping. Oil-rich Alberta levies no Provincial Sales Tax, so it's a bargain-hunter's paradise.

CALGARY

With its strong cowboy culture, this is a great place to buy cowboy boots. There are plenty of retailers, but **Alberta Boot** (614 10th Avenue S.W., tel: 403/263-4605; www.albertaboot.com) is the only manufacturer in the province, with 12,000 pairs always in stock, along with Western-style clothing. You can get a Stetson to top off the outfit at **Smithbilt Hats** (1235 10th Avenue SW, tel: 403/244-9131; www.smithbilthats.com). Another highlight is **Eau Claire Market** (200 Barclay Parade, tel: 403/264-6450; www.eauclairemarkets.com), a huge complex that is central to the Calgary experience. Aside from this, the hub of downtown shopping is on Stephen Avenue, where there's a big shopping complex. The **Mission District** has a concentration of upscale stores and **Inglewood** is good for antiques.

EDMONTON

Shopping takes on a whole new dimension in Edmonton, for this is home of the world's biggest shopping mall – **West Edmonton Mall** (▶ 82). The main downtown mall is called **Edmonton City Centre** (2000 10025-102A Avenue N.W., tel: 780/426-8400), which has more than 160 stores, but historic **Strathcona District** is the place for individual boutiques. For locally produced crafts, go to the **Alberta Craft Council** (10186 106 Street, tel: 780/488-6611 or 800/362-7238; www.albertacraft.ab.ca). Antiques-hunters will find more antiques shops here than in any other Canadian city; the largest complex in the country is the **Old Strathcona Antique Mall** (7614 Gateway Boulevard, tel: 780/433-0398), with more than 200 vendors.

WINNIPEG

Shopping here centers on the **Forks Market** (201 One Forks Market Road, tel: 204/942-6302), with a wonderful array of food stands and local arts and crafts. Good areas to look for individual stores include **Corydon Avenue, Osborne Village** and the **Exchange District**, while **Academy Road** has designer fashions and gourmet food stores. For art and crafts, check out the **Bayat Gallery** (163 Stafford Street, tel: 204/475-5873), one of Canada's largest and finest galleries for Inuit works from the Arctic regions.

SASKATOON

The main downtown mall here is **Midtown Plaza** (1st Avenue and 21st Street, tel: 306/653-8844), with more than 130 stores, or visit the **Broadway District**, with its independent storekeepers and specialty stores. First Nations items are available at the **Wanuskewin Heritage Park Gift Shop** (Wanuskewin Road and Highway 11, tel: 306/931-6767) or **The Trading Post** (226 2nd Avenue South, tel: 306/653-1769). **Riverhouse Gallery** (308 Spadina Crescent West, tel: 306/933-2399) has artists in residence.

REGINA

The heart of Regina's downtown shopping is located around **Market Square** and **Albert Street**. The **Cornwall Centre** is the biggest mall, but for more interesting retail experience, wander round **Cathedral Village** or the Old Warehouse District with their individual types of stores.

Where to...
Be Entertained

The Prairies are more than the country music capital of Canada, and cultural institutions include the Calgary Opera, Opera Saskatchewan and the Alberta Ballet, the Edmonton, Regina and Winnipeg symphony orchestras and the Manitoba Theatre for Young People. In the world of sport, try to get to a rodeo (Canadian Cowboys' Association, tel: 306/931-2700 for information). There are *Where* magazines for Edmonton, Calgary and Winnipeg, and Calgary's *Straight* is a weekly paper with listings.

CALGARY

This is a lively town, with plenty of entertainment and nightlife. Its magnificent **Epcor Centre for the Performing Arts** (205 8th Avenue S.E., tel: 403/294-7455) includes a 1,800-seat concert hall and five theaters, and there's the **Southern Alberta Jubilee Auditorium** (1415 14th Avenue N.W., tel: 403/297-8000), home to the Alberta Ballet and Calgary Opera. For live rock and blues go to **Woody's Taphouse** (225–4307 130 Avenue SE, tel: 403/257-1666), and the **Back Alley Nightclub** (4630 Macleod Trial, tel: 403/287-2500).

The **Calgary Flames** are the NHL hockey team, or you can catch some football with the **Calgary Stampeders**. Don't look for them at

Stampede Park though, because this is the race track (2300 Stampede Trail S.E., tel: 403/261-0214).

EDMONTON

Edmonton's **Francis Winspear Centre for Music** (4 Sir Winston Churchill Square, tel: 780/428-1414 or 800/563-5081) is a world-class concert hall, home of the Edmonton Symphony, and the big **Northern Alberta Jubilee Auditorium** (11455 87 Avenue N.W., tel: 780/427-2760), has a full and varied program. One of Canada's foremost arts facilities, the **Citadel Theatre** (9828 101A Avenue, tel: 780/425-1820), comprises three theaters and a theater school. Jazz fans should head for the **Yardbird Suite** (10,203 86 Avenue N.W., tel: 780/432-0428).

For sport, check out the **Edmonton Oilers** hockey team, the **Trappers** baseball team and the **Edmonton Eskimos** football team.

There are a remarkable number of first-class entertainment facilities in this cultured city, including the **Canwest Global Performing Arts Centre** (2 Forks Market Road, tel: 204/942-8898 or 877/871-6897) and the **Centennial Concert Hall** (555 Main Street, tel: 204/956-2792). Theaters include the historic **Burton Cummings Theatre** (364 Smith Street, tel: 204/956-5656), the **Manitoba Theatre Centre** (174 Market Avenue, tel: 204/942-6537 or 877/446-4500), the lavish **Pantages Playhouse** (180 Market Avenue, tel: 204/989-2889) and **Winnipeg Jewish Theatre** (123 Doncaster Boulevard, tel: 204/477-7478). An open-air **Shakespeare** season is imaginatively staged on a vast downtown rooftop (tel: 204/957-1753).

For sport seek out the **Manitoba Moose** for hockey, the **Winnipeg Blue Bombers** for football and **Assiniboia Downs** race track.

Ontario

Getting Your Bearings

Ontario stretches for 1,600km (1,000 miles) from the tundra around Hudson's Bay in the north to the vineyards of the south, and the landscapes in between are enormously varied. Water plays a great part – the province borders on all but one of the Great Lakes and there are countless smaller bodies of water. The Ottawa River forms part of the border with Québec and the mighty St. Lawrence links Lake Ontario with the open sea far away to the east.

A blazing sun goes down over the Thousand Islands

Most of the population clusters in the south, where there are two capital cities – the national capital, Ottawa, and the provincial capital, Toronto. Unusually, it is the national capital that gets overshadowed. Toronto is not only much bigger (Canada's largest city, in fact), but it's the financial, entertainment and shopping capital of the country and an exciting place to visit. Ottawa is altogether more cozy, but the government buildings by the wide Ottawa River give it more than a touch of grandeur, the National Gallery of Art is a magnificent institution, and the compact, low-rise downtown is a delight.

Ontario also has the most famous waterfall in the world (Niagara) and the only theme park in Canada that comes anywhere near to Disney (Canada's Wonderland). But the province is not all brash tourist attractions. It has some beautiful scenery, notably the Thousand Islands, Georgian Bay and the Algonquin Provincial Park, and there are many charming and interesting rural towns in its heartland.

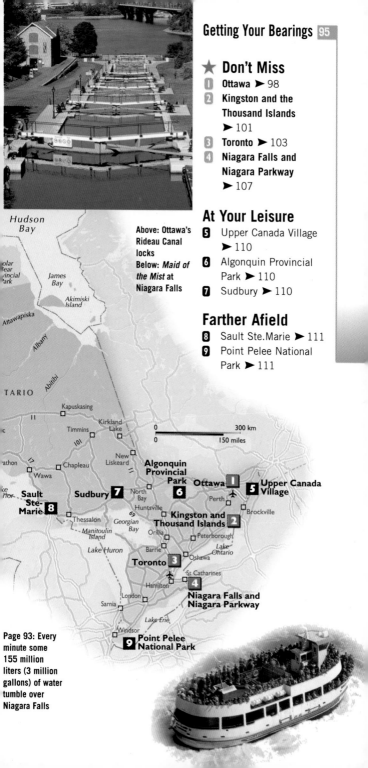

★ Don't Miss

At Your Leisure

Farther Afield

Above: Ottawa's Rideau Canal locks

Below: *Maid of the Mist* at Niagara Falls

Page 93: Every minute some 155 million liters (3 million gallons) of water tumble over Niagara Falls

From the national capital to the provincial capital, via the beautiful Thousand Islands, then on to Canada's most famous natural attraction – Niagara Falls.

Ontario in Five Days

Day One

Morning Start in ❶ **Ottawa** (➤ 98–100). Take a walk around the **Canadian Parliament Buildings** on your way to the **National Gallery of Canada**. Get a cup of coffee at the Cafétéria des Beaux-Arts, with a great river view, then stroll across town to explore **Byward Market** (left).

Lunch The Blue Cactus in Bayard Market (tel: 613/241-7061, ➤ 113) has a wide choice of light and more filling lunch dishes.

Afternoon Spend the whole afternoon at the **Canadian Museum of Civilization**, across the river in Gatineau, Québec.

Evening Catch a performance of the **sound-and-light show** that is projected onto the central façade of the Parliament Buildings (check which time your preferred language – French or Engligh – is featured).

Day Two

Morning Drive south from Ottawa on Highway 416 to the junction with Highway 401. Turn west on the 401, following the St. Lawrence River, to Gananoque. Take a cruise (right) around the beautiful ❷ **Thousand Islands** (➤ 101–102; Gananoque Boat Lines, tel: 613/382-2144).

Lunch Have lunch at Muskie Jakes Tap and Grill at the waterside Gananoque Inn (tel: 613/382-2165, $$).

Afternoon Continue west to ❷ **Kingston** (➤ 101–102) and take the **Confederation Trolley tour** (tel: 613/548-4453 or 888/855-4555) for a 50-minute overview of this lovely lakeside city. After that, visit **Fort Henry** for a living history experience.

Evening Catch a show at the historic Grand Theatre (tel: 613/530-2050) or take to the water for a dinner cruise (tel: 613/549-5544).

Day Three

Morning Continue west on Highway 401 to ❸ Toronto (➤ 103–106). Abandon your car and do all your city travel by métro and streetcar. Explore the stores and galleries of the **Harbourfront Centre** and **Queen's Quay Terminal** (left).

Lunch Have lunch at one of the restaurants in Queen's Quay Terminal, overlooking the lake.

Afternoon Head north to Dundas Street West to visit the wonderful **Art Gallery of Ontario**, then walk down to Nathan Phillips Square and City Hall before continuing to the **Eaton Centre**.

Evening Have an early dinner (of the famous ribs) at the Baton Rouge (tel: 416/593-9667, $$$) in the Eaton Centre, then catch a show in the nearby Theatre District.

Day Four

Morning Still in Toronto, get to the **CN Tower** early and spend an hour up at the top of the world's tallest free-standing structure. Back on the ground, get the ferry to the **Toronto Islands** for magnificent city views.

Lunch Have a picnic in the park on Centre Island.

Afternoon Return to the mainland and visit the **Royal Ontario Museum**.

Evening Experience more of Toronto's nightlife – perhaps a concert, or a comedy show at the famous Second City (tel: 416/343-0011).

Day Five

Morning Take Queen Elizabeth Way west from Toronto to Niagara-on-the-Lake, then follow the ❹ Niagara Parkway to ❹ Niagara Falls (➤ 107–109).

Lunch The lunch bufet at the Table Rock Restaurant (tel: 905/354-3631) offers good-value food and spectacular views of the falls.

Afternoon View the **Horseshoe Falls** from above on Table Rock, then take the **Journey Behind the Falls**. After this, get in line for the *Maid of the Mist*.

Evening Treat yourself to dinner at the Sheraton Fallsview (➤ 113) and see the falls illuminated (right).

❶ Ottawa

Canada's capital city is also one of its loveliest, its downtown area a compact mixture of grand government buildings, superlative museums and galleries, and intimate shopping areas that are full of character. The wide Ottawa River and the Rideau Canal enhance the scene, with pleasure and tour boats in summer and skating in winter.

The **Canadian Parliament Buildings**, commonly referred to as "Parliament Hill," form a High Victorian Gothic set piece with their turrets, towers and copper roofs. They stand in spacious lawns on a bluff high above the Ottawa River and are at their most impressive when seen from the water. Tours include the beautiful renovated library and the Peace Tower, with its splendid view across the city (by law no city building can be higher than this tower). The colorful Changing of the Guard ceremony is a daily event in summer, as are the after-dark sound-and-light shows.

First Nations mask at the Canadian Museum of Civilization

A short distance from Parliament Hill is the architectural masterpiece of the **National Gallery of Canada**, with its gleaming glass walls and glittering prisms allowing natural light to stream in. Not surprisingly, the gallery contains the world's largest collection of Canadian art – over 1,500 works on permanent display – including Inuit and First Nations art, the Group of Seven (▶ 43), religious art of "New France," and naïve murals from Nova Scotia. There are also European and American works, notably Barnett Newman's enormous *Voice of Fire* (1967), simply featuring three huge stripes. Its $11 million price tag is still the cause of some controversy among Canadian tax-payers. At the heart of the gallery is the Rideau Street Chapel, a dramatic presentation of French Canadian religious art, removed here to save it from demolition.

The magnificent **Canadian Museum of Civilization** lies just across the river in **Gatineau**, Québec. The extraordinary building borrows from First Nations traditions in that it has no straight lines and no corners; it also represents the geology of the nation, with fossil-rich Manitoba limestone cladding its façade. Inside, the Grand Hall is the centerpiece, with floor-to-ceiling windows rising 112m (365 feet) high. It houses a fine collection of totems, displays about traditional culture, and six Pacific Coast First Nations houses set against a forest backdrop. The entire hall is overlooked by Bill Reid's magnificent *Spirit of Haida Gwaii* sculpture. The Canada Hall uses actual-size buildings to reveal the nation's history, sometimes aided by costumed actors. It includes a Maritimes shipyard, a whaling station, a Prairies church and a French Canadian town square, complete with authentic artifacts and furniture.

Totems tower over visitors in the Canadian Museum of Civilization

The federal government buildings sit high above the Ottawa River on Parliament Hill

A new national museum opened in Ottawa in May 2005. The **Canadian War Museum**, in a superb building by the river, west of Parliament Hill, illustrates this peace-loving country's military history, going back to wars between First Nations tribes and the early struggle for supremecy between the French and British. The two world wars and subsequent peace-keeping missions are covered, and there's a collection of hardware, including tanks and airplanes.

To experience the atmosphere of the city, visit the **Byward Market** area – several historic streets around the market building are lined with stands selling fresh fruit and vegetables, crafts and clothing, and interesting little stores. There are plenty of good restaurants, cafés and pubs here too. Throughout the city there are lovely river- and canal-side paths.

TAKING A BREAK

The Café du Musée at the Canadian Museum of Civilization (tel: 819/776-7009, $) has wonderful views across the river toward Parliament Hill.

OTTAWA: INSIDE INFO

Top tips Museum hounds may well find it an advantage to purchase a **Canada's Capital Museums Passport**, from the Capital InfoCentre opposite Parliament Hill. For $30 ($75 for a family of five) it covers 15 national institutions.

Hidden gem In the **National Gallery of Canada**'s Inuit collection, seek out the remarkable *When Days are Long and the Sun Shines into the Night* (1966–69) by Jessie Oonark.

➕ 207 F3

National Capital Commission Infocentre
➕ 217 B1 ✉ 90 Wellington Street
☎ 613/239-5000 or 1-800/465-1867;
www.canadascapital.gc.ca

Parliament Buildings
➕ 217 B1 ✉ Wellington Street;
☎ 800/622-6232; www.parliamenthill.gc.ca
🕐 Mid-May to early Sep daily; closed
Jan 1, Jul 1, Dec 25 📞 Call for information

National Gallery of Canada
➕ 217 B2 ✉ 380 Sussex Drive
☎ 613/990-1985 or 1-800/319-2787;
www.gallery.ca 🕐 May–Sep daily 10–5;

Oct–Apr Tue–Sun (year-round Thu open to 8pm)

Canadian Museum of Civilization
➕ 217 A2 ✉ 100 Laurier Street,Gatineau,
Québec ☎ 819/776-7000 or 1-800/555-5621; www.civilization.ca 🕐 Daily 9–6
(Oct–Apr 5; also Thu 6–9pm) 💲 Expensive

Canadian War Museum
➕ 217 B2 ✉ 1 Vimy Place ☎ 918/776-8600, 1-800/555-5621; www.civilization.ca
🕐 May to early Oct daily 9–6; early Oct to Apr Tue–Sun 9–5 (year-round Thu until 9pm; Jul–early Sep Fri until 9pm). Closed 8–12 Jan, 25 Dec 💲 Expensive ❓ Combined tickets with Canadian Museum of Civilization 🚌 8, 86, 87, 95, 96, 97

2 Kingston and the Thousand Islands

Kingston, in a beautiful location on Lake Ontario, once had aspirations to become the capital of Canada, and though it ultimately lost out to Ottawa, the city has a legacy of fine limestone buildings and stately tree-lined streets that sets it apart from many cities of similar size. Right on the doorstep is one of southern Ontario's loveliest regions – the Thousand Islands – where the wide St. Lawrence River is scenically littered with wooded islands.

Kingston started out as a fur-trading settlement, later became a British military base and dockyard, and a temporary seat of government between 1841 and 1843. The waterfront is still full of interest, with its busy marina, sightseeing boats and the **Marine Museum of the Great Lakes**. Outside you can board the icebreaker, **Alexander Henry** (offering unique bed-and-breakfast accommodations in summer), and nearby is the **Pump House Steam Museum**, with working engines.

The city is still dominated by **Fort Henry**, built between 1832 and 1836 to protect the naval dockyard and the entrance to the Rideau Canal. The fort, staffed by costumed guides, has been magnificently restored to provide a vision of military life

At least a thousand islands dot this lovely stretch of the St. Lawrence

Ontario

in the mid-19th century, and there are wonderful river views.

Close to Kingston, Wolfe Island marks the start of the **Thousand Islands** area, which stretches downstream to Brockville Narrows. No one can agree about the true number of islands here – many of them are little more than a rock – but there is absolutely no dispute regarding its beauty, with pinkish rocks contrasting with the sparkling blue water and deep green of the foliage. Boating is, naturally, the main activity here, and sight seeing trips leave from Kingston, Gananoque Ivy Lea and Rockport. Take your passport with you as the U.S. border runs along the St. Lawrence in mid-stream, so many of the islands are U.S. territory, including the fairy-tale **Boldt Castle**, with a real-life story that is equally as heartbreaking as any fictional tale.

Boldt Castle is as romantic as the tragic story of its past

TAKING A BREAK

In Kingston, call in at the **Sleepless Goat Café** (tel: 613/545-9646, $) on Princess Street; in the Thousand Islands, **Good Time Charley's** (Gananoque, tel: 613/382-3511 or 1-800/267-9145; $) is a smoke-free family restaurant.

KINGSTON AND THE THOUSAND ISLANDS: INSIDE INFO

Top tips Kingston's **Confederation Trolley** departs hourly from Confederation Park, across from City Hall, for a 50-minute sightseeing tour (mid-May to Jun daily 10–5; Jul–early Sep 10–7; early Sep–Thanksgiving 10–2).

Hidden gem Bellevue House on Kingston's Centre Street (tel: 613/545-8666; open Jun–Labour Day daily 9–6; Apr–May and Labour Day–Oct 10–5) is an Italian villa. Costumed guides present the house as it was in 1848.

✚ 207 F2

Kingston Tourist Information
✉ 209 Ontario Street, Kingston
☎ 613/548-4415 or 1-888/855-4555;
http://tourism.kingstoncanada.com

1000 Islands Gananoque Chamber of Commerce
✉ 10 King Street East, Gananoque
☎ 613/382-3250 or 1-800/561-1595;
www.1000islandsgananoque.com

Marine Museum of the Great Lakes
✉ 55 Ontario Street, Kingston
☎ 613/542-2261; www.marmuseum.ca
🕐 Mar–mid-May Wed–Fri 10–4, Sat noon–4;

mid-May to Sep daily 10–4, by appointment Oct to mid-May; *Alexander Henry* and Pump House: mid-May to Sep only 🖐 Moderate

Fort Henry
✉ Fort Henry Drive, Kingston ☎ 613/542-7388 or 1-800/437-2233;
www.forthenry.com 🕐 Mid-May to early Oct daily 10–5 🖐 Expensive

Boldt Castle
✉ Heart Island, New York, USA
☎ 315/482-9724, 315/482-2501 or 1-800/847-5263; www.boldtcastle.com
🕐 Mid-May to mid-Oct daily 10–6:30 (Jul–Aug to 7:30) 🖐 Moderate (Canadian currency accepted)

3 Toronto

Big, beautiful, supremely confident, Toronto is the epicenter of Canada's entertainment, commercial and financial worlds. It is set on Lake Ontario, and the view from offshore of its skyscrapers, the slender CN Tower, and the big white Rogers Centre is quite breathtaking. It is ultramodern and innovative, but there is a history between the highrises.

As the entertainment capital of Canada, Toronto has a huge number of first-rate concert halls, theaters, live music venues and nightclubs. It's also a movie capital, with dozens of location shoots taking place on any day of the year – it is often used as a stand-in for New York – and you may see the movie stars hanging round upscale Yorkville on their days off.

Highlights of Toronto's modern architecture include the striking **BCE Place** (1993), north of Front Street between Yonge and Bay, and the twin curved towers of **City Hall** (1965) that dominate spacious Nathan Phillips Square, but towering above them all, in every respect, is the **CN Tower**, a city icon since 1976. The tallest free-standing structure in the world, it was originally built to improve TV reception, but the inspired addition of the observation levels quickly made it a top tourist attraction. A glass-fronted elevator whisks you at a stomach-churning speed up to the Look Out at 346m (1,136 feet) with its outdoor observatory (and a glass floor). From here an internal elevator climbs another 447m (1,465 feet) to

Baseball at the Rogers Centre, with its retractable roof open to the summer sky

the SkyPod, the world's highest man-made observatory, for views that extend to 160km (100 miles) on a clear day.

A big downtown attraction is the **Eaton Centre**, a spectacular atrium of arched glass and steel soaring above three floors of stores, restaurants and services. It is linked to the metro and the extensive PATH underground walkway system, its 12km (7 miles) of corridors lined by stores.

The oldest site in Toronto is **Fort York**, where the city was founded in 1793. Bitter fighting took place when an American army attacked the fort in 1813. Facing defeat, the Canadians ignited the remaining gunpowder and blew up the fort, but it was rebuilt immediately, and retains some structures from that time. Guides wear period uniform, and military drills are enacted in summer.

In the north of the city, the **Black Creek Pioneer Village** provides a splendid counterpoint to the modernity of downtown.

History is regularly re-created for visitors to Fort York

Original farm buildings and reconstructions form a village, all inhabited by costumed guides carrying out the crafts and chores of everyday life.

Of the handful of historic homes that are open to the public in Toronto, the most remarkable is **Casa Loma**, a conspicuous edifice of turrets, towers, Elizabethan chimneys and machicolations that has been described as a mixture of 17th-century Scottish baronial and 20th-century Fox. Sir Henry Pellatt spent a fortune to build and provide his home with every conceivable luxury and fanciful feature. Now restored and re-furnished, it's fun to explore.

Opposite: hot lakefront property, backed by the CN Tower Inset: Toronto by night, from the observation deck of the CN Tower

Toronto has a number of world-class museums, headed by the **Royal Ontario Museum** (ROM). Already the largest museum in Canada, its expansion and refurbishment program is adding almost 28,000sq m (300,000 square feet) in 27 galleries, and work was scheduled to be completed in 2007. The original heritage building is a stately presence on Queen's Park, but around the corner on Bloor Street the stunning extension explodes out of its north facade in a series of gigantic prisms – The Crystal – designed by Michael Lee-Chin. The

---

TORONTO: INSIDE INFO

Top tips The **Toronto City Pass** gives access to six of the top attractions: the AGO, CN Tower, Casa Loma, Ontario Science Centre, ROM and Toronto Zoo, and at $55 (child $37) provides great savings. Buy it at any of the attractions listed, or online at www.citypass.com.

• **Lines** for the CN Tower can be long at peak times, so plan to arrive early.
• Don't drive into downtown because traffic is heavy and parking expensive.
Public transportation is excellent and you can transfer between the subway, streetcars and buses for one fare on a one-way trip with no stopovers. If you are paying cash for your ticket, you'll need the exact change. Day passes are available in all subway stations (Toronto Transit Commission; 416/393-4636).

stands supreme. It has a superb European collection, and the Canadian Wing houses works by Lucius O'Brien, Paul Peel, and the Group of Seven (➤ 43), while the Henry Moore Sculpture Centre houses the world's largest collection of Moore's works. In 2002 Lord Thomson donated his massive art collection, which includes Rubens' *Massacre of the Innocents*. He also gave $50 million toward a building to house the works. Further donations of around $150 million enabled Frank Gehry's spectacular extension, open in 2008, to be built.

The ROM has some splendid dinosaur displays

Toronto's multicultural **neighborhoods** are great for a visit. In particular, explore upscale Rosedale, historic Cabbagetown, Greektown on the Danforth, Little Italy and the downtown Chinatown. The historic **Distillery District** is an enclave of performance venues, arts and crafts workshops and eateries, and a trip over to the lovely **Toronto Islands** is another must. Don't miss a visit to **Toronto Zoo**, a superb collection of wildlife, kept in spacious, near-natural habitats.

TAKING A BREAK

For a meal with a view, you can't beat the revolving **360 Restaurant at the CN Tower** (➤ 114), or one of the restaurants overlooking the lake at Queen's Quay Terminal.

➕ 207 E2

Toronto Tourism
➕ 221 D1 ✉ 207 Queen's Quay West
☎ 416-203-2600 or 1-800-499-2514;
www.torontotourism.com

CN Tower
➕ 220 C2 ✉ 301 Front Street
☎ 416-868-6937; www.cntower.ca
🕐 Daily 9am–10pm (10.30pm Fri–Sat)
✋ Expensive

Fort York
➕ 220 A2 ✉ 100 Garrison Road
☎ 416-392-6907 www.fortyork.ca 🕐 Daily
10–5; Sep to mid-May may close earlier.
Closed mid-Dec to Jan 2 ✋ Moderate

Art Gallery of Ontario
➕ 220 C4 ✉ 317 Dundas Street West
☎ 416-979-6648; www.ago.net
🕐 Wed–Fri noon–9, Sat–Sun 10–5:30
✋ Moderate (special exhibtions expensive); free Wed 6–9pm

Casa Loma
➕ 220, off B5 ✉ 1 Austin Terrace
☎ 416-923-1171; www.casaloma.org
🕐 Daily 9:30–5 ✋ Expensive

Black Creek Pioneer Village
➕ 221, off D4 ✉ 1000 Murray Ross
Parkway ☎ 416-736-1733; www.blackcreek.ca 🕐 May–Jun and Labour Day–Dec
Mon–Fri 9:30–4, Sat–Sun 11–5; Jul–early
Sep Mon–Fri 10–5, Sat–Sun 11–5
✋ Expensive

Royal Ontario Museum
➕ 221, off D5 ✉ 100 Queen's Park
☎ 416-586-5549 or 8000; www.rom.on.ca
🕐 Daily 10–6 (also 6–9:30 Fri) ✋ Expensive

Toronto Zoo
➕ 221 off F2 ✉ Meadowvale Road,
Scarborough ☎ 416-392-5900 www.torontozoo.com 🕐 Mid-May to early Sep daily
9–7:30; closes earlier in winter
✋ Expensive

4 Niagara Falls and Niagara Parkway

One of the most famous sights in the world, Niagara Falls is spectacular, and the sight of 155 million liters (3 million U.S. gallons) per minute of water crashing down onto the rocks below is truly awesome. The name comes from the local First Nations word for "thundering water" and it's no misnomer. If you're expecting a let-down after the big build-up, prepare to be stunned by the reality.

There are two waterfalls at Niagara – the Horseshoe (or Canadian) Falls and the American Falls across the border – which runs midstream all the way along the Niagara River. Tiny Goat Island, also American soil, separates the two cascades. Only 10 percent of the river winds up in the **American Falls**, which are 300m (1,000 feet) wide and 54m (176 feet) high. These dimensions would be impressive enough if the falls stood alone, but alongside the wide curve of the **Horseshoe Falls**, 800m (2,600 feet) wide and about 51m (167 feet) high, they are dwarfed.

To many, the most impressive sight of the Horseshoe Falls is at the top, at **Table Rock**, where the deep, dark green water slips silently over the edge. It's a compelling sight. From here, you can take the **Journey Behind the Falls**. You descend by

The *Maid of the Mist* sails close into the thundering waters of the Horseshoe Falls elevator to a short tunnel leading to a rock platform behind the falls (disposable, biodegradable waterproofs are provided).

Just about the most popular thing to do, though, is to take a trip on the **Maid of the Mist**, a little craft that chugs just a little farther than you would think advisable into the turbulent water at the bottom of the falls. Again, waterproofs are provided for the thrilling experience.

The highway that runs alongside the falls is the **Niagara Parkway**, which follows the the river for 53km (33 miles) and makes for an interesting scenic drive (▶ 182–184). Taking the Parkway in the same direction as the flow of the river, you begin at **Old Fort Erie**, where the Peace Bridge forms the border crossing to the city of Buffalo, New York. The British fort that stood here

Nothing can prepare you for the sheer power of the falls

during the War of 1812 (destroyed by the Americans in 1814) has been reconstructed as a living history exhibit, with costumed guides.

Beyond the falls, the river continues over boiling rapids, and you can descend to the riverbank for the thrilling **White Water Walk**. Next along the Parkway is the Whirlpool Bridge, another border crossing to the US and the historic **Whirlpool Aero Car**, which has been making the trip over the famous vortex in the river here since 1916.

Queenston Heights, 11km (7 miles) downstream from Niagara Falls, was the original site of the falls before erosion pushed them upstream. Queenston was the home of Canadian heroine of the War of 1812, Laura Secord, who journeyed on foot to warn the British of an imminent attack by the Americans after they ransacked her home. The charming **Laura Secord Homestead** is open to the public. The Niagara Parkway ends at **Niagara-on-the-Lake**, one of the most charming towns in Ontario, with gracious 19th-century homes and wide, tree-lined streets. At the entrance to the town the restored **Fort George National Historic Park** played an important role in the War of 1812. Beyond the town is the Niagara wine area, where several wineries welcome visitors.

NIAGARA FALLS AND NIAGARA PARKWAY: INSIDE INFO

Top tips The falls are equally impressive in **winter**, when they are partially frozen, but beware – the spray freezes in the air and can drop onto you as ice pellets.

• The **Niagara Falls Great Gorge Adventure Pass** gives admission to the Journey Behinds the Falls, White Water Walk, *Maid of the Mist*, Butterfly Conservatory, Falls Incline Railway and a day's travel on the People Mover, plus discounts on the Whirlpool Aero Car, Niagara Parks Heritage sites and Cirque Niagara. It costs $37.95 (child 6–12 $23.95) and is available at www.niagaraparks.com.

• **Information centers** are located in the Table Rock Complex, Rapids View Parking Lot, Queen Victoria Park, Murray Street and in the Maid of the Mist Plaza. They are open year-round, but hours vary seasonally.

Hidden gem A short way north of Niagara Falls on the Niagara Parkway, you'll reach the delightful **Butterfly Conservatory**, full of exotic, colorful butterlies fluttering free in a tropical rain-forest setting, alighting every so often on the lush plants. It's a great place to warm up on a winter visit, too.

TAKING A BREAK

Take an hour to lunch in the **Skylon Tower's** revolving restaurant (tel: 905/356-2651, $$$) – that's how long it takes to do the full circuit, including a superb view of the falls.

🚊 207 F1

Niagara Parks Commission
✉ 7400 Portage Road South, P.O. Box 150, Oak Hall Administrative Building, Niagara Falls ☎ 905/356-2241; www.niagaraparks.com

Niagara-on-the-Lake Chamber of Commerce
✉ 26 Queen Street, P.O. Box 1043, Niagara-on-the-Lake ☎ 905/468-1950; www.niagaraonthelake.com

Journey Behind the Falls
✉ 6650 Niagara Parkway ☎ 905/356-2241; www.niagaraparks.com ⏰ Daily from 9am. Closing varies 💲 Expensive

Maid of the Mist
✉ 5920 Niagara Parkway ☎ 905/358-0311 (recorded information) ⏰ Apr–late Oct (depending on weather) daily from 9:45–4:45. Closing varies 💲 Expensive

Old Fort Erie
✉ 350 Lakeshore Road, Fort Erie ☎ 905/356-2241; www.niagaraparks.com ⏰ Early May–early Oct daily 10–4, 5 or 6 💲 Moderate

White Water Walk
✉ 4330 Niagara Parkway ☎ 905/356-2241; www.niagaraparks.com ⏰ Mar–Oct daily from 9am 💲 Moderate

Whirlpool Aero Car
✉ 3850 Niagara Parkway ☎ 905/356-2241 ⏰ Mid-Mar to mid-Nov daily from 9am. Closing varies 💲 Expensive

Laura Secord Homestead
✉ 29 Queenston Street, Queenston ☎ 905/356-2241; www.niagaraparks.com ⏰ Early May–late Jun Mon–Fri 9:30–3:30, Sat–Sun 11–5; Jul–early Sep daily 11–5 💲 Inexpensive

Fort George National Historic Park
✉ Queen's Parade, Niagara-on-the-Lake ☎ 905/468-4257; www.pc.gc.ca ⏰ May–Nov daily 10–5, 💲 Moderate

Butterfly Conservatory
✉ 2405 Niagara Parkway ☎ 905/356-2241; www.niagaraparks.com ⏰ Daily from 9am. Closing varies 💲 Expensive

At Your Leisure

5 Upper Canada Village

When the St. Lawrence Seaway was constructed in the 1950s, the Long Sault rapids were dammed to form Lake St. Lawrence and in the process eight villages, 200 farms and thousands of homes were submerged. But not all was lost – 30 historic buildings were carefully removed and reconstructed to form Upper Canada Village. Today, the "village" looks as if it has always been here, and there is constant activity from the costumed guides, who represent all the trades and professions that a village such as this would need.

✚ 207 F2 ✉ 13740 County Road 2, Morrisburg ☎ 613/543-4328 or 1-800/437-2255; www.uppercanadavillage.com ⏰ Mid-May to early Oct daily 9–5:30 💲 Expensive

6 Algonquin Provincial Park

Algonquin Park is the very essence of the wilderness, with maple-clad hills, sparkling lakes, rivers and marshes. It is Ontario's best-known

The "Big Nickel," a famous Sudbury landmark, now located in Dynamic Earth

provincial park, and a haven for wildlife that includes bear, deer and the wolves that are often heard but rarely seen. Three attractions are right on Highway 60: the **Algonquin Aarts Centre**, with wildlife art; the **Visitor Centre**, with exhibits about the nature and human history of the park; and the **Algonquin Logging Museum**, a re-creation of a logging camp.

Algonquin Visitor Centre

✚ 207 E2 ✉ Highway 60, 43km (27 miles from west gate) ⏰ Nov–Mar daily 10–5 in summer, weekends only off season

7 Sudbury

Up in northern Ontario, Sudbury is a mining town on top of the largest known source of copper and nickel in the world. It's not pretty, and it's most prominent landmark is a 380m (1,250-foot) smokestack, but tourists flock to Sudbury. Why? To visit the outstanding **Science North**, with its exceptional hands-on displays and superb underground auditorium, and for **Dynamic Earth**, which takes visitors deep underground in a glass elevator (while watching a spectacular multimedia show) for an imaginative geological experience.

✚ 207 D2

Sudbury Tourism

☎ 705/688-7570 or 877/304-8222

Science North

✉ 100 Ramsey Lake Road ☎ 705/522-3700 or 1-800/461-4898; http://sciencenorth.ca ⏰ May–late Jun daily 9–5; late Jun–early Sep 9–6; early Sep–Apr 10–4 💲 Expensive

Dynamic Earth

✉ 122 Big Nickel Road ☎ 705/522-3701 or 1-800/461-4898; http://dynamicearth.ca ⏰ Early Mar–Oct daily 9–5 💲 Expensive

Farther Afield

8 Sault Ste. Marie

"Sault" is the French word for rapids, and Sault Ste. Marie (familiarly "the Soo"), has a turbulent mile on which the St. Mary's River drops more than 6m (20 feet). The river connects lakes Superior and Huron and forms the border between Ontario and the US state of Michigan. To bypass the rapids on the American side, four side-by-side locks were built, the last of 16 between the Atlantic Ocean and Lake Superior, and they are among the busiest (and longest) in the world. By contrast, the Canadian side has one small lock that's used for pleasure craft and a **cruise** that gets up close to the seagoing freighters.

Another trip from Sault Ste. Marie goes north on the **Agawa Canyon Train**, a 184km (114 mile) route crossing high trestle bridges, and passing pristine lakes, forest and granite rock formations. A two-hour stop is made in the canyon, which is as much as 175m (574 feet) deep.

✚ 206 C2

Tourism Sault Ste. Marie
✉ 99 Foster Drive, Sault Ste. Marie
☎ 705/759-2500;
www.sault-canada.com

Lock Tours Canada Boat Cruises
✉ Roberta Bondar Park, PO Box 325
☎ 705/253-9850 or 1-877/226-3665;
www.locktours.com ⏱ Late May to mid-Oct daily 12:30 and 3 (also Jul–early Sep 10 and 6) 💰 Expensive

Algoma Central Railway
✉ 129 Bay Street (PO Box 130), Sault Ste. Marie ☎ 705/946-7300 or 1-800/242-9287; www.agawacanyontour-train.com ⏱ Late Jun to mid-Oct tours daily 8am 💰 Expensive

9 Point Pelee National Park

On the same latitude as Rome and northern California, Point Pelee is the southernmost tip of Canada, and the 20sq km (8-square mile) national park is a triangular oasis jutting into

The boardwalk at Point Pelee opens up an otherwise inaccessible marshland

Lake Erie. It is a lush area of marsh and woodland, with plant and animal life that is unique in Canada. Each spring and fall, nearly half a million birdwatchers come to the park to view the annual migrations of thousands of birds – more than 350 species have been recorded. This is a stopping-off point for hoards of Monarch butterflies on their fall migration to Mexico.

The **Marsh Boardwalk** shouldn't be missed, a 1.5km (1-mile) walk through a sea of cattails, with observation towers at both ends.

✚ 207 E1 ✉ 407 Monarch Lane, RR1, Leamington ☎ 519/322-2365 or 1-888/773-8888; www.pc. gc.ca ⏱ Apr–Oct daily; bus to the Tip (access for visitors' vehicles Nov–Mar) 💰 Moderate

For Kids

For thrill-rides and water-based fun take them to **Canada's Wonderland** (905/832-7000; www2.paramountpa-rks.com/canadaswonderland; open late May–early Sep daily, May and Sep–Oct weekends, expensive) or **Ontario Place** on Toronto's lakeshore. For animals, you can't beat **African Lion Safari** (Cambridge; tel: 519/623-2620 or 800/461-WILD; www.lionsa-fari.com; open late Apr to mid-Oct daily; expensive), or **MarineLand** at Niagara Falls.

Where to... Stay

Prices
High season room only rates, based on two sharing a double room, excluding taxes
$ under $160 $$ $161–$300 $$$ more than $300

OTTAWA

▼▼▼ Albert House Inn $–$$

Built in 1875, this is a lovely downtown inn with old-style furniture and period decor, offering distinctive accommodations with private bathrooms, some with whirlpool tubs. It's famous for its breakfasts (included in the price), featuring both traditional and unusual items.

🚹 207 F3 ⊠ 478 Albert Street
☎ 613/236-4479, 1-800/267-1982;
www.albertinn.com

▼▼▼ Arc the Hotel $$

Just four blocks from Parliament Hill and close to the National Arts Centre, this is the city's only designer boutique hotel and is pure minimalist chic. Bedrooms are elegant and include orchids, fruit, Bulgari toiletries and deep bathtubs.

🚹 207 F3 ⊠ 140 Slater Street
☎ 613/238-2888, 1-800/699-2516;
www.arcthehotel.com

▼▼▼ Fairmont Château Laurier $$–$$$

This is the grandest hotel in Ottawa, truly château-like with its sturdy limestone walls topped by turrets. It mirrors the government buildings across the canal. Inside is pure opulence and the rooms and suites offer true comfort.

🚹 207 F3 ⊠ 1 Rideau Street
☎ 613/241-1414; www.fairmont.com

KINGSTON

▼▼▼ Hotel Belvedere $–$$

Down on Kingston's waterfront, near to City Hall, this is a fine restored mansion dating to the 1880s and preserving many original features. It's furnished in keeping with its age, with antique Canadian pieces, and modern comforts include down comforters (and whirlpool tubs in a couple of the suites).

🚹 207 F2 ⊠ 141 King Street East
☎ 613/548-1565, 1-800/559-0584;
www.hotelbelvedere.com

TORONTO

▼▼▼ Fairmont Royal York $$–$$$

The stately grande-dame of Toronto hotels, the Royal York has been hosting visiting royalty and celebrities since 1929 and is distinguished exterior is a city landmark, right opposite Union Station. Its the ultimate luxury, with original features such as hand-painted ceilings, travertine pillars and glittering chandeliers, and every modern convenience has been added, including a pool, spa and fitness center.

🚹 207 E2 ⊠ 100 Front Street
☎ 416/368-2511, 1-800/257-7544;
www.fairmont.com

▼▼▼ Palmerston Inn B&B $–$$

In a beautiful historic building, with a stately verandah, this elegant property is on a tree-lined residential street close to the fascinating University and Annex area. Rooms are individually styled, some with antiques, and all but two have private bathrooms. A full hot breakfast is included in the price.

🚹 207 E2 ⊠ 322 Palmerston Boulevard ☎ 416/920-7842;
http://palmerstoninn.com

▼▼▼ Westin Harbour Castle $$–$$$

This has got to be the best location in the city – right on the lakeshore,

Where to...
Eat and Drink

Prices
Based on the cost of a three-course dinner, excluding drinks and service.
$ under $30 $$ $30–$50 $$$ more than $50

OTTAWA

▼▼ Blue Cactus $–$$

Stylish eatery in Byward Market specializing in southwest cuisine, with Creole and Cajun seasonings, hot chili sauces and milder concoctions such as chicken marinaded in herbs and lime juice with melon orange salsa. There's also a good range of sandwiches, fajitas, wraps, burgers and pizzas for a quick lunch. Stay on for late-night jazz and soul music on weekends.

✚ 207 F3 ⊠ 2 Byward Market
☎ 613/241-7061;
www.bluecactusbarandgrill.com
🕓 Daily 11:30am–late

▼▼ Merlot $$–$$$

This revolving restaurant is on the 29th floor of the Marriott Hotel, with wonderful views. Don't be in a hurry, the full circuit takes two hours. The service is formal and the menu has fairly standard international dishes.

✚ 207 F3 ⊠ 100 Kent Street
☎ 613/783-4212; www.merelot-tawa.com 🕓 Daily 6–10, Sun 10:30am–2pm

KINGSTON

▼▼ Chez Piggy $–$$

The *Chez Piggy Cookbook* is a Canadian bestseller and if you eat

---

with superlative views, and close to the major attractions and theater district. The 977 rooms feature "Heavenly Beds" with pillow-top mattresses, and there are casual and formal restaurants and a long list of leisure amenities.

✚ 207 E2 ⊠ 1 Harbour Square
☎ tel: 416/869-1600; fax: 416/869-0573; www.westin.com/harbourcastle

▼▼ Willowdale Inn $

Newly built, this is a small, intimate boutique hotel, with contemporary suites at very competitive prices. Rooms are air-conditioned and have a kitchenette with microwave and refrigerator, and a complimentary Continental breakfast is included in the price. The North York location, just off Highway 401, is handy for out-of-town excursions, and there are good public transit services to downtown.

✚ 207 E2 ⊠ 170 Willowdale Avenue
☎ 416/850-6666 or 1-877/877-6691;
www.willowdaleinn.com

NIAGARA FALLS

▼▼ Sheraton Fallsview $$

Overlooking the Horseshoe and American falls, this is a superb modern high-rise hotel. There is a variety of room types, the best of which have nice reproduction furniture and, of course, the view.

✚ 207 E1 ⊠ 6755 Fallsview Boulevard ☎ 905/374-1077, 1-800/267-8439;
www.fallsview.com

NIAGARA-ON-THE-LAKE

▼▼ Pillar and Post Inn $$–$$$

In an 1890 building, this is one of Canada's loveliest inns, with an exceptional range of services and a spa. Rooms, each with a Victorian fireplace, are superb and have big-screen TV, Playstation and robes.

✚ 207 E1 ⊠ 48 John Street
☎ 905/468-2123, 1-888/669-5566;
www.vintageinns.com

here you'll see why. It serves up brilliantly executed home-cooking from several countries, including Turkey and Vietnam, and the staff is particularly cheerful and friendly.

✚ 207 F2 ⊠ 68R Princess Street
☎ 613/549-7673;
http://chezpiggy.com ⊙ Mon–Fri
11:30–2, 5:30–10, Sat 11:30–2:30,
5:30–10, Sun 11–2:30, 5:30–10

GANANOQUE

☞ Gananoque Inn $$–$$$

At the heart of the Thousand Islands area, this historic inn sits beside the St. Lawrence. Its sophisticated dining room serves Continental cuisine such as broiled chicken with guacamole and salad. The pub, with a patio deck, serves pasta and burgers.

✚ 207 F2 ⊠ 550 Stone Street S
☎ 613/382-2165 or 1-800/465-3101;
www.gananoque inn.com
⊙ May–Nov daily 7–10am, 11:30–2,
5:30–10; Apr and Dec Fri–Sun
5:30–10. Closed Jan–Mar

TORONTO

☞ Golden Thai $–$$

There are a lot of Thai restaurants in Toronto, but this one is up there with the best. The pad Thai here is a real triumph. The menu is huge (though portions are small), service is speedy, and the decor is warm and restful.

✚ 207 E2 ⊠ 105 Church Street
☎ 416/868-6668 ⊙ Mon–Fri
11:30–10, Sat 5–11, Sun 5–10

☞ Sassafraz $$–$$$

Soak up the atmosphere of upscale Yorkville at this trendy restaurant where, for a price, you'll dine among celebrities on imaginative French and California cuisine with an Oriental influence. Signature dishes include an intricate assiette of Australian lamb, Asian-influenced steak Miss Saigon, and a daily seafood creation.

✚ 207 F2 ⊠ 100 Cumberland Street
☎ 416/964-2222; www.sassafraz.ca
⊙ Daily 11am–2am

☞ 360 Restaurant at the CN Tower $$

This is the ultimate revolving restaurant, the highest in the world, and the quality of the food and service is equally lofty. Canadian specialties include Ontario rainbow trout, Atlantic Salmon, Alberta beef and a delicious maple syrup cheesecake. There's an excellent wine list. Surrounded by windows, you are guaranteed a spectacular view and you'll see it all in 72 minutes. The admission charge to the tower is refunded to diners.

✚ 207 E2 ⊠ 301 Front Street West
☎ 416/362-5411; www.cntower.ca/
restaurants ⊙ Daily 11–2, 4.30–10
(10:30 Fri–Sat), Sun 10:30am–2pm.
Closed lunch Jan–May

NIAGARA FALLS

☞ Mick & Angelo's Eatery and Bar $–$$

There are plenty of upscale Niagara restaurants with views of the falls, but if you want to get away from all

that for a good simple meal, this is the place. With typical Italian decor and hospitality, it's a fun place that serves great pizza, pasta, meatballs and other Italian favorites. There's a lovely patio for summer dining.

✚ 207 E1 ⊠ 7600 Lundy's Lane, at
corner of Montrose ☎ 905/357-6543;
www.mickandangelos.ca ⊙ Daily
11am–12:30am

NIAGARA-ON-THE-LAKE

☞ Shaw Café and Wine Bar $$

This place is impossible to miss with its semicircular facade projecting onto the street, fronted by a glorious patio decked with blooms. There's a range of soups, salads, sandwiches, pasta and burgers, plus such entrees as rosemary stewed beef or pan-roasted fillet of salmon

✚ 207 F1 ⊠ 92 Queen Street
☎ 905/468-4772; www.shawcafe.ca
⊙ Apr–Oct daily 10am–midnight;
Nov–Mar Mon–Thu 10–6, Fri–Sun
10–8

Where to...
Shop

You won't be disappointed in the shopping opportunities in Ontario. Toronto is home to a large number of flagship stores, Ottawa is renowned for quality and Niagara Falls for tourist kitsch, but throughout Ontario there are hidden gems to be found – individual crafts at workshops and local galleries, and boutiques with unique fashions.

OTTAWA

This is a national capital with a small-town feel, but the stores are excellent, with a good range of quality items. The busy hub of the city is around **Rideau Street**, where you'll find the **Rideau Centre** (50 Rideau Street, tel: 613/236-6565), with about 200 stores. Traffic-free **Sparks Street**, one block back from Parliament Hill, is a famous thoroughfare lined with individual stores and craft galleries. Another great attraction is **Byward Market** (▶ 100), where stands spill out of the undercover market into the surrounding streets; nearby stores are interesting too, such as the artist-run **Inuit Artists' Shop** (2081 Merivale Road, tel: 613/224-8189).

TORONTO

Toronto is heaven for shoppers, with a huge number of downtown and suburban malls and every kind of specialty store. The **Eaton Centre** (220 Yonge Street, tel: 416/598-8700), a world leader when it opened in the 1980s, is still a major tourist attraction, with around 300 stores beneath a beautiful glass roof. Another superb mall is **Queen's Quay Terminal**, on the lakeshore, an imaginative conversion of an old warehouse that is full of upscale stores and galleries. At the other end of the scale, just for the fun of it, check out **Dr. Flea's** (8 Westmore Drive, tel: 416/745-3532), an undercover flea market, and **Honest Ed's** (581 Bloor Street West, tel: 416/537-1574), a glittering temple to the great bargain.

Toronto's neighborhoods open up a treasure trove of individual stores. **Bloor-Yorkville** is the best area for upscale shopping, with a village atmosphere and leafy streets lined with fashion boutiques, antiques shops, galleries and specialty stores. There's great people-watching and celebrity-spotting in its sidewalk cafés. **St. Lawrence Market** (Front and Jarvis, tel: 416/392-7120) and **Kensington Market** (Dundas and College) are worth exploring too for their unique atmosphere, eclectic array of vendors and street entertainers.

NIAGARA FALLS

Niagara Falls is not noted as a shopping destination, though there is a factory outlet mall, **Canada One** (7500 Lundy's Lane, tel: 905/356-8989) with around 40 stores offering huge discounts on Ralph Lauren, Tommy Hilfiger, Reebok, Villeroy and Bosch and other designer labels.

Niagara-on-the-Lake has better opportunities, with some nice craft galleries and antiques shops, including **Europa Antiques** (1523 Niagara Stone Road, tel: 905/468-3130), a converted old church building full of furniture and household bits and pieces. There's also the **French Perfume Factory** (393 York Road, tel: 905/685-6666) where you can see big-name fragrances being made, and then buy them. In the surrounding area you can shop for wine at the many wineries that welcome visitors and buy delicious fresh fruit direct from the orchards or their roadside stands.

Where to...
Be Entertained

Ontario is rich in entertainment. Toronto is the entertainment capital of Canada, practically on a par with New York and London; Ottawa has the National Arts Centre and several theaters; Niagara-on-the-Lake offers the summer Shaw Festival; Stratford has its Shakespeare Festival, and www.summertheatre.org is a good source for what's on.

OTTAWA

Ottawa's **National Arts Centre** (53 Elgin Street, tel: 613/947-7000) is one of the world's largest and most comprehensive performance centers. Theaters include the **Great Canadian Theatre Company** (910 Gladstone Avenue, tel: 613/236-5196), **Ottawa Little Theatre** (400 King Edward Street, tel: 613/233-8948) and the **Centrepoint Theatre** (101 Centre-point Drive, Nepean tel: 613/580-2700). Big-name touring acts also play at **Scotia Bank Place** (1000 Palladium Drive, Kanata, tel: 613/599-0250).

The **Lynx** (baseball), **Renegades** (football), **Senators** (hockey) and **Rebels** (lacrosse) represent Ottawa's sporting scene, and there's horse racing at the Rideau Carleton track.

TORONTO

There's just too much going on in Toronto to list it all here and you should check out the listings magazines *Where* and *Now* for the full picture. Toronto's Theatre District includes the **Royal Alexandra** (260 King Street W, tel: 416/593-4142), the **Princess of Wales** (300 King Street W, tel: 416/593-4142), the **Canon** (244 Victoria Street, tel: 416/872-1212) and the **Elgin & Winter Garden** (189 Yonge Street, tel: 416/314-2871). There's also **Canstage** (26 Berkeley Street, tel: 416/368-3110), Canada's largest contemporary theater company. Big concert venues include the **Hummingbird Centre** (1 Front Street East, tel: 416/393-7429), the **Air Canada Centre** (40 Bay Street, tel: 416/815-5500), the **Roy Thompson Hall** (60 Simcoe Street, tel: 416/872-4255), the **SkyDome** (1 Blue Jays Way, tel: 416/341-3000) and **Molson Amphitheatre** (Ontario Place, tel: 416/260-5600).

There are hundreds of live music clubs, including the **Horseshoe** (368 Queen Street W, tel: 416/598-4753), **Healey's Roadhouse** (56 Blue Jays Way, tel: 416/593-2626), run by legendary guitarist Jeff Healey, **CEst What?** (67 Front Street E, tel: 416/416/867-9499).

Dance clubs jostle for position at the top; current favorites include **Baba'U** (136 Yorkville Avenue, tel: 416/515-0587), **The Government** (152 Queen's Quay E, tel: 416/869-0045), and **Fly** (8 Gloucester Street, tel: 416/925-6222), which is primarily a gay club.

Comedy is big in Toronto (Mike Myers and Jim Carrey honed their skills here). **Second City** (5a Mercer Street, tel: 416/343-0011) is the club that inspired "Saturday Night Live," and **Laugh Resort** (370 King Street W, tel: 416/364-5233) hosts top comedy stars.

Spectator sports include the **Blue Jays** (baseball), twice winners of the World Series, and the **Argonauts** (football), the **Maple Leafs** (hockey) and **Raptors** (basketball). The **Woodbine Race Track** (555 Rexdale Boulevard, tel: 416/675-1101) stages Canada's classic thoroughbred races.

Québec

Getting Your Bearings

The Maritimes have the Acadians, the Prairies have the Métis, and there's a smattering of Francophones in Ontario, but Québec is thoroughly French and immensely proud of its Gallic heritage. This gives any visit to the province an extra dimension, with signs in French, the French language ringing in your ears (though most Québecois are fluent in English too), a cosmopolitan sophistication in the cities, and a laid-back *joie-de-vivre* just about everywhere.

The province hugs both banks of the mighty St. Lawrence River as it flows east into the Gulf of St. Lawrence, and all the major cities are on or close to this busy waterway. Stretching to the north is a vast wilderness of lakes and tundra that is sparsely populated but very beautiful.

Some of the oldest settlements on the continent are here, notably the fabulous Québec City, with its intact city walls and mighty Citadelle fortress. Montréal is Canada's second city (after Toronto), a vibrant cultural and commercial center with ancient quarters and remarkably elegant modern architecture.

Out in the country, there's the vacation paradise of the Laurentian Mountains and Gaspésie, pretty rural areas of orchards and vineyards, cascading tributories flowing into the St. Lawrence, and the spectacular fall colors of the Gatineau Valley.

Péninsule d'Ungava

Chisasibi

Ea

Page 117: Québec City is split in two by a sheer escarpment that's dominated by the Château Frontenac hotel

Left: The Tremblant Resort is at the heart of the Laurentians

At Your Leisure

The rocky land-scape of the Saguenay Fjord

Kuujjuaq

Caniapiscau

Schefferville

Lac Bienville

Lac Caniapiscau

Fermont

Blanc Sablon

Romaine

Réservoir Manicouagan

Sept-Îles

Moisie

138

Île Anticosti

Gulf of St Lawrence

QUÉBEC

Lac Mistassini

Manicouagan

Baie-Comeau

St Lawrence

▲1268

Gaspé

Îles de la Madeleine

Mistissini

Forestville

Bonaventure

Matane

Chapais

167

Saguenay Fjord **4**

Chicoutimi

Rimouski

Lac St-Jean **9**

167

Clermont

Rivière-du-Loup

Parc Provincial des Laurentides

3 **Charlevoix Coast**

Réservoir Gouin

Québec City **2** **7** **Île d'Orléans**

Ste-Thècle

Beauceville

0 ————— 300 km

Trois-Rivières **6**

Lac-Mégantic

0 ————— 150 miles

Réservoir Cabonga

Les Laurentides **8**

Drummondville

Sherbrooke

117

St-Jérôme

Granby

5 **Cantons-de-l'Est**

1 **Montréal**

Gatineau

★ Don't Miss

This tour takes in the nation's second-largest city and its oldest city, then heads out along the coast for some whale-watching and a magnificent fjord cruise.

Quebec in Five days

Day One

Morning Start your visit to Montréal (➤ 122–125) at place Jacques Cartier, take a horse-drawn calèche ride (➤ left), and explore the old city. Then make your way west along rue St.-Paul to place d'Armes.

Lunch Visit the **Basilique Nôtre-Dame** during its quietest period, then eat authentic Mexican food at Casa de Mateo in rue St-François-Xavier.

Afternoon Take a look around the Vieux Port, then stop in at the Marché Bonsecour to browse the craft boutiques and have a coffee at Le Petit Paysan. Then head up to Mont-Royal to see the famous **Oratoire St.-Joseph**.

Evening Stay up on **Mont-Royal** to watch the sun go down and the lights of the city (and the Mont-Royal cross) go on. Make your way to the Latin Quarter for some French-style nightlife and cuisine.

Day Two

Morning Still in **Montréal** start in the heart of downtown at place du Canada, visit the **Cathédrale Marie-Reine-du-Monde**, then go underground to explore the Ville Souterraine (➤ below).

Lunch Pick and choose from the delicious choices of food on offer at the Marché Mövenpick at place Ville-Marie in the underground city.

Afternoon Window-shop along rue Ste.-Catherine, then head northwest to visit the **Musée des beaux-arts** on rue Sherbrooke Ouest. Take a break in the museum café.

Evening Treat yourself to dinner at Nuances (➤ 137), at the Casino down on the water-front, one of the finest restaurants in North America. Stay on to catch a show at the Cabaret or play the tables and slots.

Day Three

Morning Take Highway 40 northeast to **2 Québec City** (➤ 126–128) for a walk on Terrasse Dufferin (➤ left) and Promenade des Gouverneurs.

Lunch Reward yourself for all that walking, and have lunch in the city's oldest building at Aux Anciens Canadiens (➤ 137).

Afternoon Take the tour of the **Citadelle**, then have a quick look inside the **Basilique Notre-Dame de Québec** before taking the funicular down to the lower town. Visit the **Musée de la Civilisation**.

Evening Stay in the Basse-Ville for a stroll around its delightful narrow lanes and a meal at Panache (tel: 418/692-2211; $$–$$$) in the Auberge Saint-Antoine, to sample upscale French Canadian cuisine.

Day Four

Morning Drive northeast out of Québec City along the **3 Charlevoix Coast** (➤ 129–130), stopping at any little community that takes your fancy.

Lunch Aim to be in Baie St.-Paul around midday for lunch at Le Mouton Noir (tel: 418/240-3030, $$) on rue St.-Anne.

Afternoon Continue along the coast, stopping at La Malbaie, Port-au-Persil and the viewpoint above Baie Ste.-Catherine. Take the ferry across to **Tadoussac** and visit the **Interpretation Centre for Marine Mammals**.

Evening Have a stroll around this charming little town and a meal in the William Restaurant at the Tadoussac Hotel.

Day Five

Morning Get the earliest whale-watching trip you can, which will last about two hours. Then drive up the **4 Saguenay Fjord** (➤ 131–132, right) to **Chicoutimi**.

Lunch Have lunch at La Bougresse (tel: 418/543-3178, $) in the town center.

Afternoon Take a cruise on the fjord from Chicoutimi's waterfront.

Evening Drive to lovely **Baie Éternité** for a stroll along its waterside path.

⓪ Montréal

The capital of French-speaking Canada, Montréal is a beautiful and fascinating city, set on an island in the wide St. Lawrence River. It has a striking mixture of modern and historic buildings, some of the finest ecclesiastical architecture on the continent, and a vibrant, cosmopolitan atmosphere. It is Canada's second-largest city – after Toronto, with which there is a deal of rivalry – and the second-largest Francophone city in the world (after Paris).

Mellow Montréal is one of the most beautiful cities in the world

The first part of Montréal that many visitors see is the Dorchester Square/Place du Canada area, the commercial hub that is full of modern architecture and monuments. The real heart of the city, though, is up on **Mont-Royal** (Mount Royal), from which the city took its name. It rises 228m (750 feet) above the downtown bustle, topped by a lovely park, and is a precious oasis for residents and a place where visitors can enjoy the wonderful panorama. The Chalet and Camilien Houde viewpoints have the best views of the St. Lawrence River. On the north slope is the famous **L'Oratoire St.-Joseph** (St. Joseph's Oratory), a city landmark, which has one of the largest domes in the world.

Montréal is fascinating to explore, with its striking contrasts. For instance, you can walk for kilometers through the ultramodern **Ville Souterraine**, a vast underground network of corridors and sun-lit atriums that link stores, offices and the métro system, then emerge to stroll around **Vieux-Montréal** (Old Montréal). Founded by a little French mission in 1642, this area has been restored and revitalized and, though it is a great tourist attraction, it is also a working and residential area of great character. Touring it by horse-drawn calèche is one of the great Montréal experiences. Place Jacques Cartier is the hub, particularly lively on summer evenings.

One of the glories of Montréal is in the old city – the Roman Catholic **Basilique Nôtre-Dame de Montréal**. The twin towers, rising to more than 69m (226 feet), are a city landmark and it has a stunning interior. Magnificent wood-carving and fine statuary adorns the huge, 68m (223-foot) long nave, which is illuminated by three rose windows in the roof.

Over on rue Ste.-Catherine, its Anglican counterpart, **Christ Church** cathedral is squeezed between towering office blocks and underpinned by a large shopping center. It's a superb example of flamboyant neo-Gothic architecture with stained-glass windows from the studio of William Morris and a cross made from nails collected in the ruins of Coventry Cathedral in England after it was bombed in 1940.

Down on the river, the **Vieux-Port** (Old Port) was once the biggest grain port in North America, but was abandoned when the St. Lawrence Seaway opened in 1959. Rescued from dereliction in the late 1970s, it includes a waterfront park with superb views and leisure activities. The Montréal Science Centre is here, too, with lots of hands-on activities for children, or you can ferry them across to Île Ste.-Hélène for La Ronde, a huge amusement park, and the **Biosphère**. This huge geodesic dome tells the story of the St. Lawrence River, the Seaway and the Great Lakes, with interactive displays.

Montréal has some excellent museums and galleries, and a good place to start is **Pointe-à-Callière**, on the site where Montréal was born. The unusual museum occupies several buildings around Place Royal and Place d'Youville, with its entrance in the modern Éperon building. Head to the basement for the "Where Montréal was Born" exhibition, an underground route through an authentic archaeological site, which emerges into the Ancienne Douane buildings, built in 1836 as the city's first custom house. Place d'Youville has the 1915

The interior of the Basilique Notre-Dame is breathtaking

Youville Pumping Station, the Archaeological Field School and Mariners House, used for school groups.

Next, move on to the place des Arts complex. This is Canada's only cultural complex devoted to both the performing and visual arts, and is dominated by the elliptical facade of its concert hall. Here, too, is the **Musée d'art contemporain** (Contemporary Art Museum), the only gallery of its kind in Canada.

Opposite: Paul Kane's *Mah-Min* in the Musée des beaux-arts

The **Musée des beaux-arts de Montréal** (Montréal Museum of Fine Arts) occupies buildings on rue Sherbrooke. It's one of Canada's oldest museums, with an encyclopedic collection of art and a program of blockbuster exhibitions.

MONTRÉAL: INSIDE INFO

Top tips Visit the **Basilique Nôtre-Dame** around lunchtime, when there are fewer tour groups or attend a Mass to see the interior with all the lights on.
• Take advantage of the **mini-train** to get around the Botanical Gardens. It's free with admission and you can get on and off to explore different areas.
• An **STM Tourist Card** is excellent value, offering unlimited travel on Montréal's bus and métro network for $9 ($17 for three days). Tel: 514/280-5507.
• The **Montreal Museums Pass** gives free access to 32 museums and other attractions for three consecutive days ($35, or $45 to include public transit).

In more depth The Old Fort on Île-Ste-Hélène houses the **Stewart Museum** (20 chemin Tour-de-l'Île, tel: 614/861-6701; www.stewart-museum.org; open year-round, closed Tue early Sep–early May; moderate) devoted to the history of European settlement in Québec. For more local history, visit the **Château Ramezay** (280 rue Nôtre-Dame Est, tel: 514/861-3708; www.chateauramezay.qc.ca; open year-round, closed Mon Oct–May; moderate).

Hidden gem Tiny **rue St.-Amable**, close to rue St.-Paul, is known as the artists' street, and in summer it is lined with artists selling their canvases.

If the busy streets get too much, there's an antidote in the wonderful **Jardin botanique de Montréal** (Montréal Botanical Gardens) over in the east end. Extending to more than 73ha (180 acres), they are considered the finest of their kind in North America. Themed areas include a First Nations Garden.

Across the street is the **Parc olympique de Montréal**. Take the funicular up its distinctive spine for spectacular views. The former velodrome is now the **Biodôme de Montréal**, a remarkable indoor zoo featuring four ecosystems of the Americas – tropical rain forest, Laurentian Forest, the marine environment of the St. Lawrence and the frigid Polar World.

TAKING A BREAK

Café des Beaux-Arts (tel: 514/843-3233, $$) is an elegant bistro in the art gallery.

---

208 A1

Centre Infotouriste
218 A1 ✉ 1001 Square Dorchester
☎ 514/873-2015 or 1-877/266-5687;
www.tourism-montreal.org

Tourist Information Centre
219, off F5 ✉ 174 rue Notre-Dame Est
☎ 514/873-2015

L'Oratoire St.-Joseph
218, off A4 ✉ 3800 chemin Queen Mary ☎ 514/733-8211;
www.saint-joseph.org

Basilique Nôtre-Dame
219 F3 ✉ 110 rue Nôtre-Dame Ouest
☎ 514/842-2925 or 1-866/842-2950;
www.basiliquendm.org 🕐 Mon–Fri 8–4.30, Sat 8–4.15, Sun 12.30–4.15; sound-and-light shows Tue–Sat evenings (times vary)
💵 Inexpensive

Christ Church
218 A3 ✉ 635 rue Ste.-Catherine Ouest ☎ 514/843-6577;
www.montreal.anglican.org/cathedral

Biosphère
219, off D1 ✉ 160 chemin Tour-de-l'Île, Île-Ste.-Hélène ☎ 514/283-5000;
www.biosphere.ec.gc.ca 🕐 Jun–Sep daily 10–6; Oct–May Mon and Wed–Fri noon–5, Sat–Sun 10–5 💵 Moderate

Pointe-à-Callière
219 F2 ✉ 350 Place Royale
☎ 514/872-9150; www.pacmuseum.qc.ca
🕐 Mon–Fri 10–5, Sat–Sun 11–5 (6 late Jun–early Sep) 💵 Expensive

Musée d'art contemporain
218 B4 ✉ 185 rue Ste.-Catherine Ouest ☎ 514/847-6226; www.macm.org
🕐 Tue–Sun 11–6 (also 6–9 Wed)
💵 Moderate

Musée des beaux-arts de Montréal
218, off A4 ✉ 1379–80 rue Sherbrooke Ouest ☎ 514/285-2000 or 1-800/899-6873; www.mmfa.qc.ca 🕐 Tue 11–5, Wed–Fri 11–9, Sat–Sun 10–5 💵 Free (except temporary exhibitions)

Jardin botanique de Montréal
218, off A5 ✉ 4101 rue Sherbrooke Est
☎ 514/872-140 🕐 Jun–Sep daily; Oct–May Tue–Sun 💵 May–Oct expensive; Nov–Apr moderate

Parc olympique de Montréal
218, off A5 ✉ 4141 avenue Pierre-de-Coubertin ☎ 514/252-4141; www.rio.gouv.qc.ca 🕐 Mid-Jun to early Sep daily 9–7; Sep to mid-Jun 9–5 💵 Tower: expensive

Biodôme de Montréal
218, off A5 ✉ 4777 avenue Pierre-de-Coubertin ☎ 514/868-3000 🕐 Daily 9–5/6. Sep–Feb closed Mon 💵 Expensive

2 Québec City

Canada's oldest, and one of its most beautiful cities, Québec City has the only intact city walls in North America and some wonderful French colonial architecture. It was declared a UNESCO World Heritage Site in 1985. The city is in two parts. The upper town sits proudly atop a huge rocky promontory; the lower town nestles below, linked by the aptly named Escalier Casse-Cou (Breakneck Stairs).

The city sits on the north bank of the St. Lawrence (the Iroquois called it Kebec, the "place where the waters narrow"). For this reason, and for its high point it was chosen as a defensive settlement when hostilities between the French and English (and Iroquois) were at their height.

Opposite: maple syrup for sale

Start in the **Haute-Ville** (Upper Town), on the place d'Armes, once a military parade ground but now the focal point of this part of the city. It is dominated by the **Château Frontenac** hotel, in the style of a Loire Valley château. Entertaining guided tours are led by staff in costume.

Below: Château Frontenac

Adjoining place d'Armes is the **Terrasse Dufferin**, a wide boardwalk stretching for 670m (2,200 feet) with magnificent views across the river. It was built in 1834 to provide access over the ruins of the Château St. Louis. Major reconstruction work is ongoing, along with archaeological investigation of the underlying land. The resulting disruption will be rewarded in 2008, when people will be allowed to visit the excavations. In 2009 the terrace will be fully reinstated. Nearby is the **Promenade des Gouverneurs** (Governors' Walk), which clings to the cliffside 90m (295 feet) above the river.

QUÉBEC CITY: INSIDE INFO

Top tips Even if you have paid to take the tour, the **restrooms at the Château Frontenac** are only accessible by key card to residents. Public facilities can be found at the Infotourist Centre on place d'Armes and in the cafés on the square.
• Don't venture down to the **Basse-Ville** before 11am. Up to this time trucks are permitted to make deliveries and the narrow streets can be congested.
• For a superb view over the city and the St. Lawrence, visit the Observatoire (tel: 418/644-9841) on the 31st floor of 1037 rue de la Chevrotière.

In more depth On the Plains of Abraham, the **Musée National des Beaux-Arts du Québec** (Parc des Champs-de-Bataille; tel: 418/643-2150 or 1-866/220-2150; www.mnba.qc.ca; open Jun–early Sep daily, early Sep–May Tue–Sun; free, except temporary exhibitions) has a permanent collection devoted primarily to works by Québec artists.

Hidden gem On **rue Nôtre-Dame**, between Place-Royal and Côte de la Montagne, there is a 420sq m (4,520 square foot) *trompe-l'oeil* mural representing Québec's 400 years of history. There's an explanation board nearby.

Still a military post, home of the elite Royal 22e Régiment, the **Citadelle** (Citadel) can only be visited by joining a group tour, but it is well worth doing so. It is vast, occupying 15ha (37 acres), and was the most important fortification to be built in Canada under British rule. The tours, led by military personnel, begin on the enormous parade ground and include the small regimental museum. In summer visitors are treated to impressive traditional military ceremonies, in full dress uniform, complete with the Regimental Band and the mascot (a goat called Batisse). A word of warning: Don't be tempted to wander away from the rest of your tour group – the military frown on visitors with an independent spirit.

From here you can take a walk around all or part of the 4.5km (3 miles) of the **Fortifications**, the walls and gates that encircle the old part of the city. To learn about their construction and preservation, call in along the way at the Initiation Centre and the Esplanade Powder Magazine. Inside the northwest corner of the Fortifications is the **Artillery**

The gleaming interior of the church of Ste. Anne de Beaupré

Park National Historic Site, used by the French and English until it was taken over by Parks Canada. You can visit the Arsenal Foundry, now an interpretation center, and see the officers' quarters, a 19th-century kitchen and the officers' mess.

Return to the Terrasse Dufferin and take the Funicular down to the **Basse-Ville** (Lower Town), centered on cobblestoned Place-Royal. It's a lovely area to stroll as it is largely traffic-free and there are lots of interesting little stores. The Roman Catholic cathedral, **Cathédrale Nôtre-Dame de Québec** has an opulent interior culminating in the glowing gold-finished canopy over the altar. In summer there's an excellent sound-and-light show.

One modern building, close to the river, is the **Musée de la Civilisation.** With its copper roof pierced by stylized dormer windows, it blends nicely with the older architecture and contains diverse thematic displays devoted to civilization.

TAKING A BREAK

If you like savory or sweet crêpes, you'll love **Au Petit Coin Breton** (418/694-0758, $) on rue St.-Jean. There are also branches on boulevard Laurier and Grande Allée.

➕ 208 B1

Québec City Tourism
✉ 835 avenue Wilfrid-Laurier
☎ 418/522-0830; www.quebecregion.com

Château Frontenac Tours
➕ 217 C4 ✉ 1 rue des Carrières
☎ 418/691-2166; www.tourschateau.ca
🕐 Tours daily in summer, weekends in winter 🎟 Moderate

Citadelle
➕ 217 B3 ✉ Cote de la Citadelle, Haute Ville ☎ 418/694-2815;
www.lacitadelle.qc.ca 🕐 Apr–Oct daily by 1-hour guided tour only 🎟 Moderate

Fortifications
➕ 217 A3 ✉ 100 rue St.-Louis
☎ 418/648-7016 or 1-888/773-8888;
www.pc.gc.ca/lhn-nhs/qc/fortifications
🕐 Interpretation Centre and Powder

Magazine: mid-May to mid-Oct daily 10–5; by appointment mid-Oct to mid-May
🎟 Free; Interpretation Centre and Powder Magazine: inexpensive

Artillery Park National Historic Site
➕ 217 A4 ✉ Corner rue St.-Jean and rue d'Auteuil ☎ 418/648-4205;
www.pc.gc.ca/lhn-nhs/qc/artiller 🕐 Apr to mid-Oct daily 10–5 🎟 Inexpensive

Cathédrale Nôtre-Dame de Québec
➕ 217 C4 ✉ 10 rue de Buade
☎ 418/692-2533; www.patrimoine-religieux.com 🕐 Mon–Fri 8–4, Sat–Sun 8–6 🎟 Free

Musée de la Civilisation
➕ 217 C5 ✉ 85 rue Dalhousie
☎ 418/643-2158 or 1-866/710-8031;
www.mcq.org 🕐 Late Jun to early Sep daily 9:30–6:30; early Sep to late Jun Tue–Sun 10–5 🎟 Moderate

③ Charlevoix Coast

On the north shore of the wide St. Lawrence River, the Charlevoix is one of Québec's most beautiful and varied regions, with mountains sweeping down to the water's edge, a mixture of wild and neat rural landscapes, and charming villages nestling in the valleys. It stretches from Beaupré, northeast of Québec City, to Tadoussac, at the confluence of the Saguenay and St. Lawrence rivers, and for its unique beauty, it is a UNESCO World Biosphere Reserve.

Every June a great flotilla of whales makes its way upstream to feed in the deep waters off Tadoussac, at the mouth of the Saguenay, and a great wave of visitors arrive to view them on whale-watching boat trips. The most common species to visit these rich waters are the minke and fin whale, but occasionally a humpback will be sighted and if you're very lucky a blue whale. There's also a resident population of belugas.

Tadoussac's boardwalk overlooks the pretty harbor

The mountains of the Charlevoix were not formed by volcanic or glacial action, but by a 15-billion ton meteorite that struck the earth 350 million years ago. The resulting crater measures about 56km (35 miles), and is the largest of its kind in the world.

Heading northeast along the coast, **Baie-St.-Paul** is set amid rolling hills on a bay where the Gouffre River flows into the St. Lawrence, a site that has inspired many artists. As a result, it has many galleries and a reputation as a cultural center. Sheltering the bay is the delightfully rural **Île-aux-Coudres**, 11km (7 miles) long and 5km (3 miles) across its widest point, with exceptional views.

Baie-St.-Paul has a lovely little working harbor

Farther along the coast is **Les Éboulements**, perched 300m (980 feet) above the river, with wonderful views. Later, the road sweeps down to river level, passing through **Ste.-Irénée**, host of a prestigious music festival, then continues to the popular resort of **La Malbaie**. It's said that it was named *malle baye* ("bad bay") by French explorer Samuel de Champlain in 1608 after his ship ran aground overnight.

Baie-Ste.-Catherine and **Tadoussac** face each other across the mouth of the Saguenay at the heart of the Saguenay-St. Lawrence Marine Park, and both provide whale-watching trips. Tadoussac has a fine site on the cliffs and sand dunes of the north shore, and swells with visitors when the whales are here. Near the marina, you can visit the **Interpretation Centre for Marine Mammals** (CIMM), with some fascinating interactive exhibits, models and photographs. You can test your lung capacity against that of a whale, and listen by hydrophone to the sounds they make out in the river.

TAKING A BREAK

Call in for lunch (May–Oct only) at Au Pierre-Narcisse opposite the Arts Center in Baie St Paul (tel: 418/435-2056). There's a big terrace for outdoor eating.

CHARLEVOIX COAST: INSIDE INFO

Top tips You can **get a ferry** from St.-Siméon across the St. Lawrence River to Rivière-du-Loup on the opposite shore, with magnificent views.
• Call in at the **Eco-Musée de la Baleine**, next to St.-Simeon lighthouse before you go.
• For **whale-watching trips** you can choose between the standard, large boats that offer a good view from higher in the water, or the zippy little Zodiac inflatables that can get closer to the whales and provide a really exciting experience.

✚ 208 B2

Tourisme Charlevoix
✉ 495 boulevard de Comporté, La Malbaie
☎ 418/665-4454 or 1-800/667-2276;
www.tourisme-charlevoix.com

Tourisme Isle-aux-Coudres
✉ 1024 chein des Coudriers

☎ 418/438-2930;
http://charlevoix.qc.ca/isle-aux-coudres

Interpretation Centre for Marine Mammals
✉ 108 de la Cale Sèche, Tadoussac
☎ 418/235-4701 🕐 Mid-May to Oct noon–5 (mid-Jun to late Sep 9–8)
💵 Moderate

4 Saguenay Fjord

Flowing through a great gash in the Precambrian rock, between the Laurentian Mountains and the wilderness of northern Québec, the Saguenay is not a long river, but it is incredibly dramatic, emptying into the St. Lawrence River between Baie-Ste.-Catherine and Tadoussac. In its upper reaches, it flows out of Lac-St.-Jean and drops about 90m (295 feet) in wild and rocky rapids. Then, in its final 60km (37 miles) it transforms into a deep and majestic fjord, with sheer cliffs rising out of the water.

The best way to really appreciate the full grandeur of the Saguenay Fjord is from the water on one of the many cruises. A highlight of any cruise is the arrival at **Cap Trinité**, rising dramatically 500m (1,640 feet) out of the dark waters. In its wild and rocky setting, it is an awesome sight. The name is derived from the three ledges that punctuate its face and on the first of these, about 180m (590 feet) above the water, there is a statue of the Virgin. The statue was carved in 1881

Much of the spectacular scenery of the fjord can only be truly appreciated from the water

Cruises

Croisières La Marjolaine: Boulevard Saguenay Est (CP 203), Port de Chicoutimi, tel: 418/543-7360 or 800/363-7248; www.quebecweb.com/marjo, open Jun–Sep daily (reservations essential), expensive (under 6 free).

Croisières AML: From Tadoussac and Baie-Ste.-Catherine, tel: 418/692-1159 or 800/563-4643;, www.croisieresaml.com; open Jul–early Sep daily.

Famille Dufour Croisières: From Tadoussec; www.groupedufour.com; open Jun–Sep daily.

These little craft get closer to the whales than conventional boats

for Charles-Napoléon Robitaille, whose life had been saved twice after appeals to the Virgin. At 9m (30 feet) high, it was transported in three sections by boat then raised into position.

The cape is also accessible by land, on Route 170, about 65km (40 miles) east of Chicoutimi. Here, between Cap Trinité and Cap Éternité is the delightful little **Baie Éternité**, at the entrance to the **Parc National du Saguenay**, which protects the edges of the fjord. The village has fine views and a waterside path. From here you can hike 3km (2 miles) to the top of Cap Trinité, then descend to the statue (allow four hours).

Chicoutimi is the main center of population on the fjord and the starting point for many cruises. It was built and prospered on industry, with power generated from the rushing waters upstream, and its main tourist attraction today is the old pulp mill, **La Pulperie de Chicoutimi**. Set in a city park, it is now a museum and cultural center, with a trail through the old buildings and interesting displays. Unexpectedly, the site includes the house of artist Arthur Villeneuve, a remarkable building decorated with murals by the artist himself, which now houses exhibits on history and art.

TAKING A BREAK

La Bougresse (tel: 418/543-3178, $–$$) on the corner of rue Hotel Dieu and rue Riverin in Chicoutimi is a lively bistro serving wholesome Québecoise specialties.

SAGUENAY FJORD: INSIDE INFO

Top tips Late afternoon provides the best light for taking **photographs** from Croix de Ste.-Anne.
• Avoid hiking the trail to the top of Cap Trinité **in midsummer**, when it is plagued with mosquitoes.

➕ 208 B2

Chicoutimi Tourism
✉ 295 rue Racine Est (CP 1023), Chicoutimi ☎ 418/698-3167

Parc Narional du Saguenay
✉ 91 Nôtre-Dame, Rivière-Éternité
☎ 418/272-1556 or 1-800/665-6527;

www.sepaq.com/pq/sag/en ⊙ Mid-May to mid-Oct daily ⛊ Moderate (per car)

Pulperie de Chicoutimi
✉ 300 Dubuc, Chicoutimi ☎ 418/698-3100; www.pulperie.com ⊙ Late Jun to early Sep daily 9–6; museum only early Sep to late Jun, Wed–Sun 10–4. Closed some public holidays ⛊ Expensive

At Your Leisure

Gaspé Peninsula ➤ 185–187

Gatineau ➤ 98

5 Cantons-de-l'Est (Eastern Townships)

A land of mountains, lakes and delightful villages, the Eastern Townships have a unique mix of Anglo-Saxon charm and Québécois *joie-de-vivre*. Here the rolling wooded slopes of the Appalachian Mountains rise to nearly 1,000m (about 3,000 feet) and lakes fill the valleys.

Communities include **Knowlton**, a charming "Victorian" village brimming with craft shops, boutiques, art galleries and restaurants. Farther east, **Magog** has a wonderful setting on Lake Memphremagog, beneath Mount Orford and surrounded by the **Parc du Mont-Orford**. It's boat trips are the main draw visiting the **Abbaie St.-Benoît** on the lakeshore.

➕ 208 B1

Tourisme Cantons-de-l'Est
✉ 20 rue Don-Bosco Sud, Sherbrooke
☎ 819/820-2020;
www.cantonsdelest.com

Parc du Mont-Orford
✉ 3321 chemin du Parc, Canton d'Orford ☎ 819/843-9855 or 1-800/665-6527; www.sepaq.com/pq/mor/en 🎫 Inexpensive

Magog, in the Cantons-de-l'Est, is on the shore of beautiful Lake Memphremagog

Abbaie St.-Benoît
✉ St.-Benoît-du-Lac ☎ 819/843-4080;
www.st-benoit-du-lac.com
🕐 Mon–Sat 5am–8:30pm; store open Mon–Sat (closed 10:45–11:45 during Eucharist) 🎫 Free

6 Trois-Rivières

Where it flows into the St. Lawrence River, the St. Maurice River splits into three to flow around two islands, and it was here that Québec's second-oldest city was founded in 1634. Today, Trois-Rivières is the third-largest city in the province, and has a number of historic attractions.

The suburb of **Cap-de-la-Madeleine** is famous for its **Sanctuaire Nôtre-Dame-du-Cap**, incorporating the beautiful octagonal Rosary Basilica, which attracts half a million pilgrims each year. **Les Forges du St.-Maurice**, a little way north, was Canada's first iron-smelting works, and is now a national historic site.

➕ 208 A1

Office de Tourisme et des Congrès de Trois-Rivières
✉ 1457 rue Nôtre-Dame
☎ 819/375-1123 or 1-800/313-1123;
www.tourismetroisrivieres.com

Manoir Mauvide-Genest is a stately building on the Île d'Orléans

Sanctuaire Nôtre-Dame-du-Cap
✉ 626 rue Nôtre-Dame Est, Cap-de-la-Madeleine ☎ 819/374-2441; www.sanctuaire-ndc.ca ⊙ Daily

Forges du St.-Maurice
✉ 10,000 boulevard des Forges, Trois-Rivières ☎ 819/378-5116 or 800/463-6769; www.pc.gc.ca ⊙ Mid-May to mid-Oct daily 9:30–5:30 (4:30 in fall) 🖐 Inexpensive

7 Île d'Orléans
Wedged like a giant cork in the St. Lawrence River as it widens beyond Québec City, this beautiful and fertile island preserves some fine French architecture from the 18th century. The jewel among them is the **Manoir Mauvide-Genest**, which has been meticulously restored and populated with costumed guides, who re-create life here in former times. The island is also known for producing wine, cheese, liqueurs and preserves that can, of course, be purchased locally.
➕ 208 B1

Tourist Office
✉ 490 Côte du Pont, St.-Pierre ☎ 418/828-9411 or 1-866/941-9411; www.iledorleans.com

Manoir Mauvide-Genest
✉ 1451 chemin Royal, St.-Jean ☎ 418/ 829-2630 ⊙ May–Oct daily 10–5 🖐 Moderate

8 Les Laurentides
A land of sport, leisure, good food and *joie-de-vivre*, this is Montréal's "cottage country." The Laurentians, some of the oldest mountains in the world, are modest in height, rising to no more than 960m (3,150 feet), but are very scenic, with trees clinging precariously to their rocky slopes. The highest point is Mont Tremblant, focal point of the **Mont Tremblant National Park**, where there is now a superb alpine-style ski resort. Longer-established as a ski resort is **St.-Sauveur-des-Monts**, which has some excellent restaurants, boutiques and craft shops. **Ste.-Agathe-des-Monts** is set on lovely Lac-des-Sables (Sandy Lake), and offers popular boat cruises.
➕ 208 A1

Association Touristique des Laurentides
✉ 14142 rue de la Chapelle, Mirabel ☎ 450/224-7007 or 1-800/561-6673; www.laurentides.com

9 Lac St.-Jean
Source of the mighty Saguenay River (► 131–132), this vast, saucer-shaped lake covers 1,350sq km (850 square miles) amid flat, fertile land known for its wild blueberries. The **Village Historique de Val-Jalbert** is dominated by the magnificent Ouiatchouan Falls that once powered the pulp mill here.
  Abandoned in 1927, the village has been restored as a living history attraction, peopled by costumed actor-guides.
➕ 208 A2

Fédératon Touristique Régionale du Saguenay-Lac-St.-Jean
✉ 412 boulevard Saguenay Est, bureau 100, Chicoutimi ☎ 418/543-9778 or 877/253-8387; www.tourismesaguenay-lacsaintjean.qc.ca

Village Historique de Val-Jalbert
✉ Route 169, between Chambord and Roberval ☎ 418/275-3132 or 888/675-3132; www.sepaq.com ⊙ May–Oct daily (full animation mid-Jun to late Aug) 🖐 Expensive

Where to... Stay

Prices

High season room-only rates, based on two sharing a double room, excluding taxes

$ up to $160   **$$** $160–$300   **$$$** more than $300

MONTRÉAL

Auberge Le Jardin D'Antoine $–$$

In the heart of the Latin Quarter, this is an elegant little European-style hotel in a 19th-century building, and the bilingual owners and staff offer a friendly welcome. Rooms and suites all have queen- or king-size beds, and some of the private bathrooms have whirlpool tubs. All but two of the rooms overlook the pleasant interior courtyard. Breakfast is included in the rates.

➕ 201 A1 ✉ 2024 rue St.-Denis
☎ 514/843-4506, 1-800/361-4506;
fax: 514/281-1491;
www.hotel-jardin-antoine.qc.ca

Château Versailles $$

This is a stylish historic hotel, with original plaster moldings and huge fireplaces standing out against bold-colored walls hung with Matisse reproductions. Bedrooms have cable TV, minibar, Nintendo and coffee-makers, and are provided with bathrobes and luxury toiletries.

➕ 201 A1 ✉ 1659 rue Sherbrooke ouest ☎ 514/933-8111, 1-888/933-8111; www.versailleshotels.com

Fairmont The Queen Elizabeth $$–$$$

This grand, luxury hotel hit the world's newsreels in 1969, when John Lennon staged his famous "bed in" (in Suite 1742) and wrote and recorded "Give Peace a Chance." Lennon wasn't the first celebrity to stay here – it's hosted the rich and famous since it opened in 1958. Premier rooms and suites offer the best views. There's a modern health club, an indoor swimming pool and direct access to the underground city.

➕ 201 A1 ✉ 900 Boulevard René-Levesque ouest ☎ 514/861-3511, 1-800/257-7544; www.fairmont.com

Hotel Ruby Foos $–$$

Just off the TransCanada, this is a good option for those who prefer to be out of the city. Rooms are modern and have cable TV and coffee-makers; some also have kitchenettes, and some two-bedroom suites are available. A choice of restaurants serve seafood, Continental cuisine and sushi, and there's a fitness center.

➕ 201 A1 ✉ 7655 boulevard Decarie ☎ 514/731-7701, 1-800/361-5419; fax: 514/731-7158; www.hotelrubyfoos.com

Auberge St.-Antoine $$–$$$

Though it doesn't look it from the outside, this is a new hotel, converted from a derelict warehouse in 2003. The owners have done a superb job of creating a hotel that has enormous character, and made some bold choices in the process. You'll want to keep coming back, just to be able to stay in a different room each time.

➕ 208 B1 ✉ 8 rue St-Antoine
☎ 418/692-2211;
www.saint-antoine.com

Fairmont Le Château Frontenac $$$

Like a fairy-tale European château, with steep roofs, turrets and dormer windows, this magnificent hotel dominates its surroundings and is an integral part of the city scene. Particularly imposing seen from the lower town, it is without question the most prestigious place to stay and it's hard to believe that it was built as something so mundane as a railroad hotel. Inside it is as luxurious as you might expect of a place that has such a long list of royalty and movie stars among its clientele.

✛ 208 B1 ⊠ 1 rue des Carrières
☎ 418/692-3861, 1-800/257-7455;
www.fairmont.com

♦♦♦ L'Hôtel du Vieux Québec $

This is a fascinating building, with staircases leading this way and that before finally arriving at your room, which is likely to have sloping ceilings and exposed stone walls. It's in a great location within the old city walls and the friendly owners run free guided walks in summer.

✛ 208 B1 ⊠ 1190 rue St-Jean
☎ 418/692-1850, 1-800/361-7787;
www.hvq.com

♦♦♦ Hotel Le Priori $$

The chic modern decor sets off to perfection the brick and hardwood floors of this 18th-century building

in the Old Port. All bedrooms have private bathrooms with massaging showers, but some also have an old-fashioned tub right in the room. Suites have whirlpools, fireplaces and kitchens. The restaurant is of a high standard and the inclusive breakfasts are delicious.

✛ 208 B1 ⊠ 15 Sault-au-Matelot
☎ 418/692-3992, 1-800/351-3992;
www.hotellepriori.com

TADOUSSAC

♦♦♦ Hotel Tadoussac $

Sprawling along the bank of the St. Lawrence, this imposed red-tiled 149-room hotel is an excellent base for exploring the Charlevoix coast and Saguenay fjord and it has wonderful views. Rooms are tastefully decorated, with cable TV and coffee maker among the amenities, and the hotel has a spa and various sports facilities, including a pool.

✛ 208 B2 ⊠ 165 rue Bord de l'Eau
☎ 418/235-4421, 1-800/561-0718;
www.hoteltadoussac.com

Where to... Eat and Drink

Prices
Based on the cost of a three-course dinner, excluding drinks and service.
$ under $30 $$ $30–$50 $$$ more than $50

MONTRÉAL

♦♦♦ St.-Viateur Bagel & Café $

Be prepared to stand in line at busy times – and be prepared for the crisp, wood-oven bagels, cooked on the premises, to be well worth the wait. You can buy bags of them to take out or choose one of the sandwiches or salads and soak up the atmosphere of this vibrant area on the café's spacious terrace.

✛ 208 A1 ⊠ 5629 Monkland Avenue
☎ 514/487-8051;
www.stviateurbagel.com
⊙ Daily from 6:30am

♦♦♦ Le Commensal $–$$

French cuisine, which naturally predominates in this city, is not particularly noted for providing vegetarian options, so this chain is a welcome relief to those who prefer a meat-free diet. Home-style dishes are set out buffet style and you pay by the weight of what's on your plate. There are well-labeled vegan options too, and the staff is very knowledgeable about what they are serving. Also on rue St.-Denis, just south of rue Ontario.

✛ 208 A1 ⊠ 1204 rue McGill
College ☎ 514/871-1480; www.commensal.com ⊙ Daily 11:30–10

L'Express $$

There's a real Parisian atmosphere in this Latin Quarter bistro, from its zinc bar to its lively clientele of regulars. The menu is full of classic French favorites, such as *bouillabaisse*, steak tartare, steak-frites and seafood, and the wines are exclusively French. It's extremely popular so reservations are essential – and make sure you get directions when you call, because it's not that easy to find.

🕂 208 A1 ⊠ 3927 rue St-Denis
☎ 514/845-5333 ⏰ Mon–Fri 8am–2am, Sat 10am–2am, Sun 10am–1am

Nuances $$$

If there's one thing you expect to find in Montréal it's excellent French cuisine, and this is one of the best places of all. Part of the casino complex, it's very formal and the presentation and flavors of the food is nothing short of artistic. Dishes might include a starter of lobster chartreuse or shrimp

tempura (or caviar at $280), followed by roasted veal with cocoa-infused sauce or duck with honey and coriander seeds. There's a dress code – business smart – and an age limit of 18.

🕂 208 A1 ⊠ 5th Floor, Casino du Montréal, 1 avenue du Casino
☎ 514/392-2746, 1-800/665-2274;
www.casino-de-montreal.com
⏰ Daily 5:30–11 (11:30 Fri–Sat)

3 Amigos Resto-Bar $–$$

In an easy-to-find, downtown location, this is a Mexican/Tex-Mex restaurant that offers deliciously authentic south-of-the-border cuisine. The daily specials are particularly good value.

🕂 208 A1 ⊠ 1657 rue Ste.-Catherine ouest ☎ 514/939-3329
⏰ 11am–midnight (1am Fri–Sat)

Weinstein & Gavino's Pasta Bar Factory Co Ltd $–$$

On Montréal's busy nightclub street, this popular restaurant is always busy and always buzzing,

spilling out onto the terrace in warm weather. The menu features all the traditional Italian dishes, including an extensive *antipasti* selection, pastas, pizzas and entrées that include chicken, steak, seafood and lamb. Good value and good fun.

🕂 208 A1 ⊠ 1434 rue Crescent
☎ 514/288-2231;
www.weinsteinandgavinos.com
⏰ Daily 11–11 (midnight Thu–Sat)

QUÉBEC CITY

Restaurant Aux Anciens Canadiens $$

This is a gorgeous place – the oldest building in Québec City, dating back to 1675 – and the five separate dining rooms give it a very intimate atmosphere. The menu has some interesting dishes, such as caribou cooked with creamy blueberry wine sauce, and a ragout of boar and pig's knuckles, served with meatballs. There's lots of maple syrup in the desserts, completing the authentic Canadian experience.

🕂 208 B2 ⊠ 34 rue St-Louis, Haute-Ville ☎ tel: 418/692-1627; www.auxancienscanadiens.qc.ca
⏰ Daily noon–10

Restaurant le Parlementaire $$

Dine like a diplomat beneath glittering chandeliers in the National Assembly's imposing beaux-arts dining room. This restaurant is renowned for its regional cuisine using top-quality Québec produce, and the cost is surprisingly reasonable. Elaborate main courses might include *blanc de volaille aux épinards et fromage, grenadin de porc en croûte*, or grilled steak with mushrooms and thyme. Breakfasts are good and include omelets and crêpes.

🕂 208 B1 ⊠ National Assembly (Door No. 3) ☎ 418/643-6640;
www.assnat.qc.ca/eng/accueil/
LeParlementaire.shtml ⏰ Mon–Fri 8am–2.30pm. The restaurant may be closed without notice for government reasons

The **Marché Bonsecours** (350 rue St.-Paul Est, tel: 514/872-7730), in a magnificent building in the Old City, is headquarters of the Design Council, with two galleries and 15 boutiques selling top-quality crafts. More top-quality crafts are on show at the **Canadian Guild of Crafts** (2025 rue Peel, tel: 514/849-6091), a non-profit (which doesn't necessarily mean inexpensive) outlet for Canadian artisans.

If it's antiques you are looking for, stroll along **Antiques Row** (rue Notre-Dame Ouest, between Guy and Atwater), where down-to-earth vendors sell from decidedly unglamorous premises. There are bargains to be found.

QUEBEC CITY

This beautiful old city is home to a huge shopping mall – **Place Laurier** (2700 boulevard Laurier, tel: 418/ 651-7085), with around 350 stores – but the city is much better known for streets of

huge Grande Place, and has more than 100 stores, but the **Montréal Eaton Centre** (705 rue Ste.-Catherine Ouest, tel: 514/288-3708) tops with 175 units and is the main shopping destination in the city. **Place Montréal Trust** (1500 avenue McGill College, tel: 514/843-8000) is another bright and lofty mall in the underground city, with around 70 stores.

Montréal has three great traditional markets, each with a character all of its own. **Atwater Market** (138 avenue Atwater, tel: 514/937-7754), in a distinctive building with a tall clock tower, has fresh produce and gourmet foods; **Jean-Talon** (7070 rue Henri-Julien; tel: 514/277-1588) is a cosmopolitan treasure in the heart of Little Italy; and **Maisonneuve Market** (4445 rue Ontario Est, tel: 514/937-7754) is a 1990s building alongside the original 1936 market, the old one a cultural center for festivals and entertainment.

Where to... Shop

Québec offers a different shopping experience from anywhere else in Canada, with its distinctive French chic combined with refreshing Canadian enthusiasm and First Nations traditions.

MONTRÉAL

As Canada's second-largest city, Montréal has terrific shopping – and if you're here in winter, you'll be glad to know that much of it is sheltered from the bitter cold in the Ville Souterraine (underground city, ▶ 120). The **Complexe Desjardins** (150 rue Ste.-Catherine Ouest, tel: 514/281-1870) is the largest building in the network, centering on the

♥♥♥ Le William ($$)

Within the landmark Hotel Tadoussac, this intimate restaurant is renowned for excellent seafood, bought daily from local North Shore fishermen.

🚹 208 B2 ⊠ 165 rue Bord de l'Eau ☎ 418/235-4421, 888/222-3307 🕑 Daily

PERCÉ

♥♥♥ La Normandie $$

This waterfront dining room is renowned for some of the area's best food – and it has great views of Rocher Percé and Île Bonaventure. There's a refined atmosphere and the table d'hôte offers more than 20 main courses. Ther is also a European-style breakfast buffet.

🚹 208 C3 ⊠ Hotel La Normandie, 221 Route 123 ouest, cp129 ☎ 418/782-2112; www.normandieperce.com 🕑 Early Jun–late Sep daily 7:30–10am, 6–9pm

individual stores that will enhance the whole experience of your visit here.

The Lower Town is chock full of artisan-owned craft boutiques and galleries. **Artisans du Bas-Canada** (30 Côte de la Fabrique, tel: 418/692-2109) is a long-established showcase for the work of around 500 Canadian artists and craftspeople, including Inuit and First Nations works. At **Verrerie la Mailloche** (58 rue Sous-le-Fort, tel: 418/694-0445), near the base of the funicular, you can visit the old workshop, though it is no longer operational. Take the funicular up to visit the **Galeries d'Art Inuit Brousseau et Brousseau** (35 rue St.-Louis, tel: 418/694-1828), next door to Le Château Frontenac, a gallery dedicated to promoting the work of Inuit artists from Arctic Canada, or call in at the **5 Nations Indian Art Gallery** (20 rue Cul-de-Sac, tel: 418/ 692-1009), representing First Nations artists from across North America.

The city's **Public Market** (160 quai St.-André, tel: 418/692-2517) has a particularly good cheese selection and lots of maple syrup products alongside the usual fruit and vegetables.

Bookstores carry mostly French-language titles and some in English, but **La Maison Anglaise** (2600 boulevard Laurier, tel: 418/654-9523) only has books in English and specializes in fiction.

Montréal is the center for the Canadian **fur industry**, a contentious issue in many places, but seen here as a traditional means of supporting First Nations people – who might otherwise be forced to give their land over to oil and mineral exploitation in order to survive, causing severe ecological consequences.

Of many city furriers, **Dubarry Furs** (206 rue St.-Paul ouest, tel: 514/844-7483) has some original designs and will make to measure.

Where to... Be Entertained

Many of the theater productions here are in French, and you need a good understanding of the language to fully appreciate them, but there are some shows in English. Of course, music is universal and Québec offers some world-class performances in every genre.

MONTRÉAL

This city has everything you would expect from the second-largest French-speaking city in the world. The whole spectrum of entertainment is laid out for you, from the most prestigious classical performances to somewhat risqué night-clubs, and everything in between. The **Place des Arts** (tel: 514/842-2112) is the showpiece venue, central to Montréal's cultural life, with five halls totaling 6,000 seats and a full schedule of classical music, ballet and opera. Mega rock concerts and massive classical events are staged at the **Bell Centre** (1200 rue de la Gauchetière Ouest, tel: 514/790-1245). More intimate is the **Centre Pierre Peladeau** (300 boulevard Maisonneuve Est, tel: 514/987-6919). Montréal theaters include the **Centaur** (453 rue St.-François-Xavier, tel: 514/288-3161), home to the city's leading English-language company, with a reputation for ground-breaking productions. The **Théâtre du Nouveau Monde** (84 rue Ste.-Catherine Ouest, tel: 514/878-7878) stages classical and modern drama, **La Chapelle** (3700 rue Ste.-Dominique, tel: 514/843-7738) stages drama in French, plus roots, jazz and classical music concerts, and the **Saidye Bronfman Centre for the Arts** (5170 rue Côte Ste.-Catherine, tel: 514/739-2301) is an internationally acclaimed venue offering a wide range of productions in English and Yiddish. One of the city's premier jazz clubs is the **House of Jazz** (2060 rue Aylmer, tel: 514/842-8656), with live music nightly from big-name and local performers, plus jam sessions.

Nightlife in Montréal is really buzzing, with a huge number of nightclubs and bars, and more than 100 gay venues, including the vast **Bourbon Complex** (1474 rue Ste.-Catherine Est, tel: 514/529-6969). The **Casino de Montréal** (1 avenue du Casino, tel: 514/392-2746 or 800/665-2274) in a spectacular waterfront location, offers gaming tables, slot machines and Las Vegas-style shows.

Montréal is also world-famous for comedy because of its annual "Just for Laughs" festival, and permanent comedy clubs include **Ernie Butler's Comedy Nest** (3rd floor, Forum Pepsi, 2313 rue Ste.-Catherine Ouest, tel: 514/932-6378) and **Comedy Works** (1238 rue Bishop, tel: 514/398-9661), both of which feature top comedy names and open mike sessions.

Every other year, you get the chance to see the spectacular **Cirque du Soleil** on home ground, when the Québec company sets up its distinctive striped marquees in Montréal. Check with the tourist office for information.

Sport gets an enthusiastic following here, especially when one of the teams is playing the city's great rival, Toronto. The **Montréal Canadiens** are the hockey team, playing at the **Bell Centre** (1200 rue de la Gauchetière Ouest, tel: 514/790-1245); the **Montréal Expos** are one of only two Canadian baseball teams in the American Major League (Toronto's Blue Jays is the other), and they play to rousing support at the Olympic Stadium (4141 avenue Pierre de Coubertin, tel: 514/252-8687); and the **Alouettes** Canadian football team play at the **Percival Molson Memorial Stadium** (475 avenue des Pins, tel: 514/871-2266). The **Canadian Grand Prix** takes place at the Gilles Villeneuve circuit, accessible from the city on the métro system.

QUÉBEC CITY

Entertainment in Québec City is more low-key, but it does have the province's premier theater, the **Grand Théâtre de Québec** (269 boulevard René-Lévesque Est, tel: 418/643-8131), home to the Opera de Québec and the Québec Symphony Orchestra. Its two concert halls provide a full schedule of dance, drama and music. The **Petit Champlain** (Maison de la Chanson, 68–78 rue du Petit-Champlain, tel: 418/692-2631) is an atmospheric little theater in a converted warehouse, staging concerts by French-speaking performers. There are a couple of places where you can experience a truly French evening listening to Québecois *chansons*: **Les Yeux Bleus** (1117 1/2 St.-Jean, tel: 418/694-9118), which also has some pop music; and the **Café des Arts** (1000 rue St.-Jean, tel: 418/694-1499), where *chansons* shares the bill with jazz, poetry readings and mime.

The **Terrasse d'Orsay** (65 rue de Buade, tel: 418/694-1582) is a lovely old pub-restaurant with a great terrace and entertainment from a solo singer in summer. If you're visiting in winter, drive out to the famous Ice Hotel's nightclub, **N'Ice** (143 route Duchesnay, Ste.-Catherine-de-la-Jacques-Cartier, tel: 418/875-4522) which is as hot as it can be at a constant -2°C (28°F). This remarkable hotel is built anew every winter from blocks of ice.

Atlantic Provinces

Getting Your Bearings

Add together the Atlantic provinces of New Brunswick, Prince Edward Island and Nova Scotia and you wouldn't achieve the size of just one of the other provinces of Canada. And yet, here on the eastern seaboard, you will find a concentration of some of Canada's oldest settlements, a history that shaped the whole country, and a fascinating mixture of cultures that encompasses a large number of Acadian French and communities of Scottish descent (Nova Scotia means "New Scotland"). Put Newfoundland and Labrador into the mix and you'll get evidence of the earliest Viking visitors, the first footfall of explorer John Cabot (though Nova Scotians may disagree), and the great wave of immigrants who came here from Ireland during the Great Famine.

The character of this part of Canada is quite different from the rest of the country, with Atlantic salt in the air, fiddle music in the blood, and a slower pace of life, even on the city streets. The scenery is breathtaking, with rocky coastlines, beautiful beaches, dense forests, wide river valleys and vast stretches of wilderness in Newfoundland and Labrador. The land supports a variety of wildife, including moose, bear and caribou, while whales, seals and dolphins inhabit the coastal waters. Quaint seaside towns of colorful clapboard buildings sit on pretty coves, and, aside from Halifax, the provincial capitals are small and low-rise, with quiet tree-lined streets and fascinating historic corners.

The climate is generally warm in summer, although coastal areas are prone to mists and strong winds. In winter it's milder here than in many parts of Canada, but snowfall is among the highest in the country, making it excellent for cross-country skiing, dog-sledding and snowmobiling. Winter and summer, the place is lively with festivals and other events.

Bluenose II recalls a glorious maritime past

★ Don't Miss

At Your Leisure

The Cabot Trail around the north of Cape Breton Island features breathtaking coastal scenery

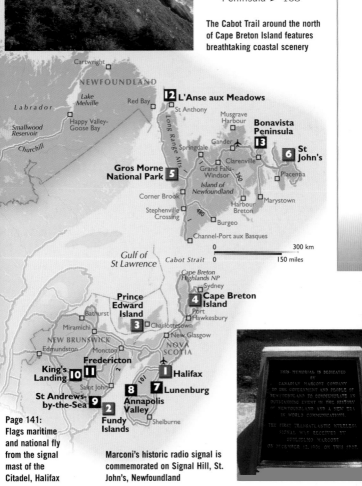

Page 141: Flags maritime and national fly from the signal mast of the Citadel, Halifax

Marconi's historic radio signal is commemorated on Signal Hill, St. John's, Newfoundland

Get an overview of the Maritimes, including provincial capitals, national parks and historic settlements, spectacular coastlines, and a few oddities of nature along the way.

Atlantic Provinces in Nine Days

Day One

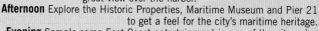

Morning Begin in **1** Halifax (➤ 146–147), up on the Citadel, then head down to the Waterfront for a boat trip of the harbor (➤ right).
Lunch Have lunch at Salty's (➤ 160), with a great view over the harbor.
Afternoon Explore the Historic Properties, Maritime Museum and Pier 21 to get a feel for the city's maritime heritage.
Evening Sample some East Coast entertainment in one of the city pubs.

Day Two

Morning Drive to **8** Annapolis Royal (➤ 156) and see its two National Historic Sites.
Lunch Stop at Ye Olde Towne Pub (tel: 902/532-2244), near the wharf.
Afternoon Continue to Digby for the ferry across the Bay of Fundy to Saint John, New Brunswick, take a look at the Reversing Falls at low or high tide, then continue west to spend the night at Back Bay.

Day Three

Morning Take the ferry to the **2** Fundy Islands (➤ 148), first to Deer Island, then on to Campobello to explore the **Roosevelt International Park**.
Lunch Have a picnic in the park.
Afternoon Return to the mainland and overnight at Saint John. Return to Reversing Falls (if the tide is right) to see them flow the other way.

Day Four

Morning Drive east on Highway 1, then take the 114 down through the **Fundy National Park** to Alma, then east along the Fundy Coast Drive. Visit the Hopewell Rocks along the way, then continue to Moncton.
Lunch Tuck in to some tapas or choose from the lunch menu at Sasha's (tel: 506/854-8748) at Robinson Court in downtown Moncton.
Afternoon Stop off at Magnetic Hill, to experience the weird sensation of freewheeling "uphill" then take Highway 15 out through Shediac and Cap-Pele. Follow signs for **3** Prince Edward Island (➤ 149–150) and stop at the visitor center on the New Brunswick side for a view of Confederation Bridge. Drive across the bridge and head up to overnight in Cavendish.

Day Five

Morning Visit the **PEI National Park** and **Green Gables House**.
Lunch On Route 6, east of Green Gables House, the
Friendly Fisherman (tel: 902/963-2234 or 2669,
1-866/963-2234; $) has some terrific seafood choices,
plus sandwiches, burgers, wraps and salads.
Afternoon Drive down to the provincial capital of
Charlottetown for a quick look round, then head for Wood
Islands on the south coast and take the ferry to Caribou on
the Nova Scotia mainland.
Evening Drive east to spend the night at Antigonish.

Day Six

Morning From Antigonish, continue on the 104 to cross
the Canso Causeway onto **4 Cape Breton Island**
(► 151–152). Visit the interesting little town of Baddeck, then follow the
Cabot Trail (► 188–190) northwest to Cheticamp.
Lunch Among Cheticamp's many restaurants, the Co-op Artisinale (tel:
902/224-3207, $) is an interesting choice, on the site of an Acadian
craft center, serving traditional Acadian dishes.
Afternoon Continue on the Cabot Trail, passing through the spectacular
scenery of the **Cape Breton Highlands National Park**, looping around the top
of the island and down the other side through Ingonish.
Evening Spend the night in North Sydney and try to get to a Cape Breton
ceilidh to experience their unique brand of Celtic music.

Day Seven

Morning Take the morning ferry from North Sydney to Port aux Basques,
Newfoundland (6 hours), and drive up to **Deer Lake** for the night.

Day Eight

Morning Start early and drive northwest for a quick look at **5 Gros Morne
National Park** (► 153), taking Highway 430 at Wiltondale along the north
shore of Bonne Bay. Retrace your route to Deer Lake, pick up supplies for
a picnic, and set off east on the TransCanada Highway toward St. John's.
Lunch Choose a scenic spot to enjoy your picnic.
Afternoon Continue the long drive to **6 St. John's** (► 154–155).
Evening At 9:30pm join the fun guided Ghost Tour (tel:709/685-3444).

Day Nine

Morning Drive up **Signal Hill** for the spectacular view along the coast.
Lunch Choose between a range of seafood and steaks and eat them over-
looking the harbor at Rumpelstiltskin's (tel: 709/579-6000; $–$$) in the
Quality Hotel Harbourview on Hill O'Chips.
Afternoon Take a whale-watching trip from the harbor.
Evening Wander around the historic streets near the harbor.

❶ Halifax

The international gateway to the Maritimes, Halifax is a lively city that sits on the second-largest natural harbor in the world (after Sydney, Australia). Historic buildings line a waterfront that has been bustling with activity since the mid-18th century. Behind the waterfront, glittering modern high-rise offices mark it as a prosperous provincial capital, but it has a distinct East Coast laid-back atmosphere.

Begin your exploration up at the **Halifax Citadel National Historic Site**, not just for its historic importance, but also for the spectacular view over the city and harbor. The site was fortified from the mid-18th century, when Halifax was one of the four major overseas naval stations of the British Empire: This was the nerve center of the city's defenses, a massive star-shaped bastion that was completed in 1865, and despite the development of the modern city it still dominates the skyline. In summer you'll be greeted by guides in uniform and hear the pipes and drums of a military band. You can tour the restored buildings and talk with "inhabitants," who are skilled at portraying military life of the 1860s.

Eventually, everyone gravitates toward the **waterfront**. A 4km (2.5-mile) walkway links the historic buildings, restaurants, craft stores and museums, there's a little food market and the renowned Alexander Keith brewery (tours available), and always activity on the water.

Between 1928 and 1971 the Halifax waterfront was the first thing seen by more than a million immigrants as they disembarked, and one of the immigration sheds has been restored as the **Pier 21 National Historic Site**. With the aid of a dramatic multimedia presentation and interactive displays, it provides a wonderful evocation of the emotional experiences of wartime evacuees, refugees, war brides and people who were just coming in search of a better life.

The sea has always played a major part in the culture and heritage of the city, and the **Maritime Museum of the Atlantic** here is the largest and oldest of its kind in Canada. Located in an 1879 chandlery, it has a collection of full-size and model ships (some floating) and seafaring artifacts, plus displays about maritime history. There's also an excellent film about the Halifax Explosion in 1917, when a collision in the harbor involving a French arms ship caused the greatest man-made explosion the world had seen prior to Hiroshima. Docked behind the museum is a restored World War II corvette, **HMCS *Sackville***, one of many that escorted north Atlantic convoys. Visitors can tour the vessel, including the engine and boiler rooms, crew's quarters and wheelhouse.

Actor-guides bring to life the military history of the Citadel

Opposite: the harbor is a lively mix of tourist and working boats in summer

TAKING A BREAK

Salty's on the Waterfront (➤ 160) has wonderful harbor views and excellent seafood.

HALIFAX: INSIDE INFO

Top tips The **FRED** (free rides everywhere downtown) shuttle bus runs daily 10:30–5:30, every 40 minutes, from early July to late October. The route includes the waterfront and Citadel Hill.
• The **ferries that cross over to Dartmouth**, on the opposite side of the harbor, provide a wonderful view back toward the city and cost less than the many sightseeing boat trips that are available from Halifax.

🕂 209 D2

Scotia Square Visitor Centre
✉ 5251 Duke Street ☎ 902/424-4248;
www.halifaxinfo.com

Waterfront Visitor Info Centre
✉ Sackville Landing ☎ 902/424-4248

Halifax Citadel National Historic Site
✉ P.O. Box 9080, Station A ☎ 902/426-5080; www.ppc.gc.ca 🕐 Early May–Oct daily 9–5 (to 6 pm Jul–Aug)
🎟 Expensive

Pier 21 National Historic Site
✉ 1055 Marginal Road ☎ 902/425-7770;
www.pier21.ca 🕐 May–Nov daily
9:30–5:30; Dec–Mar (daily during March

break) Tue–Sat 10–5; Mon–Sat 10–5
🎟 Moderate

Argyll Visitor Centre
✉ 1598 Argyle Street at Sackville Street
☎ 902/490-5946

Maritime Museum of the Atlantic
✉ 1675 Lower Water Street ☎ 902/424-7490; http://museum.gov.ns.ca/mma
🕐 May–Oct daily 9:30–5:30 (Sun from 1pm May and Oct); Nov–Apr Tue–Sat 9:30–5, Sun 1–5 (closed yeare-round Tue 8pm)
🎟 Moderate (Nov–Apr inexpensive)

HMCS *Sackville*
✉ Lower Water Street ☎ 902/429-2132 (902/427-2837 in winter) 🕐 Jun–Oct daily 10–5 🎟 Expensive

2 Fundy Islands

The three Fundy Islands – Campobello, Deer Island and Grand Manan – provide a wonderful haven for wildlife and seabirds and are the perfect place to unwind in tranquil surroundings.

Deer Island, nearest to the New Brunswick shore, is home to about 900 residents who make their living from lobsters, clams and farmed salmon. If time is limited, head straight down to Deer Island Point on the southern tip to view the **Old Sow Whirlpool**, the largest in the Western Hemisphere.

Campobello Island sits right up against the US border and is famous as the vacation spot for the Roosevelt family. Young Franklin Delano spent childhood summers here and eventually acquired his own home, now the centerpiece of the **Roosevelt Campobello International Park**, with 1,130ha (2,800 acres) of parkland and rocky shores.

The Roosevelt "Cottage" on Campobello is in Dutch Colonial style

The third and largest island is **Grand Manan**, with lofty cliffs, rugged scenery and a dulse (edible seaweed) industry.

TAKING A BREAK

Take a **picnic** – there are tables at Deer Island Point and in the Roosevelt Park.

✚ 208 C1

Tourist information
Deer Island: Lord's Cove, Deer Island
For ferry service tel: 506/747-7007
Campobello: Roosevelt Campobello
International Park Visitor Centre,
tel: 506/752-2922
For ferry service tel: 506/747-2159 or
1-877/747-2159

Grand Manan: 1141 Route 776, Grand
Manan, tel: 506/662-3442
For ferry service tel: 506/662-3724

Roosevelt Cottage and Visitor Centre
✉ Route 774, Campobello ☎ 506/752-2922
🕐 Mid-May to mid-Oct daily 10–6; park and
grounds open daily during daylight hours
🎫 Free

FUNDY ISLANDS: INSIDE INFO

Top tips The **Old Sow Whirlpool** off Deer Island is at its peak three hours before high tide during the new and full phases of the moon.
• **Swimming** is not recommended anywhere on the Fundy Islands.

3 Prince Edward Island

Canada's smallest province is a rural idyll, with rolling farmlands, a gracious provincial capital, beautiful beaches washed by the warmest waters north of the Carolinas and succulent seafood. It's the home of Anne of Green Gables and the historic birthplace of the Confederation of Canada, and remains unassuming even though it's on the list of top five islands in North America.

Access to Prince Edward Island (generally shortened to PEI, or simply "The Island") is easier since the **Confederation Bridge** opened. The longest bridge over salt water in the world, at 13km (8 miles), it links the island to New Brunswick across the Northumberland Strait and makes for a thrilling drive. There's also a ferry from Caribou, Nova Scotia.

The provincial capital, **Charlottetown**, is a charming place with quiet tree-lined streets, historic buildings, a pleasant waterfront and growing popularity as a cruise ship destination. It's here that you'll find **Founders' Hall**, which commemorates the foundation of the nation of Canada. It began with the arrival on this very spot in 1864 of 23 colonial politicians from across the land. Using modern technology, the exhibition here tells the story of Canada from its inception to the creation of the Territory of Nunavut in 1999.

Charlottetown is a stately and historic provincial capital

Green Gables House reflects the popularity of the stories about Anne

The main resort area on the island is **Cavendish**, a paradox of a place that has on the one hand a magnificently unspoiled section of protected coastline and on the other a cluster of brash, family-oriented attractions around the town itself. The **Prince Edward Island National Park** encompasses long, sandy beaches, grassy dunes, red sandstone cliffs, wetlands and forests.

You won't get far here without seeing a reference to *Anne of Green Gables*, the classic children's book by Lucy Maud Mont-gomery, and its centenary in 2008 will be vigorously celebrated. Devotees come in droves to **Green Gables House**, within the national park, the inspiration for her graphic portrayal of rural life. **Avonlea** is re-created nearby with actors taking the parts of Anne and her friends.

TAKING A BREAK

Charlottetown's **Gahan House** (➤ 160) has above average pub food and six ales brewed on the premises.

✚ 209 D2

Charlottetown Information Centre
✉ 178 Water Street, Charlottetown
☎ 902/368-4444 or 1-800/463-4PEI

Founders' Hall
✉ 6 Prince Street, Charlottetown
☎ 902/368-1864; www.foundershall.ca
🕐 Mid-May to late Jun daily 9–5 or 6; late Jun–late Aug Mon–Sat 8–8, Sun 8–5; late Aug to mid-Sep Mon–Sat 8–6, Sun 8–5; mid-Sep to early Oct daily 8–5; rest of Oct Mon–Fri 9–3:30; Nov and Mar–Apr Mon–Fri 10–3 💷 Moderate

Prince Edward Island National Park
✉ Off Route 2, between Cavendish and

Dalvay ☎ 902/672-6350; www.pc.gc.ca
🕐 Year round; full services late Jun–late Aug; Greenwich Interpretation Centre late Jun–early Oct 9–4:30 (to 6 late Jun–late Aug); Cavendish Visitor Centre daily late May to mid-Oct 💷 Day pass: moderate

Green Gables House Heritage Place
✉ Route 6, Cavendish ☎ 902/963-7874 (Parks Canada); www.pc.gc.ca 🕐 May–Oct daily noon–4; Nov–Apr Wed 10–4 or by appointment 💷 Moderate

Avonlea
✉ 8779 Route 6, Cavendish ☎ 902/968 3050; www.avonlea.ca 🕐 Mid-Jun to Aug daily 9–5, early Jun and Sep daily 10–4 💷 Expensive

---

PRINCE EDWARD ISLAND: INSIDE INFO

Top tips Public transit on PEI is limited to Charlottetown's fledgling bus system, and, though guided tours are available, a car is essential.
• In season you'll see billboards all over the island advertising **Lobster Suppers**, often run by the local church or community association. They are open to visitors, and offer great lobster (at low prices) and good company.

Hidden gem An unexpected find is the **Rossignol Estate Winery** (tel: 902/962-4193; www.rossignolwinery.com; May–Oct Mon–Sat 10–5, Sun 1–5; call ahead in winter), at Little Sands, where you can tour the winery, farm and vineyard.

4 Cape Breton Island

Cape Breton's most famous resident, Alexander Graham Bell, said about the island: "I have traveled the globe. I have seen the Canadian and American Rockies, the Andes and the Alps and the highlands of Scotland, but for simple beauty, Cape Breton outrivals them all." It is indeed one of the most beautiful islands in the world, with forest-clad mountains, glittering lakes and a spectacular coastline.

Cape Breton has an interesting blend of cultures, with its Mi'kmaq communities, its descendants of Scottish settlers, and its strong Acadian (French) presence. It also has a world-famous tradition of fiddle music and step-dancing.

At the very heart of the island is **Baddeck**, which Alexander Graham Bell made his home. The **Alexander Graham Bell National Historic Site** is a jaw-dropping exhibition illustrating the full extent of the man's genius, including his invention of the telephone, his part in the first manned flight in Canada, and the world speed record he achieved on nearby Bras d'Or Lake.

From Baddeck set out on the **Cabot Trail**, one of the most scenic drives in the world (► 188–190). On the way you'll pass through **Chéticamp**, a stronghold of Acadian French culture on the island and one of the places to get a whale-watching trip (also at Pleasant Bay, Bay St. Lawrence and

The Cabot Trail features one magnificent view after another

Ingonish). A little way north of Chéticamp, you enter the **Cape Breton Highlands National Park**, a spectacular area of densely wooded mountains and spectacular coastal vistas. At Pleasant Bay the **Whale Interpretive Centre** has life-size whale models and interactive displays. Another highlight of the Cabot Trail, over on the east coast, is **Ingonish**, with its superb beach.

The Fleur de Lis Trail along Cape Breton's southeastern coast leads to the remarkable **Fortress of Louisbourg**. Built by the French in 1713, this national historic site was a fortified town of several thousand settlers, an important trade center with a military stronghold protecting the approach to the Gulf of St. Lawrence. It was at the forefront of the struggle between the French and English and changed hands many times. About 25 percent of the original settlement has been reconstructed and more than 60 buildings are populated by costumed interpreters.

The Fortress of Louisbourg saw plenty of action in the French-English struggle for Canada

TAKING A BREAK

On the west coast, call in at the **Rusty Anchor** ($) at Pleasant Bay for superb lobster; on the east, **Keltic Lodge** (tel: 800/565-0444, $$$) at Ingonish is a popular choice.

✚ 209 E2

Cape Breton Tourism
✉ 96 Highway 4, Port Hastings
☎ 902/625-4201; http://novascotia.com

Alexander Graham Bell National Historic Site
✉ Chebucto Street, Baddeck ☎ 902/295-2069; www.pc.gc.ca ◷ Jun daily 9–6; Jul to mid-Oct 8:30–6; May and mid- to late Oct 9–5; Nov–Apr by appointment ⚑ Moderate

Cape Breton Highlands National Park
✉ 902/224-2306; www.pc.gc.ca ◷ Year round; info centers: mid-May to mid-Oct

⚑ Moderate; free mid-Oct to mid-May

Whale Interpretive Centre
✉ 104 Harbour Road, Pleasant Bay
☎ 902/224-1411 ◷ Mid-May to Oct daily 9–6 (to 8pm mid-Jun to early Sep)
⚑ Inexpensive

Fortress of Louisbourg National Historic Site
☎ 902/733-2280; www.pc.gc.ca
◷ May–Jun and Sep–mid-Oct daily 9:30–5:30; Jul–Aug 9–6 ⚑ Expensive

---

CAPE BRETON: INSIDE INFO

Top tips If you're planning to go on a **whale-watching trip,** look for one that offers guaranteed sightings. There's still a slight chance the whales won't cooperate, but if that happens, you get another trip for free.

5 Gros Morne National Park

Dramatic geological events created the spectacular land-scapes of Gros Morne National Park and it's global geological importance has made it a UNESCO's World Heritage Site.

This landscape can best be appreciated from the top of flat-topped, 806m (2,650-foot) **Gros Morne Mountain**, a day's hike. Other ways to enjoy the park include boat trips that dip in and out of fjords and sea caves or cross tranquil lakes, notably supremely beautiful **Western Brook Pond**, actually a large lake. Scenic drives round Bonne Bay include the **Discovery Centre** on the southern stretch (Route 431), where you can learn more about the area and its wildlife, and the excellent **Visitor Centre** on the northern arm (Route 430), en route to Rocky Harbour.

Lobster Cove Head Lighthouse keeps shipping safe

TAKING A BREAK

Try the **Seaside Restaurant**, Trout River (tel: 709/451-3461, \$\$\$), or **Fisherman's Landing**, Rocky Harbour (tel: 709/458-2711, \$\$).

✚ 209 D4

Gros Morne National Park Headquarters
✉ Rocky Harbour ☎ 709/458-2417;
www.pc.gc.ca/pn-np/nl/grosmorne
🕐 Mon–Fri 8–4:30; park entrance kiosk mid-May to mid-Oct daily 10–6 💲 Moderate

Discovery Centre
✉ Woody Point ☎ 709/453-2490, ext 229

🕐 Mid-May to mid-Jun and Sep to mid-Oct daily 9–5; mid-Jun to Aug 9–6 (also 6–9pm Wed and Sun 💲 Inexpensive

Visitor Centre
✉ Route 430 🕐 May and late Oct Mon–Fri 9–4; Jun–early Sep daily 9–9; mid-Sep to mid-Oct daily 9–5. Closed Nov–Dec

GROS MORNE NATIONAL PARK: INSIDE INFO

Top tips Gros Morne Mountain is **closed to hikers** until the beginning of July to let the soil dry out after the snow, and give plantlife a chance to establish itself.
• The boat trip on **Western Brook Pond** (☎ 709/458-2016) is unmissable.

6 St. John's

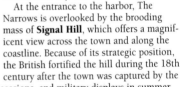

Out on the edge of the continent, the provincial capital of Newfoundland has a spectacular setting on a superb natural harbor. Here you follow in the wake of centuries of visitors, from the "discoverer" John Cabot (in 1497) to fishermen, merchants and others in search of rich pickings. Today's visitors find a strong sense of history, a vibrant culture and a very friendly welcome.

The narrow streets around the harbor are lined with brightly painted wooden houses, and the waterfront is always busy with ships from many nations. Seafaring is in the blood here, and the population, mainly of Irish descent, has a distinctive accent and a dry wit.

Picturesque clapboard buildings rise steeply above the harbor

At the entrance to the harbor, The Narrows is overlooked by the brooding mass of **Signal Hill**, which offers a magnificent view across the town and along the coastline. Because of its strategic position, the British fortified the hill during the 18th century after the town was captured by the French on three occasions, and military displays in summer commemorate those days. It was also an obvious choice for Marconi, when looking for a site to receive the first transatlantic wireless signal, beamed from Poldhu in Cornwall, England. Today, the hill is topped by Cabot Tower, erected in 1897 to mark the 400th anniversary of John Cabot's landing. At the base of Signal Hill, Quidi Vidi is an historic area that is worth exploring.

Above right: strategically placed Queen's Battery, above the Narrows and the Inner Harbour

Tunneled into the rock beneath Signal Hill, the **Johnson Geo Centre** is a thrilling attraction that explores the geology of the planet with simulated earthquakes and volcanic eruptions. Newfoundland attracts scientists from all over the world to study the evidence of plate tectonics on the island, and to examine rocks that date back to the birth of the earth 4.5 billion years ago. Here you can see why they get excited.

Rising colorfully above the St. John's townscape, **The Rooms** is a $40 million cultural center, opened in 2005, which brings the Provincial Museum, Art Gallery and Archives together under one roof. The architecture is striking and unusual, re-creating on a huge scale the traditional old "rooms" – little waterside buildings where fish processing was carried out. There's a great view from here, too.

St. John's has two cathedrals and both are worth a visit. The **Anglican Cathedral of St. John the Baptist**, designed

ST. JOHN'S: INSIDE INFO

Top tips Consult the **weather forecast** before you venture up Signal Hill. Not only do you need a clear day to enjoy the panorama, but a light breeze down in the town often transforms into a howling gale up on the summit.
• The **Eastern Newfoundland National Historic Sites Pass** is a two-day pass that includes any two of the following: Signal Hill, the Ryan Premises, Castle Hill, Hawthorne Cottage and Cape Spear. Contact Parks Canada, tel: 709/722-5367 for information.
• **Icebergs** drift close to the shore between about April and June; time it right (probably June) and you'll spot whales offshore too.

by Sir George Gilbert Scott, is a superb example of ecclesiastical Gothic, and the **Basilica Cathedral and Museum** has a splendid collection of church art and artifacts.

TAKING A BREAK

Traditional Newfoundland food can be enjoyed anytime at **Oscar's** on Duckworth Street (tel: 709/579-7050, $$) – open 24 hours, 364 days a year.

✚ 209 F4

St. John's Tourist Office
✉ 2nd Floor, City Hall Annex, 35 New Gower Street ☎ 709/576-8106 ⏰ Mon–Fri 9–4:30

Signal Hill National Historic Site
☎ 709/772-5367; www.pc.gc.ca ⏰ Mid-May to mid-Jun and Sep to mid-Oct daily 8:30–4:30; mid-Jun to Labour Day 8:30–8; mid-Oct to mid-May Mon–Fri 8:30–4:30
🎟 Inexpensive

Johnson Geo Centre
✉ 175 Signal Hill Road ☎ 709/737-7880; www.geocentre.ca ⏰ Mon–Sat 9:30–5, Sun 1–5. Closed mid-Oct to mid-May Mon
🎟 Expensive

The Rooms
✉ 9 Bonaventure Avenue ☎ 709/729-0917; www.therooms.ca ⏰ Jun to mid-Oct daily 10–5 (also 9–5 Wed–Thu); mid-Oct to May call for hours 🎟 Moderate; special exhibitions expensive

Anglican Cathedral of St. John the Baptist
✉ 16 Church Hill ☎ 709/726-5677; www.sji.ca/cathedral ⏰ Jun–Sep daily; off season by appointment

Basilica Cathedral and Museum
✉ 200 Military Road ☎ 709/726-3660; www.stjohnsarchdiocese.nf.ca ⏰ Daily 9–4 by appointment

At Your Leisure

Supremely beautiful, the little town of Lunenburg has a strong maritime heritage

7 Lunenburg

Lunenburg is just about the loveliest town in eastern Canada – if not in the whole country, and its historic core is now a UNESCO World Heritage Site. The town still adheres to its original plan, and the streets are lined by colorful, beautifully preserved buildings, many dating back to 1760.

It is for its fishing heritage that the town is best known, not least for the prowess of the schooner *Bluenose*, the unbeaten champion of the North Atlantic fishing fleet from 1921 to 1942, which features on the back of the dime coin. Sadly sold off when she retired from duty, she has been replaced by an accurate replica, **Bluenose II**, which divides its time between Lunenburg, various ports of call and and the open sea, and sometimes offers coastal cruises.

On the waterfront you'll find the **Fisheries Museum of the Atlantic**, with three floors of displays and outdoor floating exhibits.

🕂 209 D1

Visitor Information Centre
✉ Blockhouse Road ☎ 902/634-8100 or 888/615-8305; www.explorelunenburg.ca

Bluenose II
✉ At the Fisheries Museum, when in Lunenburg ☎ 902/634-1963 or 1-800/763-1963; www.bluenose2.ns.ca
🕐 Cruises on certain days. Call for information 🎟 Expensive

Fisheries Museum of the Atlantic
✉ 68 Bluenose Drive ☎ 902/634-4794; http://museum.gov.ns.ca/fma
🕐 Mid-May to Oct daily 9:30–5:30 (Jul–Aug to 7); Nov–Apr Wed 9–4
🎟 Moderate

8 Annapolis Valley

The Annapolis Valley is known for its apple orchards, charming small towns, and the site of the earliest permanent European settlement in North America. Its main attraction is **Annapolis Royal**, where you'll find the **Fort Anne National Historic Site**, built by the French in 1702. It was the most fought-over settlement in the country during the struggle between the British and the French.

About 10km (6 miles) to the west, French colonists led by Samuel de Champlain settled in 1605, three years before Jamestown in the US was established. Here the **Port Royal National Historic Site** is a faithful reconstruction of the original settlement, where interpreters portray the lives of early colonists.

➕ 209 D1

Fort Anne National Historic Site
✉ PO Box 9, Annapolis Royal ☎ 902/532-2397 (532-2321 off season); www.pc.gc.ca/lhn-nhs/ns/fortanne
🕐 Mid-May to mid-Oct daily 9–5:30
💵 Inexpensive

Port Royal National Historic Site
✉ P.O. Box 9, Annapolis Royal ☎ 902/532-2898 (2321 off season); www.pc.gc.ca/lhn-nhs/ns/portroyal
🕐 Mid-May to mid-Oct daily 9–5:30
💵 Inexpensive

🟒 St. Andrews-by-the-Sea
On a tiny promontory that juts out into Passamaquoddy Bay, this is Canada's oldest seaside resort, a pretty little town with a picturesque harbor, where whale-watching boats are moored alongside fishing charters and pleasure boats. Just back from the harbor, Water Street has remained largely unchanged for more than 200 years. It's lined with art and craft galleries, antiques stores and fashion boutiques, and intermingled with these are little cafés and restaurants. In the heart of town is the lovely 11ha (27-acre) **Kingsbrae Garden**, with views over the bay and Minister's Island. You can visit **Minister's Island** by driving across the ocean floor at low tide.

➕ 208 C1

Kingsbrae Garden
✉ 220 King Street ☎ 506/529-3335 or 866/566-8687; www.kingsbraegarden.com 🕐 Mid-May to early Oct daily 9–6,
💵 Moderate

🔟 King's Landing
A 20-minute drive west of Fredericton on the Riverside Trail (Highway 2) leads to **King's Landing**, a superb reconstruction of a Loyalist settlement on a large riverside site. It has entire farms, complete with animals and workshops, furnished homes with cultivated gardens, a church, a working sawmill, and a splendid pub, the King's Arms, where you can taste a unique beer and eat traditional food in the upstairs restaurant. The whole place is populated by costumed interpreters, who engage visitors in authentic conversations of the day. If you get footsore exploring it all, take a wagon ride.

➕ 208 C2 ✉ 20 King's Landing Road ☎ 506/363-4999 or 506/363-4959 (info-line recording); www.kingslanding.nb.ca 🕐 Jun to mid-Oct daily 10–5
💵 Expensive

🔟 Fredericton
The provincial capital of New Brunswick is a lovely, compact city on the banks of the wide St. John River, and it's easy to explore on foot. The atmosphere is gracious small-town with a touch of importance and the downtown area is full of interesting little stores and good restaurants. In the heart of the city is the historic **Garrison District**, where the British army were quartered from 1784 until Canada's independence in 1867. The buildings have been adapted to house museums, artisans' workshops, craft stores, cafés and other amenities, all arranged around Officer's Square, which hosts Changing of the Guard ceremonies, open-air theater and free concerts. A short distance west, opposite the Legislative Assembly Building (open), is the **Beaverbrook Art Gallery,** with a fine collection of works by Canadian and British artists.

➕ 208 C2

Beaverbrook Art Gallery
✉ 703 Queen Street ☎ 506/458-8545
🕐 Daily 9–5:30 (also 5:30–9 Thu)
💵 Expensive

🔟 L'Anse aux Meadows
On the northern tip of Newfoundland a discovery was made in the 1960s

Vikings came to Newfoundland to harvest the plentiful lumber and fish its rich waters

that not only has national significance, but is important to the history of the entire continent – archeological evidence that the Vikings were here around 1,000 years ago. Excavations revealed three homes and a number of workshops, and the site is now a National Historic Site and a UNESCO World Heritage Site. The first Norsemen stayed for only a short time, but others came in their wake and used the dwellings they had built as a summer base for collecting the plentiful gifts of nature – fish, wild grapes and lumber.

The little Norse encampment has been accurately reconstructed, and is populated by costumed guides, who carry out demonstrations of ancient crafts. The log houses show how the Vikings would have lived, and the visitor center has a film about the excavations and some of the artifacts.

🕂 209 D5 ⊠ PO Box 70, St-Lunaire-Griquet; 30km (18 miles) north of St. Anthony on Route 436 ☎ 709/623-2608; www.pc.gc.ca 🕐 Jun to mid-Oct daily 9–5 (also mid-Jun to early Sep 5–6pm) 🎟 Expensive

🔢 Bonavista Peninsula
"Oh, buona vista!" (Oh, happy sight!) were supposedly the words of explorer John Cabot when he made

his first landfall in North America here in 1497. Some dispute the actual location where he stepped onto the continent, but none would argue with the sentiment. Bonavista has breathtaking views, especially at the Cape, where waves pound the rocky shoreline beneath one of Canada's most picturesque lighthouses, hundreds of puffins flock around the nearby cliffs, and you can often see whales offshore. The **Cape Bonavista Lighthouse Provincial Historic Site**, fully restored after three lightning strikes set fire to it in 2001, has costumed guides to show you around.

In addition to sending news back across the Atlantic of his "New found land," Cabot alerted the fishermen of Europe to the huge shoals of cod that populated the waters here, starting off a centuries-long fishing industry. The **Ryan Premises National Historic Site**, in a restored, 19th-century fish-merchant's premises in Bonavista, tells the story.

🕂 209 F4

Cape Bonavista Lighthouse
⊠ Route 230, Bonavista ☎ 709/ 468-7444 🕐 Mid-Jun to early Oct daily 10–5:30 🎟 Inexpensive

Ryan Premises
⊠ PO Box 1451, Bonavista ☎ 709/ 468-1600; www.pc.gc.ca 🕐 Mid-May to mid-Oct daily 10–6 🎟 Inexpensive

Where to... Stay

Prices
High season room only rates, based on two sharing a double room, excluding taxes
$ up to $160 $$ $160–300 $$$ more than $300

HALIFAX

▼▼▼ Halliburton House Inn $$

In the center of Halifax, this is a lovely and comfortable historic property, elegantly furnished with antiques. All rooms have private bathrooms (some with whirlpool) and goose-down comforters. In winter, the library is a great place to relax by the open fire. Innovative Canadian cuisine is served in the four-room restaurant. Less mobile guests should bear in mind that there's no elevator.

➕ 209 D2 ⊠ 5184 Morris Street
☎ 902/420-0658, 1-888/512-3344;
www.thehalliburton.com

▼▼▼ Westin Nova Scotian $$

With views of the harbor or Point Pleasant Park, this modern hotel has a lovely waterfront site. Rooms feature pillow-top beds and there's an indoor swimming pool, spa and fitness suite. A free shuttle service to downtown is run on weekdays.

➕ 209 D2 ⊠ 1181 Hollis Street;
902/421-1000; 888/679-3784;
www.westin.ns.ca

PRINCE EDWARD ISLAND

▼▼▼ The Inns on Great George $$–$$$

Several properties in Charlottetown's National Historic District have been converted into this beautiful inn,

which maintains a 19th-century style throughout. The best rooms have a Jacuzzi and fireplace, but all are elegant. The central building, called The Pavilion, houses the breakfast room and fitness center.

➕ 209 D2 ⊠ 58 Great George Street, Charlottetown ☎ 902/892-0606, 1- 800/361-1118;
www.innsongreatgeorge.com

▼▼▼ Cavendish Beach Cottages $$

Within the national park, overlooking a beautiful sandy beach, this small, tasteful complex offers bright, air-conditioned cottages, decorated in natural pine, with its fully-equipped kitchens (including dishwasher) and barbecue.

➕ 209 D2 ⊠ RR2, Hunter River, Cavendish ☎ 902/963-2025;
www.cavendishbeachcottages.com

CAPE BRETON ISLAND

▼ Parkview Motel $

You get a real Acadian welcome at the Chiasson family's motel, which lies along the Cheticamp River at the entrance to the Cape Breton Highlands National Park. Rooms have two double beds, full bathroom and satellite TV, and deluxe rooms have better views and such extras as microwaves and refrigerators. The dining room serves fresh seafood and steaks.

➕ 209 D3 ⊠ 16546 Cabot Trail (P.O. Box 117), Cheticamp
☎ 902/224-3232, 1-877/224-3232;
www.parkviewresort.com

ST. JOHN'S, NEWFOUNDLAND

▼▼▼ Leaside Manor Heritage Inn $$

Named one of the most romantic destinations in Canada, this inn has exceptionally pretty rooms, many with four-poster beds and Jacuzzis. Wonderful breakfasts and 24-hour complimentary beverages.

➕ 209 F4 ⊠ 39 Topsail Road
☎ 709/722-0387, 1-877/807-7245;
www.leaside.nf.ca

Where to... **159**

Where to...
Eat and Drink

Prices

Based on the cost of a three-course dinner, excluding drinks and service
$ under $30 $$ $30–$50 $$$ more than $50

HALIFAX

▼▼▼ Bish World Cuisine $$–$$$

Chic modern decor and a mouth-watering menu distinguish this fine waterfront restaurant. International influences and local ingredients create such dishes as Thai lobster and coconut corn chowder, butter poached lobster on a Romesco fish stew, or cornbread-stuffed roasted pork loin with pecan butternut squash hash. Desserts include maple walnut tart with cinnamon crème fraîche. The wine list has New World and European bottles.

🛧 209 D2 ⊠ Bishop's Landing, 1475 Lower Water Street ☎ 902/425-7993; www.bish.ca ⏰ Mon–Sat 5:30–10 Closed Sun

▼▼▼ Salty's on the Waterfront $–$$

Right on the waterfront, on a 19th-century wharf, this restaurant has a spectacular view across the harbor. The decor is suitably nautical and fresh Atlantic seafood is the focus, including Nova Scotia lobster. Lighter meals available downstairs.

🛧 209 D2 ⊠ 1869 Upper Water Street ☎ 902/423-6818; www.saltys.ca ⏰ Daily 11:30–10

PRINCE EDWARD ISLAND

▼▼ Gahan House Brewery $

This great brewpub not only has a half-dozen excellent ales brewed on the premises, it also serves up some of the best pub food in the Maritimes. The signature dish is the Brown Bag Fish and Chips, with batter made using their own ale. Groups of more than four can get a brewery tour (call in advance).

🛧 209 D2 ⊠ 126 Sydney Street, Charlottetown ☎ 902/626-2337; www.peimenu.com/brewing ⏰ Mon–Sat 11–closing, Sun 4–10

CAPE BRETON ISLAND

▼▼ Baddeck Lobster Suppers $–$$

The Maritimes are famous for their lobster suppers, and here the authentic experience is available in a friendly informal restaurant that offers excellent value. In addition to fresh Atlantic lobster, the specialties are hot-planked salmon and baked ham, and all entrees come with unlimited (yes, really) amounts of fresh seafood chowder, mussels, potato salad and homemade bread.

🛧 209 E3 ⊠ 17 Ross Street, Baddeck ☎ 902/295-3307; http://baddeck.com/lobstersuppers ⏰ Early Jun to early-Oct daily 11:30–1:30, 4–9

ST. JOHN'S, NEWFOUNDLAND

▼▼ Bianca's $$

Fresh local ingredients are cooked with flair in this stylish restaurant. Start with a shrimp and crab bisque, an interesting salad, or a seafood appetizer, then tuck into fillet of caribou with sour cherries and shallots; osso bucco; or pan-roasted duck with spiced red wine and sun-dried indigo plum glacee. The lunch menu is shorter, but with excellent choices.

🛧 209 F4 ⊠ 171 Water Street ☎ 709/726-9016; www.biancas.net ⏰ Mon–Fri 11:30–2:30, 5:30–10, Sat–Sun 5:30–10

Where to... Shop

There's really only one big city in the Maritimes, and that's Halifax, but it doesn't have a monopoly on great shopping. Each of the provincial capitals has at least one good shopping mall, plus interesting individual and specialty stores.

NOVA SCOTIA

Halifax is the international gateway to the region for many visitors, and it has excellent shopping. The hub is around Spring Garden Road and South Park Street, lined with fashion stores, galleries and craft shops. The Historic Properties on the waterfront include specialty boutiques, and Cable Wharf has Canada's only traditional crystal factory, Nova

Scotia Crystal (Lower Water Street, tel: 902/492-0416).

For reading matter, seek out John W. Doull (1684 Barrington Street, tel: 902/429-1652), with a huge stock of books. Farther along this street is a store that reflects a different aspect of "New Scotland." The Plaid Place (1903 Barrington Street, tel: 902/429-6872) sells kilts, sweaters and other highland goods.

Halifax's biggest shopping mall is the Halifax Shopping Centre (7001 Mumford Road, tel: 902/454-8666). More interesting, perhaps is the Granville Mall near the harbor, in a group of 19th-century buildings. Gloscap Heritage Centre (65 Treaty Trail, tel: 902/843-3496) out at Truro has First Nations Crafts.

PRINCE EDWARD ISLAND

A popular souvenir is the PEI Dirt Shirt, a T-shirt dyed using the famous red soil. It looks better than it sounds. Another PEI product is the delicious Cow's Ice Cream.

The capital, Charlottetown, has a historic, low-rise downtown area, based on Queen Street, with lots of individual stores. On Richmond Street, traffic-free in summer, Victoria Row has craft and gift stores. The Confederation Court Mall (tel: 902/894-9505) is the largest mall (with around 50 stores), while down on the waterfront, Peake's Wharf offers clothing, craft and gift stores. Farther out is the Charlottetown Mall (670 University Avenue, tel: 902/368-8854) and the PEI Factory Shops (TransCanada Highway, North River Causeway), discount outlets offering low prices on big-name lines.

NEWFOUNDLAND AND LABRADOR

St. John's is where you'll find Newfoundland's best shopping, with craft shops and art galleries, including the Craft Council (49 Duckworth Street, tel: 709/753-2749). Look especially for textile crafts at a number of workshops

and stores. On the harbor, the Murray Premises are home to boutiques, while the city's main shopping mall is the Avalon Mall (48 Kenmouth Road, tel: 709/753-7144) with over 140 outlets.

NEW BRUNSWICK

Fredericton is a charming city that has preserved its downtown area as a pleasant place to wander among individual stores. The historic Garrison District includes River Valley Crafts and Artisan Gift Shops (tel: 506/460-2837) and Botinicals (65 Shore Street, tel: 506/454-7361), great for quality souvenirs. Boyce's Farmers' Market (665 George Street, tel: 506/451-1815) has more than 200 vendors. Of the malls, Regent Mall (1381 Regent Street, tel: 506/452-1005) is the brightest and best, with more than 115 stores and services. However, the biggest mall in the Atlantic Provinces is Champlain Place over at Moncton.

Where to...
Be Entertained

NOVA SCOTIA

Halifax is the prime spot for entertainment in Nova Scotia, but many towns have good theaters: the lovely, historic **King's Theater** at Annapolis Royal (209 St. George Street, tel: 902/532-7704); the **Bauer** at Antigonish (St. Francis-Xavier University, tel: 902/867-3333); the grand **Savoy** at Glace Bay, Cape Breton (116 Commercial Street, tel: 902/564-6668); the **Decoste Entertainment Centre** at Pictou (Water Street, tel: 902/485-8848); and **Th'Yarc** in Yarmouth (76 Parade Street, tel: 902/742-8150).

In **Halifax**, the principal venues are the **Dalhousie Arts Centre** (6101 University Avenue, tel: 902/494-3820), home of Symphony Nova Scotia, and the 1915 **Neptune Theatre** (1593 Argyle Street, tel: 902/429-7070 or 800/565-7345).

Nightlife in Halifax ranges from the **Casino Nova Scotia** (1983 Upper Water Street, tel: 902/425-7777), to places like the **Lower Deck Pub** (Upper Water Street, tel: 902/425-1501), for traditional Maritimes music. **Niche** (corner of Spring Garden Road, Barrington Street, tel: 902/422-6280) provides live entertainment and a good menu, then you can go on to their sister nightclub, **Pacifico** until the early hours.

PRINCE EDWARD ISLAND

PEI draws visitors for its tranquility and rural charm, but it is certainly not devoid of entertainment. One of the island's biggest attractions is a musical based on *Anne of Green Gables*, a perennially popular feature of the **Charlottetown Festival**. For live music in the provincial capital, try the **Olde Dublin Pub** (131 Sydney Street, tel: 902/892-6992) for traditional Celtic music.

NEWFOUNDLAND

With its strong Irish and English heritage, this province is reeling (literally) with traditional Celtic music. In **St. John's** on any night of the week, you can stroll along the main streets (George Street in particular) and hear it wafting from many of the pubs. There are pubs that feature country or rock music, too. **O'Reilley's** (15–17 George Street, tel: 709/722-3735) is one of the best places for Irish music.

Big concerts are staged at **Mile One Stadium** (tel: 709/576-7657), in the heart of downtown. The **Arts and Culture Centre** (Allandale Road and Prince Philip Drive, tel: 709/729-3900) has a varied program, while classical music is staged at the **Cochrane Street United Church** (tel: 709/722-3023). **Bowring Park Amphitheatre** (off route 1, tel: 709/576-8415) has varied open-air entertainments.

NEW BRUNSWICK

Fredericton is a lively provincial capital with lots to do. The main theater is the modern **Playhouse** (686 Queen Street, tel: 506/458-8344). In summer there's outdoor entertainment in **Officer's Square** (575 Queen Street, tel: 506/460-2129). Nightlife is provided by city bars such as **Dolan's** (349 King Street, tel: 506/454-7474) and the **Right Spot/20-20 Club** (403 Regent Street, tel: 506/457-9887) in the old station building, which has a pool room, a sports bar and a venue featuring 1960s music.

The North

Getting Your Bearings

The North is a vast area of rugged mountains, endless wilderness, forests, lakes and waterways, even desert, as well as impressive highways running through some truly remarkable scenery. The area is divided into the Yukon, adjoining the American state of Alaska, the Northwest Territories, and Nunavut, Canada's newest territory, created in 1999 from the eastern part of the Northwest Territories. The Yukon is Gold-Rush country, where at the end of the 19th century prospectors rushed in to stake their claim to the riches hidden in the gold fields of the Klondike. Many of the attractions – the cities, the museums, the highways – owe their existence to this incredibly brief period in history.

But nature has provided more than enough of its own attractions in the North. This is the land of the *aurora borealis* and the midnight sun; a land where temperatures range from an icy -40°C (-40°F) in winter to a very respectable 25°C (77°F) in summer. The wildlife is wonderful, the sport varied and plentiful, the shopping unique – the craftwork of the First Nations peoples is treasure indeed.

And as if that wasn't enough, throughout the year there are entertainments in the form of festivals, sporting events, celebrations of the changing of the seasons and First Nations gatherings.

Beaufort Sea

Banks Island

Amundsen Gulf

Tukluk Nogait National Park

6 Inuvik

Eagle Plains

Peel

Fort Good Hope

Coronation Kugluktuk (Coppermine

1 Dawson City

Stewart Crossing

Yukon

YUKON

Great Bear Lake

Mackenzie

Kluane National Park

4 Alaska Highway

Haines Junction

NORTHWEST TERRITORIES

Mackenzie Mts

Wrigley

2 Whitehorse and White Pass

Skagway

Teslin

Watson Lake

5 Nahanni National Park

Liard

Yellowknife

3 ✈

Great Slave Lake

Fort Providence

Fort Smith

Mer Isl.

Opposite: Driving the Alaska Highway is still an adventure

Ellesmere Island

Right: First Nations art and crafts reflect the nature of the northern lands

Axel Heiberg Island

Queen Elizabeth Islands

Parry Islands

Devon Island

Lancaster Sound

Somerset Island

Prince of Wales Island

Gulf of Boothia

Boothia Peninsula

Baffin Bay

Davis Strait

Baffin Island 7

Auyuittuq National Park

Nettilling Lake

Cumberland Sound

Melville Peninsula

Foxe Basin

NUNAVUT

Southampton Island

Hudson Strait

| 0 | 500 km |
| 0 | 250 miles |

Hudson Bay

□ *Arviat (Eskimo Point)*

Nueltin Lake

Page 163: It's not always the "frozen North," but severe winters only add to the spectacular beauty

The North is a huge area with vast distances between the main sites, so travel by small plane is the best option. The only major Yukon airport is at Whitehorse, so this is the best place to use as your base. As attractions in the Yukon are seasonal, the itinerary suggested here is for the summer season, mid-May to mid-September.

The North in Eight Days

Day One

Morning Fly from **2** Whitehorse (➤ 170) up to **1** Dawson City (➤ 168–169) via the local air service.

Lunch/Afternoon You're here to experience Gold-Rush fever, so do it in style with lunch at Klondike Kate's (➤ 175, above left), then wander around the historic buildings.

Evening Visit **Diamond Tooth Gertie's** casino, even if you don't want to gamble, then take a drive up to the **Midnight Dome** to enjoy the sunset and the view.

Day Two

Morning Still in Dawson City, visit the **Tr'ondek Hwech'in Dänojà Zho Cultural Centre** for a taste of life before the Gold Rush. Catch a reading of the works of Jack London or Robert Service in the cabins where they lived.

Lunch Buy picnic food at Bonanza Market (2nd Avenue and Princess; tel: 867/993-6527) and eat it by the Yukon River in town or up on Midnight Dome, with magnificent views.

Afternoon/Evening Return to Whitehorse and see the **Frantic Follies** show (➤ 176).

Day Three

Leave Whitehorse very early to follow the **Golden Circle Drive** (➤ 191–192, right). Aim for an overnight stop in Haines City.

Day Four

Continue on the Golden Circle Drive. Allow yourself time to explore
Skagway (➤ 170) before driving over the White Pass back to Whitehorse.

Day Five

Fly to **8** **Yellowknife** (➤ 171) and enjoy a leisurely pre-prandial stroll along
the shores of Great Slave Lake.

Evening Try some northern food creatively cooked at L'Heritage Restaurant
Français (➤ 175), then walk it off in one of the city parks.

Day Six

Morning Visit the **Diavik Diamond Mines Visitor Centre** in Yellowknife.

Lunch All kinds of food, from light snacks to meals based on caribou or
Arctic char can be enjoyed at L'Attitudes (Yellowknife Inn, Central Square
Mall, tel: 867/873-2603)

Afternoon Stroll around the Old Town –
make sure you soak up the atmosphere
along Ragged Ass Road, and finish up
at the Pilots' Monument, the highest
point, for views over the city and the
Great Slave Lake.

Evening Enjoy the food and more views at
the Wildcat Café (➤ 175).

Day Seven

Morning Visit the **Prince of Wales Northern
Heritage Centre** (➤ 171).

Lunch Eat at the Heritage Café within the
heritage center (Mon–Fri 11:30–2;
tel: 867/873-0205)

Afternoon Treat yourself to some shopping, then relax by taking a trip on a
river steamer.

Evening Have supper at The Prospector (3506 Wiley Road, tel: 867/920-
7639, $), right on the water's edge – you might be treated to the sight of
float planes landing or taking off right in front of you.

Day Eight

Fly back to Whitehorse or carry on to your next destination.

⬛Dawson City

Dawson is an extraordinary city, where the few short years that saw the Yukon Gold Rush at the end of the 19th century are frozen in a collection of meticulously preserved historic buildings. Here is the stuff of old black-and-white movies – you'll find clapboard houses, costumed characters and a casino with the irresistible name of Diamond Tooth Gertie's.

Above and right: visitors still pan for gold nuggets

To get a real feel of those manic years of feverish endeavor, imagine arriving in Dawson via the "Gold Rush Route" – the Klondike Highway – followed by the 100,000 or so prospectors who virtually stampeded their way north to pan for gold. Stretching from Skagway in Alaska, it was covered on foot or horseback as far as Whitehorse (➤ 170), then the final leg to the Klondike gold mines – more than 500km (300 miles) – was by boat on the Yukon River.

Gold was discovered here in 1896, but the rush was over within three years, and Dawson almost died with it, even losing its status as capital of Yukon Territory to Whitehorse in 1950. However, its role as a part of Canadian heritage was recognized, and a rescue operation began on some of its historic buildings. These now form the Dawson Historic Complex, a National Historic Site including the Old Post Office, Commissioner's Residence, Palace Grand Theatre, and the Robert Service Cabin, where the "bard of the Klondike" penned his still-popular verses.

Dawson is not just about the Gold Rush. It has a thriving First Nations tribe, the Han Hwech'in, celebrated at the **Tr'ondek Hwech'in Danajo Zho Cultural Centre**; downstream on the Yukon River, the annual Mooseshide Gathering is a festival of the tribe's traditions. And if you're a fan of the writer Jack London – whose novels include *The Call of the Wild* (1903) and *White Fang* (1905) – or the poet Robert Service (➤ 16–17), whose fondness for alliteration inspired him to write *Songs of a Sourdough* (1907) and *Rhymes of a Rebel* (1952), you might like to catch a reading of their works in the re-created cabins where they lived on 8th Avenue.

TAKING A BREAK

Klondike Kate's (➤ 175) offers Canadian and ethnic food in an original Gold-Rush building.

DAWSON CITY: INSIDE INFO

Top tips The **best time to visit** Dawson is during the summer months, from mid-May to mid-September. This is mainly because the attractions, and some of the hotels and restaurants, are only open during this period, and also there are some great annual events to enjoy, such as the **Yukon Gold Panning Championships**, a music festival and some fun happenings at Diamond Tooth Gertie's, where the opening and close of the season are celebrated in style.
• **Follow the Dome Road** out of Dawson for 8km (5 miles) to the top of the Midnight Dome (884m/2,900 feet), for a wonderful view over the city and the surrounding mountains, sunlit until late at night. On June 21, the summer solstice, you can see the sun at midnight.

➕ 210 B4

Klondike Visitors' Association
✉ P.O. Box 389 ☎ 867/993-5575, 1-877/465-3006; www.dawsoncity.org

Tourism Yukon Visitor Reception
✉ Corner of Front and King streets ☎ 867/993-5566;
http://travelyukon.com ⏰ Mid-May to early Oct daily 8–8

Dawson Historic Complex
✉ P.O. Box 390 ☎ 867/993-7200; www.pc.gc.ca ⏰ Daily; Jun to mid-Sep
summer program 💵 Moderate; various combined tickets available

Tr'ondek Hwech'in Dänojà Zho Cultural Centre
✉ Downtown, opposite Visitor Information Centre ☎ 867/993-6768;
www.trondek.com ⏰ May–Sep daily 10–6; Oct–Apr by appointment
💵 Moderate (ticket valid 2 days)

Jack London Cabin
✉ 8th Avenue ⏰ Mid-May to mid-Oct daily at 11:30 and 2:15; mid-Oct to
mid-May check with the Klondike Visitors' Association 💵 Inexpensive

The view from
Midnight Dome
over Dawson
City and the
Yukon River

2 Whitehorse and White Pass

Whitehorse may not be the prettiest place in the world, but it's an excellent base for exploring the Yukon. It's another Gold-Rush town, where prospectors stopped off to negotiate the troublesome obstacles of Miles Canyon and the Whitehorse Rapids. The problem was solved by building a railway, and the town continued to do well even after the Gold Rush was over. There are some good museums to visit and a fantastic range of artists live and work here – including painters, sculptors, potters, carvers and quilters.

Follow the **Golden Circle Drive** (► 191–192) from Whitehorse, and you will climb up to White Pass, a steep ravine heading south-west between Whitehorse and Skagway. It's impressive, especially Dead Horse Gulch, where there are the bones of more than 3,000 pack horses, which were unable to survive the harsh conditions.

Skagway, in Alaska, is in a glorious position at the head of the Lyn Canyon waterway, and it's much as it was 100 years ago. The Klondike Goldrush National Historic Park is a living museum.

A dog-sled race sets off from the main street in Whitehorse

TAKING A BREAK

The **Talisman** (► 175) on Whitehorse's Wood Street is family-friendly café, serving home baking.

✚ 210 B2

Whitehorse Yukon Visitor Information Centre
✉ 100 Hanson Street ☎ 867/667-3084; http://travelyukon.com
🕓 Mid-May to early Oct daily; Oct to mid-May Mon–Fri

WHITEHORSE AND WHITE PASS: INSIDE INFO

Top tips You'll need your **passport** to visit Skagway, which is over the United States border in Alaska.

3 Yellowknife

If you like diamonds with your gold, head for the vibrant, cosmopolitan city of Yellowknife, on the northeast shore of the Great Slave Lake, dubbed "the Diamond Capital of North America." Once a boom town for gold prospectors, it switched to diamond-mining as its main industry in the 1990s.

Yellowknife, capital of the Northwest Territories, was named by a traveler in 1770, after the "yellow knives" (copper-blades) used by the native Dongrib Dene peoples. In spite of the industry, it's not all modern tall buildings – a stroll around the **Old Town**, where miners once lived in tents or wooden shacks, takes you right back through history.

This is the place to connect with **nature** – the forests and wilderness around Yellowknife are unspoiled and great for wildlife watching – and to view the midnight sun in summer and the *aurora borealis*. It's fabulous, too, for fresh-air activities – walking, cycling, sailing, swimming, fishing, canoeing – or you can take a leisurely trip on a river steamer and just soak it all up.

To get a good feel of the whole area, from the traditions and lifestyles of the local First Nations peoples to life after the discovery of gold and diamonds, head for the **Prince of Wales Northern Heritage Centre**.

TAKING A BREAK

Take your camera and head for the **Wildcat Café** (► 175) in an original log building overlooking Back Bay – the views are as good as the northern specialties.

First Nations culture is evident throughout the North region

➕ 211 F2

Prince of Wales Northern Heritage Centre
✉ PO Box 1320; off Highway 4 near Northern

Frontier Visitors' Centre ☎ 867/873-7551; http://pwnhc.learnnet.nt.ca 🕐 Jun–Aug daily 10:30–5:30; Sep–May Mon–Fri 10:30–5, Sat–Sun noon–5 💲 Moderate

YELLOWKNIFE: INSIDE INFO

Top tips Learn all about the mining, cutting and polishing of diamonds at the **Diavik Diamond Mines Visitor Centre** (5007 50th Avenue; tel: 867/669-6500; Mon–Fri 10:30–5, Sat–Sun noon–5)

At Your Leisure

The "signpost forest" at Watson Lake continues to grow as visitors add their home towns

4 Alaska Highway

The Alaska Highway starts at the Mile Zero marker in Dawson Creek, BC and runs for 2,400km (1,488 miles) to Delta Junction, Alaska, USA. It was built at incredible speed (it took just over seven months to complete) as a joint Canadian/US venture during World War II to protect Alaska by linking it to mainland America.

It's a marathon journey to cover the whole highway, so if time is limited you could just drive a short stretch. If you head southeast of Whitehorse, after 420km (262 miles) you'll reach **Watson Lake**, where there's an interpretive center, a Northern Lights Centre and an amazing "forest" of signposts. The first one was "planted" by a homesick US Army soldier in 1942, pointing his way home, and the idea has been taken up by more than 42,000 travelers since.

On the way you'll pass through **Teslin** – take a look in the George Johnson Museum, where there's a wonderful collection of early 20th-century photographs of the local Tlingit people, taken by George Johnston (1884–1972).

➕ 210 C2

Northern Rockies Alaska Highway Tourism Association
✉ PO Box 6850, 9923 96 Avenue, Fort St. John, British Columbia ☎ 250/785-2544

5 Nahanni National Park

Some planning is needed to visit this glorious wilderness in the southwest Northern Territories, because you can only reach it by chartering a seaplane. You'll get a fantastic view of the sheer rocky peaks of the **Cirque of the Unclimbables**, the 92m (302-foot) **Virginia Falls** (twice the height of Niagara), and the deep canyons.

This remote national park protects sections of the Mackenzie Mountains and was the first designated UNESCO World Heritage Site. The park is centered around the **South Nahanni River** – the place to go for white-water rafting. There are incredible hot springs here, such as **Rabbitkettle**, which is at a constant 20°C (68°F).

➕ 211 D2 ✉ P.O. Box 348, Fort Simpson ☎ 867/695-3151; www.pc.gc.ca ⏰ Mid-Jun to mid-Sep daily; Park Office: mid-Jun to mid-Sep daily 8–noon, 1–5; mid-Sep to mid-Jun Mon–Fri 8:30–noon, 1–5

Farther Afield

The aptly named Igloo Church is a unique landmark in Inuvik

6 Inuvik

You reach Inuvik by plane from Yellowknife or via the 735km (455-mile) **Dempster Highway**. Inuvik lies in the delta of the Mackenzie River, and is the largest Canadian settlement north of the Arctic Circle. The delta's islets and channels attract migratory wildfowl and fish; herds of caribou migrate here to calve, and polar bears live in the vast tundra.

Inuvik's population of 3,400 – mostly Inuvailut and Gwich'in – live by hunting, sport hunting and ecotourism. Attractions include white-water rafting, kayaking, hiking or wildlife viewing or, in winter, snowmobile, dogsled or snowshoe trips and *aurora borealis* viewing.

You won't be able to miss the town's biggest landmark, the circular **Igloo Church of Our Lady of Victory** on Mackenzie Road. Built in 1958, the white walls are marked to resemble blocks of ice. Inside you'll see the *Stations of the Cross* by local Inuit artist, Mona Thresher.

211 D5

Western Arctic Visitor Centre
Mackenzie Road 867/777-7237/4727; www.iti.gov.nt.ca Mid-May to mid-Sep daily 9–8

7 Baffin Island

Baffin Island forms the major part of **Nunavut**, which means "our land" in the Inuit language. Three-quarters of the island's land mass lies north of the Arctic Circle, and the landscape is wild, rugged and glaciated, with vast areas of tundra. Here again, you'll find great opportunities for sport and wildlife spotting. The Inuit have lived here for 5,000 years, but don't expect to see them living their traditional lifestyle – they have mostly shunned their nomadic existence in favor of conventional homes and offices. As a tourist, however, you can stay in a igloo, if you wish!

213 D3

Unikkaervik Visitor Centre
Iqaluit, Nunavut 867/979-4636; www.nunavuttourism.com

Wildlife to Spot on a Boat Trip

- Polar bears
- Whales
- Narwhals
- Seals
- Walruses

Where to... Stay

Prices
High season room only rates, based on two sharing a double room, excluding taxes
$ up to $160 $$ $160–$300 $$$ $more than $300

If you're visiting in the summer, it's best to book ahead, and remember that some attractions and a number of hotels are only open from around mid-May to mid-September.

▼▼ Dawson City Bed and Breakfast $

This is a lovely heritage home, overlooking the Klondike and Yukon Rivers and within walking distance of the downtown attractions. Cozy rooms, some with private bathrooms, have cable TV with VCR or DVD, and high speed Internet is available. After the all-you-can-eat breakfast, you can borrow bicycles and fishing rods to use all those calories.

🕂 210 B4 ✉ 451 Craig Street
☎ 867/993-5649, 1-800/697-6539;
www.dawsonbb.com

▼▼ High Country Inn $–$$

This inn has four floors of rooms with great views, from standard doubles to luxurious suites with Jacuzzis or kitchenettes, but it still manages to retain a country atmosphere. Other facilities include private bathroom, cable TV and a modem outlet. You'll know you're at the right place when you spot the 12m (40-foot) wooden Mountie guarding the door. There's a good menu of northern specialties – fresh fish, caribou steak, venison – served in the restaurant or the less formal bar.

🕂 210 B2 ✉ 4051 4th Avenue;
☎ 867/667-4471, 1-800/554-4471;
www.highcountryinn.yk.ca

▼▼ Midnight Sun Inn $

Oozing friendly hospitality, the Midnight Sun offers four individually styled theme rooms (Persian, Egyptian, Victorian and Yukon) with private bathrooms, cable TV, bathrobes, telephones and high speed Internet access. There's also the thoughtful provision of a private lounge, with hot drinks and a fruit basket, big-screen TV, laundry facilities, stove and microwave. A delicious hot breakfast is included in the price.

🕂 210 B2 ✉ 6188 6th Avenue
☎ 867/667-2255, 1-866/284-4448;
www.midnightsunbb.com

▼▼ Chateau Nova $$

This is a fine modern hotel with big-city standards of comfort twinned with such up-to-the-minute facilities as internet connection and telephones with voice mail in the rooms. All the rooms are large and elegant and have private bathrooms. The walls of the hotel are adorned with wonderful archive images of early explorers, emphasizing how lucky guests are that the days are gone when travelers had to sleep outside with the mosquitoes. The Mill Wright Restaurant serves excellent Northern food and is famed for its Sunday brunches. The hotel has a fitness center where you can work out, or you can indulge yourself with a relaxing treatment in the spa.

🕂 210 B2 ✉ 4401 50th Avenue;
☎ 867/873-9700, 1-877/839-1236;
www.chateaunova.com

Where to...
Eat and Drink

Prices

Based on the cost of a three-course dinner, excluding drinks and service

$ under $30 $$ $30–$50 $$$ more than $50

DAWSON CITY

Amica's Ristorante $

You can dine on good-value Italian food at this laid-back venue with a view of the Yukon River. As well as the good choice of pasta dishes and pizzas, there are simple fish dishes such as baked salmon, salads and more complex offerings with a European flavor, such as mussels in white white. At lunchtime there are sandwiches too.

➕ 210 B4 ✉ 401 Craig Street
☎ 867/993-6800 ⏰ May–Sep daily 11–11; Oct–Apr Mon–Fri 11–2, 5–10

Klondike Kate's $

It's fun to eat in this authentic Gold-Rush building (1904), which opens early (try the $4.99 breakfast special) and closes late. Canadian and ethnic dishes can be enjoyed inside or on the covered, heated patio.

➕ 210 B4 ✉ Corner of 3rd Avenue and King Street ☎ 867/993-6527; www.klondikekates.ca ⏰ Mid-May to mid-Sep daily 6:30am–11pm

WHITEHORSE

The Cellar Steakhouse and Wine Bar $$–$$$

An elegant dining room in the Edgewater Hotel serving imaginative steaks, chicken, seafood and pasta – look for the Fillet Neptune, a tenderloin steak topped with crab, asparagus and hollandaise sauce, and the Alaska king crab (don't miss this if you're a fan of crab) with lemon and clarified butter.

➕ 210 B2 ✉ Edgewater Hotel, 101 Main Street
☎ 867/667-2572, 1-877/484-3334; www.edgewaterhotelwhitehorse.com ⏰ Tue–Sat 5–10

Talisman Café $–$$

First Nations owned and operated, this is a cozy and friendly place, within the Riverview Hotel. It offers generous portions of international dishes, hearty breakfasts are also served and there's a lovely garden area for outside dining on warm summer days.

➕ 210 B2 ✉ 2112 2nd Avenue ☎ 867/667-2736 ⏰ Summer Mon–Sat 7am–8pm, Sun 8–4; rest of year Mon–Sat 8–4 (7 Thu–Fri), Sun 8–2

YELLOWKNIFE

L'Heritage Restaurant Français $$–$$$

The place to go for elegant French dining in downtown Yellowknife. Traditional Northern foods such as caribou, muskox and arctic char are given a French twist with exotic sauces, and there's an excellent range of wines to go with them.

➕ 211 F2 ✉ 5019 49th Street, 2nd level ☎ 867/873-9561 ⏰ Tue–Sat 5–10

Wildcat Café $

Good food and fabulous views in this original log cabin overlooking Back Bay. It's tiny and gets very crowded, but it's a Yellowknife must. The menu changes daily, but usually includes Northern specialties such as caribou, muskox and local fish; the fresh pie and coffee are legendary.

➕ 211 F2 ✉ 3904 Wiley Road; ☎ 867/873-8850 ⏰ Mon–Fri 11–10, Sat–Sun 10–10. Closed mid-Sep to May

Where to... Shop

As you might expect, the shopping opportunities in this area tend to center around local gold and crafts and keeping warm. Whitehorse, Dawson City, Yellowknife and Iqaluit are the principal oases amid this vast retail wilderness.

CLOTHING

n Iqaluit, the Inuit culture is reflected in the exclusive sealskin garments at **Rannva Design** (Apex Beach, Old Hudson Bay Building 3606, Iqaluit, Nunavut, tel: 867/979-3183). Perhaps it's the long dark days of winter, perhaps it's the inspirational landscape, but whatever the reason, there are some

excellent crafts to look for in the north, including carvings, pottery, paintings and jewelry. Check out **Midnight Sun** (205C Main Street, Whitehorse, tel: 867/668-4350; www.midnightsunyukon.com) or **North End Gallery** (118-1116 First Avenue, Whitehorse, tel: 867/393-3590; www.northendgallery.ca)

GOLD

For genuine gold nuggets, original jewelry designs and other souvenirs, try Klondikde Nugget and Ivory (990 Front Street, Dawson City, tel: 867/993-5432;www.knis.ca) or Goldsmiths (106 Main Street, Whitehorse, tel: 867/667-7340).

BOOKS

Mac's Fireweed Books (203 Main Street, Whitehorse, tel: 867/668-6104) has a wide selection of books about the Yukon.

Where to... Be Entertained

FOLLIES AND FESTIVALS

Though it's not all can-can dancers and old-style humor – the **Yukon Arts Centre** (Yukon College Campus, Whitehorse, tel: 867/667-8574) has an eclectic program – the Gold-Rush theme is definitely to the fore in the Yukon's entertainment scene. There are plans to develop an arts and entertainment area on the waterfront, but in the meantime you can see a play at the Guild Theatre (27 14th Avenue; tel: 1-867/633-3550) or gamble at **Diamond Tooth Gertie's** (Queen Street, Dawson City; tel: 867/993-5525). Vaudeville is also the theme at **Frantic Follies** (Westmark Whitehorse Hotel, 200 Wood Street, Whitehorse, tel: 867/668-2042).

Music festivals take place year-round, from the **Frostbite Music Festival** (www.frostbitefest.com) – cool in every way – to the **Dawson City Music Festival** (www.dcmf.com), which takes place under the midnight sun.

SPORT

There are plenty of sporting events throughout the year. In winter, time your visit to coincide with a **sled dog race** (www.yukonquest.com or www.thepercy.com); the long days of summer are ideal for such events as **midnight sun golf tournaments** (www.topoftheworldgolf.com) or the Yukon River Quest, the longest **canoe and kayak race** in the world (www.polarcom.com/riverquest).

Tours

1 INSIDE PASSAGE CRUISE

Tour

Canada's western coast is dotted with islands, and early explorers soon found a way through these safe, sheltered waters. Today, it is one of the most spectacular cruise routes in the world, with rocky mountains rising straight out of the ocean, prettily wooded islands and magnificent glaciers breaking into the waves. Whales, dolphins, porpoises, sea lions and seals inhabit the waters, bald eagles are among about 100 species of bird that fly overhead, and you may spot bears on the mainland shore. In summer the entire trip is completed in daylight.

DISTANCE 288km (180 miles) **TIME** 15 hours
START POINT Port Hardy, Vancouver Island; ferry departs 7:30am ✚ 202 B2
END POINT Prince Rupert, arrival 10:30pm ✚ 202 B4

1–2
At the northern tip of Vancouver Island, **Port Hardy** is your departure point, the largest town in the area and a center for all kinds of outdoor activities. It's worth arriving

a day early to explore its waterside nature path, take a forestry industry tour, or browse its art and craft galleries. Sailing out of the harbor, you soon enter the Queen Charlotte

Strait, the only stretch of open ocean on the voyage. It can be rough at times, but it doesn't last for long and the ferry soon enters the calmer waters of Fitzhugh Sound (also known as the Discovery Coast).

The first island on the left side is Calvert Island, 32km (20 miles) long and between 3 and 16km (2 and 10 miles) wide. It is thickly wooded on its western side, its highest point is Mt. Buxton (1,045m/ 3,430 feet), and to the north is the Hakai Provincial Recreation Area, for marine activities such as sea kayaking, salmon fishing and wilderness camping. It's British Columbia's largest marine park, encompassing a group of islands of outstanding natural beauty. The town you will see on

There is a resident population of orca off Vancouver Island

Hecate Strait

Banks Island

Pitt Island

Grenville Channel

Princess

Butedale ☐

4

BRITISH COLUMBIA

Skeena Valley

Prince Rupert ☐ 5

16

37

☐ Terrace

☐ Kitimat

C o a s

3–4

Milbanke Sound is a prime fishing spot, with shoals of herring and salmon on their spawning runs. Fishing boats vie with the resident orca (killer whale), visiting humpback whales, Steller sea lions, northern fur seals and bald eagles for the catch. From here, the ferry soon tucks into the lee of Price and Swindle islands, where forests inhabited by bears grow right down to the high tide mark, reflecting prettily in the water. Narrow Meyers Pass separates Swindle from the larger **Princess Royal Island**, which has a much-indented coastline and a dense growth of rain forest. But the island is most famous as a habitat of the white Kermode bear that is only found in this region.

4–5

Continuing north between Gill and Gribbell islands, the ferry enters the 89km (55-mile) long Grenville Channel, only 600m (1,970 feet) wide at its narrowest point, for the most dramatic scenery of the entire voyage. Thickly forested mountains rise steeply from water that is so deep the boats can get close inshore. Finally, the ferry enters the harbor at **Prince Rupert** (▶ 66).

the right is **Namu**, which had a thriving cannery until the 1980s. You can still see the cannery buildings, built out over the water.

2–3

The ferry snakes between King Island, Hunter Island and Campbell Island on its way north. On Campbell Island, **Bella Bella** is the biggest settlement in the area, home to the Heiltsuk First Nations, who have an interpretive center here. Beyond Campbell Island, the ferry sails into Milbanke Sound.

There are huge numbers of bald eagles in British Columbia

Information

BC Ferries: ✉ 1112 Fort Street, Victoria,
☎ 250/386-3431 or 1-888/223-3779; www.bcferries.bc.ca
🕓 Mid-May to end Sep $116, child (5–11) $58, under 5 free; reduced rates off season. Fuel surcharge $16.20 for each passenger. Vehicles are charged extra – call for rates. All quoted prices are subject to change.

2 THE ICEFIELDS PARKWAY

Drive

DISTANCE 230km (142 miles) **TIME** 1 day
START POINT Lake Louise village ✚ 203 E2
END POINT Jasper ✚ 203 D3

Traversing the Banff and Jasper national parks (▶ 60–64), the Icefields Parkway is one of the most spectacular drives in the world, opening up ever-changing vistas of vertiginous peaks, strings of dazzling blue lakes, glittering waterfalls, great river valleys and the glaciers that give the parkway its name. Just driving this route is enough to take your breath away, but the route also provides easy access to some of the highlights of the Banff and Jasper national parks, many of which are just a short walk from the designated parking areas.

1–2
Start at **Lake Louise** village (stock up with snacks and water here). Take Route 1 north, then turn right onto Route 93 (Icefields Parkway). After a couple of kilometers you'll pass through the national park entry point (stop to buy a park pass, if you don't already have one) before embarking on the Parkway.

2–3
Beginning in the Bow Valley, the route climbs steadily for the first 16km (10 miles), and scenic treasures begin to unfold when tiny Herbert Lake, backed by Mt. Temple, then **Hector Lake** appear to the left. Both have parking with viewpoints. Some 34km (21 miles) from Lake Louise you'll catch sight of **Crowfoot Glacier**, so named because it looked like a giant, icy claw gripping the rocks. Soon, Bow Lake (with a pleasant lakeshore walk) and Bow Glacier comes into view. When you reach the Bow Summit, at 2,088m (6,850 feet) the highest point on the parkway, turn left for the **Peyto Lake viewpoint**, with a panorama sweeping out over pine forests to the azure lake below.

3–4
Descending beyond the Bow Summit, there are wonderful views of the peaks of the Continental Divide, with Upper Waterfowl Lake in the foreground. When you have driven

72km (45 miles) from the beginning of the parkway, you'll reach the start of a short trail leading into the narrow **Mistaya Canyon**. Drive another 5km (3 miles) north to cross the wide, rocky valley of the North Saskatchewan River (fuel up here – it's the last until Jasper 130km/81 miles).

There are spectacular lake and mountain views all along the Icefields Parkway

follows the course of the river through the narrow gorge. Later come the even more spectacular **Athabasca Falls**. The Athabasca contains the greatest volume of water of any river in the Rockies, and here it cascades about 21m (70 feet).

Continue for 30km (19 miles) to end your journey at **Jasper** (▶ 63–64).

When to Go

The road is open all year, weather permitting, but many services along the way are only open April through October. Avoid high summer, when the route is busy with tour buses.

Places to Visit

Icefield Centre ☎ 877/423-7433 ◷ May to mid-Oct daily 9–5, (Jun 27–Sep 2 to 6pm).

Taking a Break

The **Crossing Resort** (tel: 403/761-7000, $–$$) at Saskatchewan River Crossing has food all day.

4–5

Beyond the river are views of the yellowish-hued Mt. Wilson, and then the valley narrows, with waterfalls tumbling down its rocky flanks, before reaching the Big Bend. Viewpoints here look out over Cirrus Mountains and Bridal Veil Falls, and there's a path to the Panther Falls. Up on the plain above, there's a steep 2.5km (1.5-mile) walk along Parker Ridge for a breathtaking view of the Saskatchewan Glacier.

5–6

The parkway exits Banff National Park at **Sunwapta Pass** and goes directly into the Jasper National Park and the Columbia Icefield. Beneath the snow-capped mountains is a moonscape of rocks and moraine interspersed with huge glaciers, with streams that grow into rushing rivers and waterfalls and feed turquoise lakes. Call in at the Icefield Centre, which has masses of information. It's worth stopping here, especially for the two-hour Ice Explorer Tour (tel: 877/423-7433; expensive) onto the **Athabasca Glacier**, 6km (4 miles) long and 1km (0.6 mile) wide. Alternatively, you can walk to the glacier's edge from the parking lot at **Sunwapta Lake**,

where marker posts show how the glacier has retreated over the years.

6–7

Farther north the road follows the wider flood plain of the Sunwapta River, and the two main attractions are waterfalls. The first is the **Sunwapta Falls**, where a trail

3 NIAGARA PARKWAY
Drive

This beautiful drive opens up wonderful sights and interesting contrasts. There's the world-famous Niagara Falls, of course, with its thundering waters and power plants (and huge numbers of visitors), but there are also tranquil stretches of water, delightful old towns and villages full of history, and large areas of vineyards and orchards producing the Niagara region's renowned wines and fruits.

DISTANCE 53km (33 miles), not including detours
TIME 1 day, including stops for sightseeing
START POINT Old Fort Erie ✚ 207 F1
END POINT Niagara-on-the-Lake ✚ 207 E1

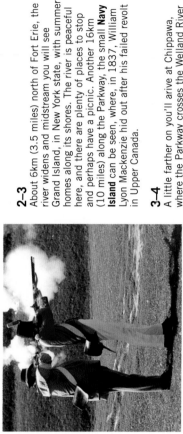

Old Fort Erie recalls the days of British-American hostilities during the War of 1812

1–2
The drive begins at the Mather Arch by the **Peace Bridge**, the border crossing from the US, which links Fort Erie, Canada with Buffalo, New York across the Niagara River. It is one of four international bridges across the river. Close by is **Old Fort Erie** (➤ 108), a reconstruction of a British fort that was built during the War of 1812 and destroyed by the Americans in 1814. It has a wonderful site, with views over Lake Erie and Buffalo.

2–3
About 6km (3.5 miles) north of Fort Erie, the river widens and midstream you will see Grand Island, in New York state, with summer homes along its shores. The river is peaceful here, and there are plenty of places to stop and perhaps have a picnic. Another 16km (10 miles) along the Parkway, the small **Navy Island** can be seen, where, in 1837, William Lyon Mackenzie hid out after his failed revolt in Upper Canada.

3–4
A little farther on you'll arrive at Chippawa, where the Parkway crosses the Welland River near its confluence with the Niagara. The Dufferin Islands are a cluster of islets linked by bridges, forming a park with lovely walks. After this, you'll see the control works that

Lake Ontario

Niagara-on-the-Lake

0   10 km
0   5 miles

opposite Table Rock, and explore all that **Niagara Falls** has to offer (▶ 107–109).

6–7

Drive the 2km (1.2 miles) to the **Rainbow Bridge**, another crossing to the US. Soon the Parkway passes the Whirlpool and White Water Walk (▶ 108), where you can get close to the turbulent waters below the falls. If you continue for another 3km (2 miles), you can hike down into the gorge for free at **Niagara Glen**. A short distance farther on are the Niagara Parks Botanical Gardens and Butterfly Conservatory, maintained by the students of the School of Horticulture here. Covering 40ha (100 acres), the gardens are a riot of color in summer.

7–8

Some 2km (1.2 miles) beyond here the Parkway passes impressive **generating stations** on both banks of the river. More attractive is the Floral Clock, a 12m (40-foot) working clock with 20,000 small plants decorating its surface. Another 1km (0.6 mile) along is Queenston Heights Park and the Brock Monument, on the top of the Niagara

The botanical gardens at Niagara are a testament to the favorable summer climate of southern Ontario

divert the river below ground to the hydro-power plants beyond Niagara Falls.

4–5

The Niagara River picks up pace north of Chippawa, traveling at nearly 100kph (60mph) in its downhill journey through great rapids toward the falls. Excitement builds too, with the anticipation of the sights to come, especially when the spray starts to hit the windshield.

5–6

Just 2km (1.2 miles) beyond Chippawa, you arrive at Table Rock and the **Horseshoe (Canadian) Falls** (▶ 107). You can park

escarpment. Here, during the War of 1812, British commander Isaac Brock was killed in battle and his monument stands 50m (165 feet) tall above the site. A little farther on, you can detour into Queenston (▶ 108) to visit the home of Canadian heroine, Laura Secord, who embarked upon a long walk to warn the British that an American attack was imminent after they ransacked her home.

8–9

Beyond Queenston Heights, the vast orchards and vineyards of the Niagara wine region open out, and you can detour to a number of wineries for tours and tastings. Eventually, the Parkway ends in **Niagara-on-the-Lake** (▶ 108), one of the loveliest towns in Ontario. Settled by Loyalists after the American Revolution, it was the first capital of Upper Canada, but was burned to the ground by the Americans during the War of 1812. Visit nearby Fort George National Historic Park (▶ 108) for a glimpse of military life in those days. The town was rebuilt soon afterwards, and it is this era that is recalled in its gracious homes and wide, tree-lined streets. The town is also well known for its summer Shaw Festival (see ▶ 116).

Niagara-on-the-Lake is a delightful set-piece of charming homes and craft and antiques shops

Taking a Break

There are a number of options with views of the falls at Niagara Falls. One of the best for families is the **Edgewaters Tap and Grill** (tel: 905/356-2217, $) within a lovely floral park. Just outside Niagara-on-the-Lake, the Riverbend Inn (tel: 905/468-8866, $–$$) is a beautiful Georgian mansion amid vineyards offering lunch, dinner and an 11am–11pm lounge menu.

When to Go

June and September are the best months, when the weather is good and the biggest summer crowds have not yet built to their peak. The falls are impressive in winter, but if you drive the route after October and before late May, some of the attractions will not be open.

Places to Visit ▶ 107–109

Information
Niagara Parks Commission (▶ 109)

Niagara Economic and Tourism Corporation
✉ 2201 St David's Road (P.O. Box 1042), Thorold ☎ 905/984-3826 or 1-800/263-2988; www.tourismniagara.com

Niagara-on-the-Lake Chamber of Commerce (▶ 109)

Shaw Festival 10 Queens Parade, Niagara-on-the-Lake ☎ 905/468-2172; www.shawfest.com

4 GASPE PENINSULA

Drive

This drive follows the spectacular coastline of the Gulf of St. Lawrence, with deep coves, craggy capes and pretty little fishing villages along the way. It explores the extraordinary cliffs of the Forillon National Park, with later views of the famous pierced rock at Percé. At the very beginning of the route, just before the descent into the town of Grande-Vallée, there is a wonderful view over the village and its bay.

DISTANCE 236km (147 miles), not including detours
TIME 1 day, 2 to allow sufficient time in Percé
START POINT Grande-Vallée ➕ 208 C3
END POINT Grand-Rivière ➕ 208 C3

1–2
As you drive through **Grande-Vallée**, notice the covered bridge across the Grande-Vallée River and the parish church, high on the cape. From the village, take Route 132 east, twisting and turning around the coast. Waves smash on the rocks, seagulls fly overhead, and one tiny fishing village succeeds another, all clustered in sheltered coves. After 65km (40 miles) you reach **Rivière-au-Renard**, an important fishing center.

2–3
Here the route enters the **Forillon National Park**, which preserves 245sq km (94sq miles) of the peninsula, encompassing mountains and coastline with seabird colonies. Continue for 10km (6 miles) to **L'Anse-au-Griffon**, a small agricultural and fishing community. Here, Le Manoir LeBouthillier, built in the 1850s for a wealthy cod merchant, is open to the public.

Covered bridges, sometimes quite lengthy, are a feature of French Canada

3–4
From here it's 11km (7 miles) to **Cap-des-Rosiers**. Samuel de Champlain visited the cape in 1631 and made a note in his journal about the wild rose bushes, and they still flourish here. Canada's tallest lighthouse, 34m (112 feet) high, is here. The route turns

Places to Visit
Manoir LeBouthillier ✉ 578 Boulevard Griffon (CP 37), L'Anse-au-Griffon
☎ 418/892-5150 ⏰ Mid-Jun to early Oct daily
💲 Moderate

Forillon National Park ✉ 122 Boulevard de Gaspé, Gaspé ☎ 418/368-5505; www.parkscanada.gc.ca/forillon 💲 Moderate

inland through the national park. Make a left onto a park road, signed Cap Bon Ami, for a round-trip detour of 12km (7.5 miles). Stop at the Interpretive Centre after 2km (1.2 miles) to walk the short Discovery Trail (about 20 minutes). You can also get boat trips from the wharf to view seabirds and seals. Then continue to **Cap Bon Ami** to view the tilted limestone cliffs.

4–5

Return to Route 132, turn left and continue across the peninsula through the mountains. There's a great viewpint after 8km (5 miles), looking out toward Percé. When you've driven 11km (7 miles) from Cap-des-Rosiers, turn left on a park road, signed Grande Grave for a 13km (8-mile) round-trip detour to this former cod-processing center. Some of the buildings have been restored and are open to the public (mid-Jun to mid-Oct daily). The detour continues to Anse aux Sauvages for a hike out to the tip of Cap Gaspé (8km/5 miles round trip).

5–6

Return to Route 132 and continue for 11km (7 miles) to the Penouille Peninsula and Information Centre, where there is a fine

sandy beach and you can stretch your lets on a 4km (2.5-mile) trail. After this, the route exits the national park to wind around the Baie de Gaspé, crossing a long bridge over the Dartmouth River estuary. There are some terrific backward views as you climb away from the river. Eventually, 20km (12 miles) beyond Penouille, you'll enter **Gaspé**, the commercial heart of the peninsula and a historic spot, where French explorer Jacques Cartier claimed the land for France.

The road down into Percé has a wonderful view, with the whale-like Bonaventure Island offshore

Information

Association Touristique Régionale de la Gaspésie ⌖ 357 Route de la Mer, Ste.-Flavie ☎ 418/775-2223, 1-800/463-0323; www.tourisme-gaspesie.com

Office du Tourisme et des Congrès du Gaspé ⌖ 27 Boulevard York, Gaspé ☎ 418/368-6335; www.tourismgaspe.org

Information Touristique de Percé ⌖ 142 Route 132, Percé ☎ 418/782-5448; www.rocherperce.com

Boat Trips

Bateaux de Croisières Julien Cloutier (Forillon and Ile Bonaventure) ⌖ 395 Route 132 Ouest (CP 467), 9 rue de Quai, Percé ☎ 418/782-5606 (Cap-des-Rosiers in season) or 1-877/782-2161 (Percé) ⌚ Mid-May to mid-Oct daily 💲 Expensive

Les Bateliers de Percé (Ile Bonaventure) ⌖ 162 Route 132 (CP 278), Percé ☎ 418/782-2974 or 1-877/782-2974 ⌚ Mid-May to late Oct daily 💲 Expensive

Les Traversiers de l'Île Inc. (Île Bonaventure) ⌖ 9 rue de Quai, Percé ☎ 418/782-5526 (in season) or 1-866/782-5526 ⌚ Mid-Jun to late Sep daily 💲 Expensive

Taking a Break

At **La Maison du Pêcheur** (155 place du Quai, Percé; tel: 418/82-5331; Jun–Oct, $–$$) there's a terrific choice of fresh seafood, meat dishes and pizzas.

6–7

Leave Gaspé via the bridge over the York River, then turn left with Route 132, with views across the bay. The route detours inland around the St.-Jean River estuary and continues to Douglastown, 25km (15.5 miles) from Gaspé, and, in another 23km (14 miles), **Pointe-St.-Pierre**. Here, make a left opposite the Episcopal church on to rue du Quai, which leads to the water's edge for a fine view of the Rocher Percé (Percé Rock) and Île Bonaventure (Bonaventure Island).

7–8

Back on the main route, there's a scenic 7km (4.3-mile) stretch to Barachois, with constant views of the rock, then it disappears as you begin the steep, winding descent into **Percé**. Finally, and dramatically, you breach the last hill and the great rock is directly below. In this spectacular area that shows its geological upheavals all too clearly, there is none so impressive as the Rocher Percé, a massive chunk of limestone

88m (289 feet) high and 438m (1,437 feet) long, with a hole right through it. You can walk out to the rock at low tide.

8–9

Leaving Percé, halt awhile at the viewpoint on Cap Blanc, 2km (1.2 miles) out of town, for another magnificent view of the rock and Mont-Ste.-Anne. In another 7km (4.3 miles) you will reach the little town of **L'Anse-à-Beaufils**, and 7km (4.3 miles) beyond here is **Cap d'Espoir**, with a final view of Rocher Percé.

Then the route heads west to end at **Grande-Rivière**, known for its salmon-rich waters.

5 THE CABOT TRAIL

Drive

Cape Breton (▶ 151–152) is one of the most beautiful islands in the world, and the Cabot Trail encircles one of the most scenic parts of the island, incorporating the mountains and forests of the Cape Breton Highlands National Park and a spectacular coastline. It is named after the 15th-century explorer, John Cabot, who is said to have landed on the northern tip of the island in 1497.

DISTANCE 292km (181 miles)
TIME Allow 2 days
START/END POINT Baddeck ♦ 209 E3

character of the drive changes markedly, and you will notice that all the place names are in French here, for this area is populated largely by French-speaking Acadians. Look for their flag – a French tricolor with a gold star.

1–2

Leave **Baddeck** (▶ 151) on Highway 105 west in the direction of the Canso Causeway, to skirt the lovely Bras d'Or Lake. At Nyanza, reached after 8km (5 miles), make a right, signed "Cabot Trail" and drive for 52km (32 miles) through agricultural countryside, following the Margaree River to **Margaree Harbour**. Here, where the river flows into the Gulf of St. Lawrence, you turn north along the coast. The

Information

Cape Breton Highlands National Park
⊠ Ingonish Beach ☎ 902/224-2306;
www.pc.gc.ca/capebretonhighlands
⏰ Visitor center: mid-May to mid-Oct daily 9–5 (late Jun to late Aug 8–8); park: always accessible
💲 Park fee moderate

2–3

Continue north for 24km (15 miles) until you reach **Chéticamp**, the center of Acadian culture – visit the Coopérative Artisinale Acadienne (Acadian Crafts Cooperative), which has a good selection of locally produced hooked rugs (made by a group of ladies known as "Happy Hookers") and other items. With its sheltered harbor, Chéticamp is one of the places where you can go whale-watching.

3-4

About 8km (5 miles) north of Chéticamp, the route enters the **Cape Breton Highlands National Park** (▶152), with an excellent information center. From here, the highway winds around the coast on one of the most spectacular parts

Cape Breton's renowned fall colors are just beginning to appear as a backdrop to the lovely Neil's Harbour

of the drive, with stunning views, then curves inland, up through thickly forested mountains. There are regular parking areas where you can stop for a walk. The highest ground is at French Mountain (455m/1,495 feet) and Mackenzie Mountain (355m/1,165 feet), and after this, a series of dramatic hairpin bends winds down to **Pleasant Bay**. This is another whale-watching center, with a Whale Interpretive Centre above the harbor.

4-5

The Cabot Trail leaves the coast here, heading inland for 14km (8 miles) and climbing the slopes of North Mountain (457m/1,500 feet) to the **Lone Shieling**, a tiny stone replica of a Scottish croft amid a beautiful maple forest. The cottage is a reminder of the many Scottish settlers who came to the island following the Highland Clearances during the 18th and 19th centuries. Their presence on the island has given it a strong culture of music and dance – and a whiskey distillery. Beyond here, the route descends into the Aspy Valley and follows the river to **Aspy Bay** on the northeast coast.

Taking a Break

A good place to eat on the northwest stretch of the Cabot Trail is the **Rusty Anchor** (tel: 902/224-1313, $), just south of Pleasant Bay. It has a lovely ocean-view terrace. Along the other coast, the **Atlantic Restaurant** at the Keltic Lodge resort (tel: 902/285-2880 or 1-800/565-0444, $$) is a good place for lunch.

---

20 km
10 miles
0 0

North Sydney

St Ann's Bay
7
Tarbotvale
312
St Ann's
South Gut St Ann's
105
125
Baddeck
1
8
St Andrews Channel
223
Middle River
Nyanza
Finlayson
Northeast Margaree
Margaree Forks
19
395

school on the North American continent to teach the Gaelic language and traditional Scottish arts and crafts. This was also home to the Cape Breton Giant – Angus MacAskill (d.1863), who grew to be 2.35m (7 feet 9 inches) tall. From here it's just 19km (12 miles) back to **Baddeck**.

When to Go

Cape Breton, jutting out into the Atlantic Ocean, is famous for the dense fog that rolls in off the ocean. Wait for a clear day to see the island at its most magnificent. The fall colors are spectacular, and the roads are less busy at this time (except during the Celtic Colours Festival in October).

Places to Visit

Coopérative Artisanale Acadienne ⊠ 15067 Main Street, Chéticamp ☎ 902/224-2170; www.co-opartisanale.com ⓒ Daily mid-May to mid-Oct; Tue–Thu pm off-season

Museum of the Gaelic College of Celtic Arts and Crafts ⊠ P.O. Box 80, Englishtown ☎ 902/295-3411; www.gaeliccollege.edu ⓒ Early Jun–Sep ⏲ Inexpensive

5-6

Turning inland once again, the chances of spotting a moose are good, especially at dawn or dusk. After 34km (21 miles) there's a very worthwhile detour to the charming fishing village of **Neil's Harbour**, and 6km (4 miles) beyond here is pretty **Black Brook Cove**, with a lovely beach and coastal walks. In another 6km (4 miles) Lakies Head Lookout has wonderful views of Cape Smokey and Middle Head. For the next 20km (12 miles) the lovely communitites and beaches of the **Ingonish** (▶ 152) area are dotted along the coast, with Ingonish Island offshore.

The wooded mountains sweep down to the sea between Presquile and Petit Etang

6-7

After 22km (13.5 miles) you'll begin the dramatic drive up over **Cape Smokey**, rising 366m (1,200 feet) out of the ocean, its summit often obscured by the swirling mists that give it its name. From the lookout at the top, there's a spectacular view over the Ingonish villages around the bay. The drive down the other side of the cape is even more dramatic, returning you to sea level. From here, the route continues southward along the Gaelic coast, another recognition of the strong Scottish heritage on the island. The

Bird Islands can be seen offshore, and they are aptly named, forming a safe nesting ground for a huge numbers of birds.

7-8

After 23km (14 miles) take a detour on Route 312 and cross a narrow inlet by ferry to join Highway 105 (the TransCanada Highway) and rejoin the Cabot Trail. You can simply stay on the Cabot Trail, but this is a more scenic alternative. Either way, you will end up in **South Gut St. Ann's**, which is home of the only

6 GOLDEN CIRCLE

Drive

This route follows in the footsteps of the prospectors of the Klondike Gold Rush through some of the most unspoiled landscapes in the world, with high mountain peaks, glaciers, bright blue lakes and even a tiny desert.

DISTANCE 483km (300 miles)
TIME At least 2 days, more to allow for hiking
START/END POINT Whitehorse 🞧 210 B2

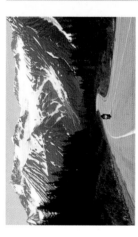

Haines Highway is never too crowded with traffic

1–2
Leave **Whitehorse** (▶170) via 4th Avenue and Two Mile Hill to join Route 1, the **Alaska Highway** (▶172). The initial section – by Yukon standards at least – is not that special, but as you approach Haines Junction, after 160km (100 miles), the horizon becomes jagged with the peaks of the St. Elias Mountains. **Haines Junction** is a popular base for the **Kluane** (pronounced *kloo-wa-nee*) **National Park**.

2–3
From Haines Junction, head south on the Haines Highway (Route 3), skirting the east-

ern edge of the Kluane National Park. After 27km (16.5 miles) turn right to **Kathleen Lake**, where there's a wonderful 10km (6-mile) hike into the mountains. Stay on Route 3 for 17km (10.5 miles) to access the short Rock Glacier Trail. From here it's 7km (4.3 miles) to **Klukshu**, a First Nations camp that's only occupied June through early November (best visited during the salmon run).

Information
• The route crosses the US border, so make sure you have all the necessary documentation for the vehicle and its passengers.
• Keep your fuel topped up – there are some long distances between filling stations.

Whitehorse Tourism ✉ 2121 Second Avenue, Whitehorse ☎ 867/667-6401; www.visitwhitehorse.com

Skagway Convention and Visitors Bureau
☎ 907/983-2854; www.skagway.org

Haines Convention and Visitors Bureau
☎ 907/766-2234; www.haines.ak.us

3–4
In another 40km (25 miles) or so, the route crosses into British Columbia amid superb mountain scenery, climbing steadily to the

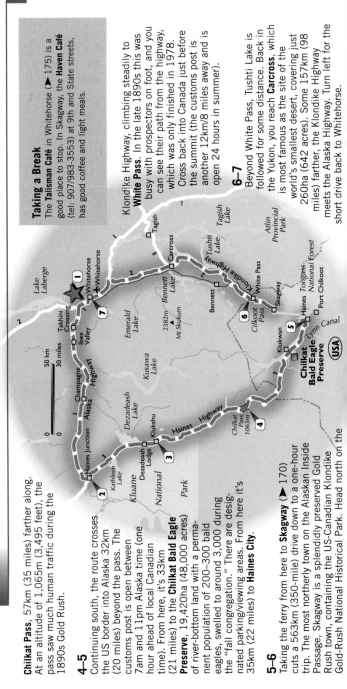

Taking a Break

The **Talisman Café** in Whitehorse (➤ 175) is a good place to stop. In Skagway, the **Haven Café** (tel: 907/983-3553) at 9th and State streets, has good coffee and light meals.

Klondike Highway, climbing steadily to **White Pass**. In the late 1890s this was busy with prospectors on foot, and you can see their path from the highway, which was only finished in 1978. Cross back into Canada just before the summit (the customs post is another 12km/8 miles away and is open 24 hours in summer).

6–7

Beyond White Pass, Tushti Lake is followed for some distance. Back in the Yukon, you reach **Carcross**, which is most famous as the site of the world's smallest desert, covering just 260ha (642 acres). Some 157km (98 miles) farther on, the Klondike Highway meets the Alaska Highway. Turn left for the short drive back to Whitehorse.

Chilkat Pass, 57km (35 miles) farther along. At an altitude of 1,065m (3,495 feet), the pass saw much human traffic during the 1890s Gold Rush.

4–5

Continuing south, the route crosses the US border into Alaska 32km (20 miles) beyond the pass. The customs post is open between 7am and 11pm Alaska time (one hour ahead of local Canadian time). From here, it's 33km (21 miles) to the **Chilkat Bald Eagle Preserve**, 19,420ha (48,000 acres) of river-bottom land with a permanent population of 200–300 bald eagles, swelled to around 3,000 during the "fall congregation." There are designated parking/viewing areas. From here it's 35km (22 miles) to **Haines City**.

5–6

Taking the ferry from here to **Skagway** (➤ 170) cuts a 563km (350-mile) drive down to a one-hour trip. The most northerly town on the Alaskan Inside Passage, Skagway is a splendidly preserved Gold Rush town, containing the US-Canadian Klondike Gold-Rush National Historical Park. Head on the

Practicalities

GETTING ADVANCE INFORMATION

- British Columbia: www.hellobc.com
- Alberta: www1.travelalberta.com
- Saskatchewan: www.sasktourism.com
- Manitoba: www.travelmanitoba.com
- Ontario: www.ontariotravel.net
- Québec: www.bonjourquebec.com
- New Brunswick: www.tourismnbcanada.com
- Newfoundland/Labrador: www.newfoudlandlabradortourism.com
- Nova Scotia: http://noviascotia.com
- Prince Edward Island: www.gov.pe.ca
- Northwest Territories: www.explorenwt.com
- Yukon: http://travelyukon.com
- Nunavut: www.nunavuttourism.com

BEFORE YOU GO

WHAT YOU NEED

- ● Required
- ○ Suggested
- ▲ Not required
- △ Not applicable

Some countries require a passport to remain valid for a minimum period (usually six months) beyond the date of entry – contact their consulate or embassy or your travel agent for details.

	UK	Germany	USA	Canada	Australia	Ireland	Netherlands	Spain
Passport/National Identity Card	●	●	●	●	●	●	●	●
Visa (regulations can change – check before booking)	▲	▲	▲	▲	▲	▲	▲	▲
Onward or Return Ticket	●	●	▲	▲	●	●	●	●
Health Inoculations (tetanus and polio)	▲	▲	▲	●	▲	▲	▲	▲
Health Documentation (▶ 198, Health)	▲	▲	▲	●	▲	▲	▲	▲
Travel Insurance	●	●	▲	○	●	●	●	●
Driver's Licence (national)	●	●	●	●	●	●	●	●
Car Insurance Certificate	△	△	●	●	△	△	△	△
Car Registration Document	△	△	●	●	△	△	△	△

Anyone convicted of a drunken-driving or other offense within the last ten years, may not be allowed into Canada without submitting a "Ministers Permit" to show they are deemed "rehabilitated." Information available at: www.cic.gc.ca/english/applications/rehabil.html

WHEN TO GO

Toronto

High season Low season

JAN	FEB	MAR	APR	MAY	JUN	JUL	AUG	SEP	OCT	NOV	DEC
-4°C	-3°C	1°C	8°C	14°C	19°C	21°C	21°C	18°C	12°C	6°C	-1°C
❄	❄	☁	🌧	🌧	☀	☀	☀	⛅	☁	🌧	❄

☀ Sun   ☁ Cloud   🌧 Wet   ⛅ Sun/Showers   ❄ Cold

Weather varies considerably between the different climatic zones in this huge country. In most parts **summers** are reliably warm and can get very hot – in southern Ontario, for instance, it often exceeds 30°C (86°F). It's pleasantly fresher on the coasts, though these areas are prone to sea mists. Even in the far north it's warm in summer, and there's the added bonus of 24-hour daylight. **Winters** are punishingly cold in most areas. BC is the only province in which the average winter temperature remains above freezing point, with little snowfall along the coast (but a good deal of rain); with temperatures dropping as low as -40°C (-40°F) in the Prairies and the North. The Atlantic Provinces have relatively mild winters too, but also get some of Canada's highest levels of snowfall, and coastal regions may be battered by North Atlantic storms.

GETTING THERE

By Air The major international airports in Canada are in Toronto, Montréal and Vancouver, with international flights also handled at Ottawa, Québec City, Halifax, Edmonton, Winnipeg and Calgary. **Air Canada** (tel: 1-888/247-2262; www.aircanada.com) is the national airline.

From the US: A number of US airlines have scheduled flights to the major Canadian cities, including American Airlines, Continental Airlines, Delta, Northwest Airlines, United Airlines and US Airways.

From the UK: **British Airways** has regular scheduled flights to Vancouver, Toronto and Montréal, and **Air Canada** has flights from London Heathrow to all the major Canadian cities.

From the rest of Europe: From France, **Air France** flies from Paris to Montréal, Ottawa and Toronto, and **Corsair** operate a summer service from Paris direct to Montréal, Québec and Moncton, New Brunswick. From Germany, **Lufthansa** have direct flights from Frankfurt to Toronto, Montréal and Vancouver and from Munich to Toronto and Montréal. They also offer code-share flights to such destinations as Ottawa, Calgary and Québec City.

From Australia and New Zealand: **Qantas** flies to Toronto, Ottawa, Québec City, Montréal, Winnipeg, Calgary and Vancouver.

Air New Zealand have scheduled flights to Toronto and Vancouver.

TIME

 Canada spans six time zones: Atlantic Standard Time (GMT+4); Eastern Standard Time (GMT+5); Central Standard Time (GMT+6); Mountain Standard Time (GMT+7); Pacific Standard Time (GMT+8); Newfoundland and part of Labrador are a half-hour ahead of Atlantic Standard.

Daylight Saving Time operates in all provinces except Saskatchwewan from the first Sunday in April until the last Sunday in October.

CURRENCY AND FOREIGN EXCHANGE

Currency Canada's currency is the Canadian dollar, divided into 100 cents. **Bills** are printed in English and French in the following dollar denominations: $5, $10, $20, $50 and $100 (the latter can be hard to use – people are suspicious because of forgeries). **Coins** come in denominations of 1, 5, 10 and 25 cents, and 1 and 2 dollars. The dollar coin is called the "loonie" after the bird featured on one face; the two-dollar is called the "twonie." US dollars are often accepted on a one-for-one basis, but as the US dollar is worth more it makes sense to exchange it for Canadian currency.

The best way to take money is as **travelers' checks** made out in Canadian dollars, which are widely accepted as cash and change is given in cash.

Exchange rates are best in banks, and there is no limit to the amount of Canadian or foreign currency that can be exchanged or brought into and out of the country. You can withdraw money from most Canadian **ATMs** with a credit or debit card, but you'll need to know your PIN.

Sales tax is not usually included in displayed prices in stores.

GMT	Canada (Ottawa)	USA New York	Germany	Spain	Australia
12 noon	7am	7am	1pm	1pm	Sydney 10pm

WHEN YOU ARE THERE

CLOTHING SIZES

UK	Rest of Europe	Canada/USA	
36	46	36	**Suits**
38	48	38	
40	50	40	
42	52	42	
44	54	44	
46	56	46	
7	41	8	**Shoes**
7.5	42	8.5	
8.5	43	9.5	
9.5	44	10.5	
10.5	45	11.5	
11	46	12	
14.5	37	14.5	**Shirts**
15	38	15	
15.5	39/40	15.5	
16	41	16	
16.5	42	16.5	
17	43	17	
8	34	6	**Dresses**
10	36	8	
12	38	10	
14	40	12	
16	42	14	
18	44	16	
4.5	38	6	**Shoes**
5	38	6.5	
5.5	39	7	
6	39	7.5	
6.5	40	8	
7	41	8.5	

NATIONAL HOLIDAYS

1 Jan	New Year's Day
Mar/Apr	Good Friday and Easter Monday
Mon before 25 May	Victoria Day
1 Jul	Canada Day
First Mon in Sept	Labour Day
Second Mon in Oct	Thanksgiving
11 Nov	Remembrance Day
25 Dec	Christmas Day
26 Dec	Boxing Day

Government offices and banks are closed, but some stores are open. Various provincial holidays are also observed.

OPENING HOURS

- ○ Shops
- ● Offices
- ● Banks
- ● Post Offices
- ● Museums/Monuments
- ● Pharmacies

8am 9am 10am noon 1pm 2pm 4pm 5pm 7pm

□ Day ■ Midday ■ Evening

Stores Mon–Sat 10–6, Sun noon–6, but many stores, especially in major malls, are open until 9pm. Food stores susually open at 8am.

Banks Usually open Mon–Fri 10–4, but hours can vary and some stay open until 5 or 6 some days.

Post offices Generally open Mon–Fri 8:30–5:30; some open Sat 9–noon.

Museums Hours can vary widely, but are usually Tue–Sun 10–5; closed on public holidays. Some museums have late opening one evening a week, with free admission after 5:30 on that day.

Pharmacies Most open Mon–Sat 9–6; 24-hour or at least a late night service is usually available somewhere in major towns and cities.

EMERGENCY NUMBERS

POLICE 911

FIRE 911

AMBULANCE 911

NOTE:
In Yukon, Northwest Territories, Nunavut and Vancouver Island, dial 0 for operator and and say you have an emergency

PERSONAL SAFETY

Canada is a low-crime country and visitors need not be overly concerned about personal safety, but a few precautions can avoid unfortunate incidents.

- Carry money in a belt.
- Don't leave bags or other valuables visible in your car.
- Don't wear expensive jewelry or carry large amounts of cash.
- Leave your passport and valuables in the hotel safe.
- At night walk only along well-lit streets and avoid parks and train stations.
- Report any crime to the police and note the crime reference number.

Police assistance:
 911 from any phone

TELEPHONES

Local calls cost 25 cents for any length call from public pay phones; longer-distance calls, which generally need to be prefixed with a "1", connect to an operator who will tell you how much the call will cost. Within a province you only dial the area code if the province has more than one.

Public phones are widely available and accept coins, credit cards and pre-paid phone cards. US telephone credit cards are also accepted.

International Dialing Codes
Dial 011 followed by

US:	no country code required
UK:	44
Ireland:	353
Australia:	61
Spain	34

POST

Post offices are usually open Mon–Fri 8:30–5:30 and some larger stores and train stations have mail outlets; you can buy stamps in some convenience stores. Canada is not noted for speedy mail delivery, but Priority Post offers a next-day delivery within Canada.

ELECTRICITY

The power supply is 110 volts AC (60 Hz), the same as in the U.S. Sockets take two-prong, flat-pin plugs. An adaptor is needed for appliances with two-round-pin and three-pin plugs. European appliances also need a voltage transformer.

TIPS/GRATUITIES

Tipping is widespread; it's usually calculated on the pre-tax amount for food service. As a general guide:

Restaurants (service not included)	15 percent
Bar Service	15 percent
Tour guides	optional ($1 per person)
Hairdressers	15 percent
Taxis	15 percent
Chambermaids	optional
Porters	optional ($1 per bag)
Room service	10 percent

UK
☎ 613/237-1530

USA
☎ 613/238-5335

Australia
☎ 613/236-0841

Germany
☎ 613/232-1101

Spain
☎ 613/747-2252

HEALTH

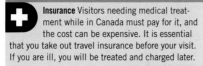

Insurance Visitors needing medical treatment while in Canada must pay for it, and the cost can be expensive. It is essential that you take out travel insurance before your visit. If you are ill, you will be treated and charged later.

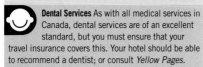

Dental Services As with all medical services in Canada, dental services are of an excellent standard, but you must ensure that your travel insurance covers this. Your hotel should be able to recommend a dentist; or consult *Yellow Pages.*

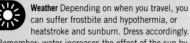

Weather Depending on when you travel, you can suffer frostbite and hypothermia, or heatstroke and sunburn. Dress accordingly. Remember: water increases the effect of the sun by reflection. Carry mosquito repellant in summer.

Drugs Medicines can be bought at drugstores and most towns and cities have at least one 24-hour pharmacy. Bring sufficient supplies of regular medications, but bring your prescription too, in case you need further supplies. It's also wise to note the generic name of any prescription medicines that you take, because they may be sold under a different name in Canada.

Safe Water Tap water is safe, except in some campgrounds. Boil back-country spring water (10 mins) – it may contain parasites.

CONCESSIONS

Students/children Many hotels offer reductions or free accommodations for children sharing parents' rooms; many restaurants have a children's menu or provide smaller portions. **Via Rail** offers free travel for under 2s and half-price for children 2–11; student rail passes give discounts of 10–50 percent. There are discounts on admission to museums and attractions, though age categories vary.

Seniors Many museums and attractions offer discounts to seniors; age limits range from over 55 to over 65 years. There are also concessionary fares on public transportation.

TRAVELING WITH A DISABILITY

Facilities and access for wheelchair-bound visitors is generally good throughout Canada, and many hotels have specially adapted rooms, but it is always wise to check in advance. A good source of information is the **Access to Travel** website (www.accesstotravel.gc.ca), set up by the government to assist people with disabilities to travel around Canada. You can also contact the **Canadian Paraplegic Association** (CPA) (1101 Prince of Wales Drive, Suite 230, Ottawa, Ontario K2C 3W7; tel: 613/723-1033; fax: 613/723-1060; www.canparaplegic.org).

CHILDREN

Hotels and restaurants are generally child-friendly, but diaper-changing amenities are by no means universal.

RESTROOMS

These can be found in public buildings, museums, malls and transportation terminals. Patrons can use restrooms in bars and restaurants.

CUSTOMS

Wildlife souvenirs sourced from endangered species may be illegal. Check your country's regulations.

CANADIAN LANGUAGES

Canada has two official languages – English and French. The reasons for this are historical. French settlement in the St. Lawrence Valley started in the early 17th century. No English-speaking settlers arrived until after the British conquest of 1760. At the time of Canadian Confederation in 1867, the English- and French-speaking populations were more or less equal in size. Today, less than a quarter of Canadians speak French as their mother tongue (6.7 million out of 31 million).

The country has large communities of peoples of other nationalities and languages, but none has official recognition.

FRENCH-SPEAKING COMMUNITIES

French Canadians are in every province, but their greatest concentration is in the province of Québec, where they comprise more than 85 percent of the population. These are the people known as the Québécois. French-speaking people form more than a third of the population of New Brunswick, and are also prominent in Nova Scotia and Prince Edward Island—these are the Acadiens, the first European settlers to colonize this part of Canada. Following dispersal by the British, many Acadiens wound up in Louisiana in the US, where they became know as "Cajuns."

Ontario has a sizable French-speaking population distributed between Toronto and in the eastern part of the province, who are known as Franco-Ontariens.

Manitoba's distinct French-speaking community is in St.-Boniface, and these people are known as Franco-Manitobins. There are also small French-speaking communities in Saskatchewan, Alberta and British Columbia.

THE FRENCH LANGUAGE

If you speak the French of France, you will find that the language of Québec has a strong and highly recognizable accent – as close to the language of the mother country as the Texas accent is to the English spoken in the UK.

The French spoken by the Acadiens is different again. For instance, *oui* sounds like "why," and *non* is pronounced "nah." The word for "and" is more likely to be *pi* than *et*. If you have a good ear, you can detect other differences and a softer accent. It resembles the French of old France more than the dynamic language that you will hear in French Montréal.

Differences of vocabulary that can cause unfortunate misunderstandings include words used for meals. In Québec, you eat *déjeuner* first thing in the morning, *dîner* at lunchtime, and *souper* in the evening. In France, breakfast is *petit-déjeuner*, the lunchtime meal is *déjeuner*, and *dîner* is the evening meal. You need to know the origin of your French-speaking hosts if you are invited for *dîner* or you may arrive for the wrong meal.

OTHER LANGUAGES

The official Canadian census of 2001 recorded a population of just over 31 million, of whom more than 17.4 million spoke English as their mother tongue and 6.7 million spoke French. The third-largest language group was Chinese, with over 850,000 people (with a great concentration of these in British Columbia), followed by Italian and German, with just under half a million each.

Polish, Spanish, Portuguese, Punjabi, and Arabic were the mother tongue of about 200,000 people each. Dutch, Filipino, Greek and Vietnamese are each spoken by about 100,000 individuals.

Of First Nations languages, Cree has the most speakers, with 73,000. Inuktitut (the language of the Inuit) is spoken by about 29,000 people.

USEFUL WORDS AND PHRASES

FRENCH	ENGLISH
bonjour / bonsoir / bon nuit	good day / good evening / good night
au revoir	goodbye
oui / non	yes / no
merci / bienvenue	thank you / you're welcome
s'il vous plaît	please
Comment ça va?	How are you?
Très bien, merci	Very well, thank you
Ça va?	How's it going? (more colloquial)
douanes / frontière	customs / international border
autoroute / chemins / rue	highway / road / street
arrêt	stop (road sign)
aéroport	airport
métro / autobus / taxi	subway / bus / taxi
gare / train / billets	station / train / tickets
entrée / sortie	entrance / exit
droit / gauche	right / left
tout droit	straight ahead
nord / sud / est / ouest	north / south / east / west
matin / après-midi	morning / afternoon
soir / nuit	evening / night
Où est le restaurant / l'hôtel?	Where's the restaurant / the hotel?
le menu / table d'hôte	the menu / table d'hote (fixed-price meal
L'addition / la facture, s'il vous plaît	The check (bill), please
Combien?	How much?
déjeuner / dîner / souper / le thé	breakfast / lunch / dinner / tea
banque	bank
toilettes	washrooms / toilets
cinéma / théâtre / concert	cinema / theater / concert
librairie / bibliothèque	bookstore / library
cathédrale / église	cathedral / church
musée / galerie d'art	museum / art gallery
centre d'achat / boutique de souvenirs	shopping mall / souvenir store
édifice / place	building / city square
hôtel de ville / palais de justice	city hall / courthouse
fontaine / chute(s)	fountain / waterfall
rivière / fleuve	river / major river
ruisseau / lac	stream / lake
montagne / colline / vallée / falaise	mountain / hill / valley / cliff
baie / champ / île	bay / field / island
ville / cité / village	town / city / village
maison / pont / jardin	house / bridge / garden
salle / porte / fenêtre	room / door / window
moulin / belvédère	mill / viewpoint

INUKTITUT	PRONUNCIATION	ENGLISH
Qanuipit?	Ka-nwee-peet?	how are you?
Qanuingittung	Ka-nweeng-ni-toon-ga	I'm fine
Qujannamiik	Coo-yan-na-mee-ick	thankyou
Ilaali	Ee-lah-lih	you're welcome
Ii	Ee	yes
Aakka or aagaa	Ah-ka or Ah-ga	no
Qatsituqqa?	Cat-see-to-kaw?	how much is it?

Atlas

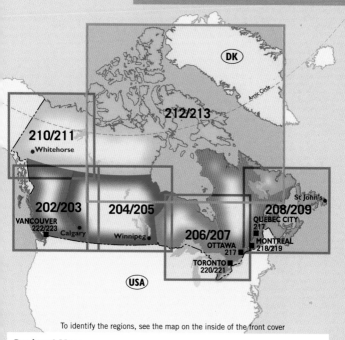

To identify the regions, see the map on the inside of the front cover

Regional Maps

▬▬▬	Major route	▫	City / Town
▬▬▬	Motorway (Expressway)		National park
▬▬▬	Main road	▣	Featured place of interest
▬▬▬	Other road	▪	Place of interest
------	International boundary	✈	Airport
------	State boundary	▲	Peak

202/211
0 ————— 150 km
0 ————— 75 miles

212/213
0 ————— 300 km
0 ————— 150 miles

City Plans

▬▬▬	Motorway (Expressway)
▬▬▬	Major route
▬▬▬	Other road
■	Important building
■	Park
◾	Place of interest
𝒊	Tourist information
●	Metro
✝	Church

218/219
0 ————— 150 metres
0 ————— 150 yards

220/221
0 ————— 300 metres
0 ————— 300 yards

222/223
0 ————— 300 metres
0 ————— 300 yards

Scales for Ottawa and Québec are shown within the plan frames

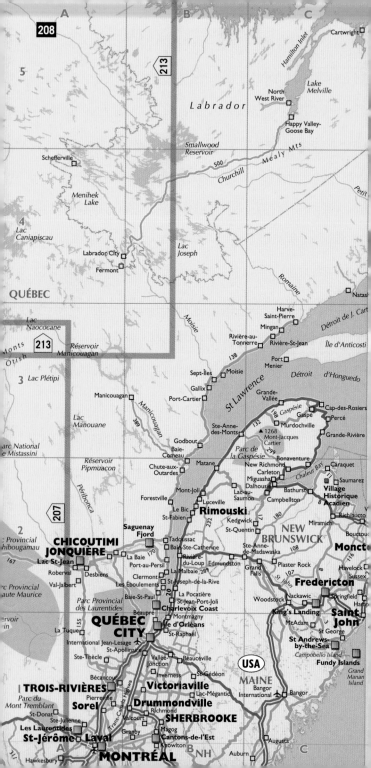

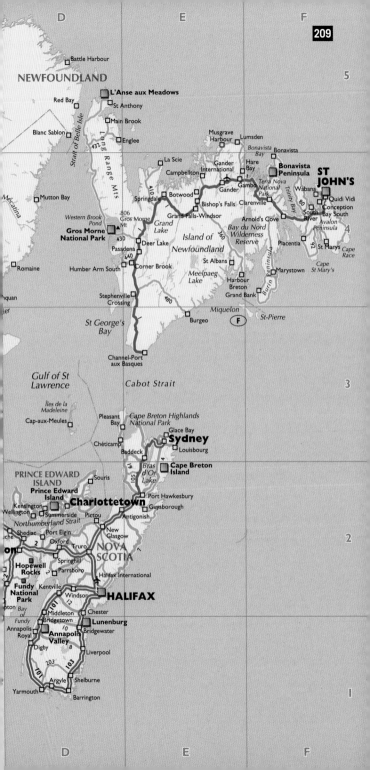

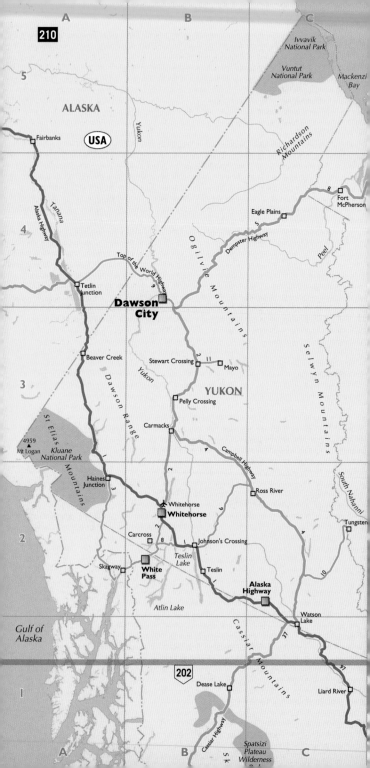

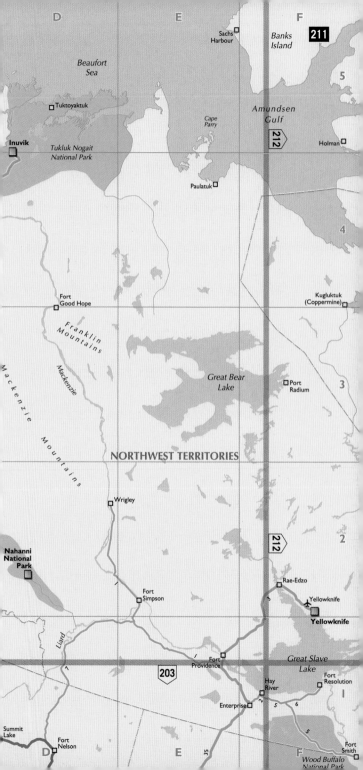

Ellesmere
Island

Axel
Heiberg
Island

Queen Elizabeth
Islands

Melville
Island

Parry
Islands

Devon
Island

Victoria
Melville
Sound

Qausuittuq
(Resolute)

Lancaster Sound

Pond
Inlet

Banks
Island

Somerset
Island

Ikpiarjuk
(Arctic Bay)

undsen
Gulf

Prince
of
Wales
Island

Gulf of Boothia

Victoria
Island

Boothia
Peninsula

Igloolik

Taloyoak

Melville
Peninsu

Kugluktuk
(Coppermine)

Ikaluktutiak
(Cambridge Bay)

King
William
Island

Ursuqtuq
(Gjoa Haven)

Coronation Gulf

211

Naujat
(Repulse Bay)

NUNAVUT

Back

Garry
Lake

Sou

Qamanittuaq
(Baker Lake)

2

Aylmer
Lake

Thelon

Dubawnt
Lake

Rae-Edzo
Yellowknife

NORTHWEST
TERRITORIES

Yellowknife

Great Slave
Lake

204

205

ay River

Fort Resolution

Arviat
(Eskimo Point)

Fort Smith

Nuelтин
Lake

Wood
Buffalo
National
Park

Uranium City

Lake
Athabasca

Stony
Rapids

Cape Churchill

Churchill

Churchill

ALBERTA

SASKATCHEWAN

Wollaston
Lake

Reindeer
Lake

MANITOBA

Fort
McMurray

A

B

Southern
Indian Lake

C

Lynn Lake

GREENLAND

DK

Baffin
Bay

Kangiqlugaapik
(Clyde River)

Davis Strait

Baffin
Island

Auyuittuq
National Park

Nettilling
Lake

Pangnirtung

Prince
Charles
Island

Cumberland Sound

Foxe
Basin

Amadjuak
Lake

Apex

Labrador
Sea

Kingait
(Cape Dorset)

Kimmirut

Frobisher Bay

Hudson Strait

Cape Chidley

1729
▲ Mt Caubvick

hampton
land

Coral
arbour

Quaqtaq

Ungava
Bay

Fisher   Strait

Coats
Island

Ivujivik

Mansel
Island

Péninsule
d'Ungava

NE

Kuujjuaq

Caniapiscau

208

Hudson
Bay

Inukjuak

QUÉBEC

Schefferville

Lac
Caniapiscau

F

Lac
Bienville

Labrador City

Fort
Severn

Kuujjuarapik

Réservoir

Atlas Index

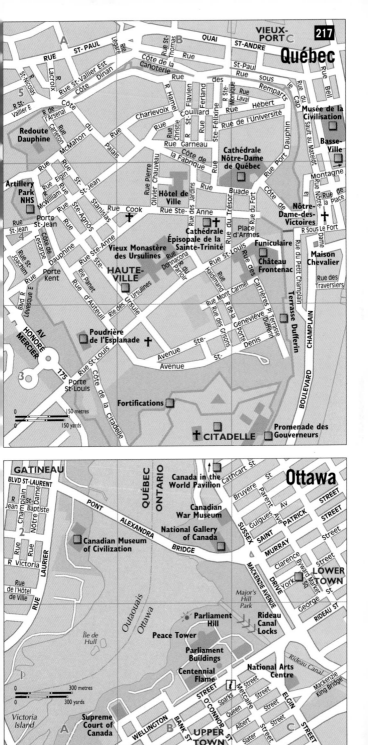

Québec

217

RUE ST-PAUL
QUAI ST-ANDRÉ
VIEUX-PORT
Côte de la Canoterie
RUE St-Nicolas
St-Nicolas
Lacroix
Rue St-Vallier Est
Côte Dinan
Rue St-Thomas
Rue
St-Paul
Rue
Rue sous le Cap
Rue du Cap
Rue Sault au Matelot
Rue Bell
Musée de la Civilisation
Redoute Dauphine
R de l'Arsenal
Rue de Carleton
Côte du Palais
McMahon
Charlevoix
R Hamel
Flavien
Couillard
Ferland
des Remparts
Rue Laval
Rue Hébert
R Ste-Monique
Rue St-Félixine
Rue Ste-Famille
Rue de l'Université
Dauphine
Rue du Port
Basse-Ville
R St-Vallier E
Artillery Park NHS
McWilliam
Rue Elgin
Rue St-Jean
Rue Ste-Agnès
Rue Christie
Rue Garneau
Côte de la Fabrique
Rue Pierre Olivier Chauveau
Rue des Jardins
Cathédrale Nôtre-Dame de Québec
Buade
Côte de la Montagne
Nôtre-Dame-des-Victoires
Rue Nôtre Dame
Porte St-Jean
Rue Stanislas
Rue Cook
Hôtel de Ville
Rue
Rue Ste-Anne
Place d'Armes
R Sous Le Fort
Rue de la Place
Porte Kent
Rue de Joachim
Rue St-Jean
Lescarde
Dauphine
Rue Ste-Anne
Rue St-Anne
Cathédrale Épiscopale de la Sainte-Trinité
Rue St-Louis
Funiculaire
Château Frontenac
Maison Chevalier
Rue du Petit Champlain
Blvd R Lévesque
Rue d'Auteuil
Vieux Monastère des Ursulines
HAUTE-VILLE
Rue Donnacona
Rue du Parloir
Rue des Ursulines
Rue Haldimand
Rue Mont Carmel
Rue des Carrières
Pl Terrasse
Terrasse Dufferin
Rue des Traversiers
AV HONORÉ MERCIER
Rue d'Auteuil
Rue des Grisons
Rue de la Porte
Rue Geneviève
Rue St-Denis
CHAMPLAIN
Poudrière de l'Esplanade
Avenue Ste-
Avenue
Porte St-Louis
175
Rue St-Louis
Côte de la Citadelle
Fortifications
BOULEVARD
CITADELLE
Promenade des Gouverneurs

0   150 metres
0   150 yards

Ottawa

GATINEAU
BLVD ST-LAURENT
QUÉBEC
ONTARIO
Canada in the World Pavilion
Cathcart St
R Jean
Champlain
St-Dame
Baptiste
Nôtre
Victoria
PONT ALEXANDRA BRIDGE
Bruyère St
Parent Av
Guigues Ave
SUSSEX
SAINT
PATRICK STREET
STREET
RUE
LAURIER
Rue de l'Hôtel de Ville
Canadian Museum of Civilization
Canadian War Museum
National Gallery of Canada
MURRAY
Clarence
MACKENZIE AVENUE
York
LOWER TOWN
Byward Market Sq
George
RIDEAU ST
Île de Hull
Outaouais
Ottawa
Major's Hill Park
Parliament Hill
Peace Tower
Rideau Canal Locks
Rideau Canal
Victoria Island
Parliament Buildings
Centennial Flame
National Arts Centre
MacKenzie King bridge
WELLINGTON
STREET
Sparks
Street
O'CONNOR ST
Metcalfe
Queen
Albert
Slater
Street
ELGIN
STREET
BANK ST
Supreme Court of Canada
UPPER TOWN

0   300 metres
0   300 yards

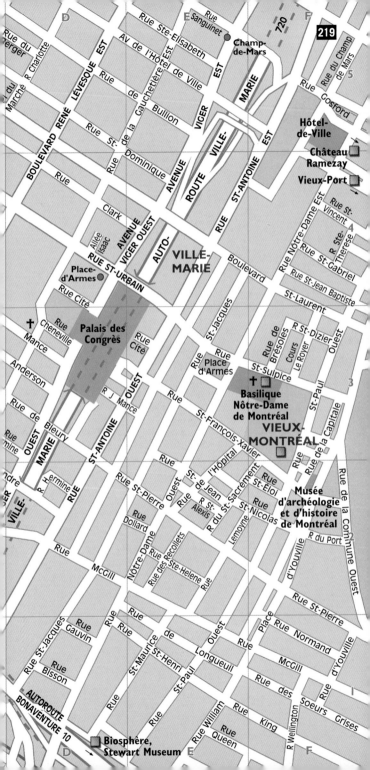

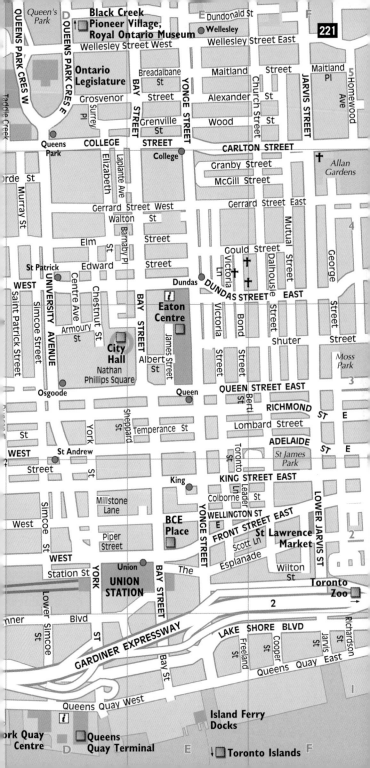

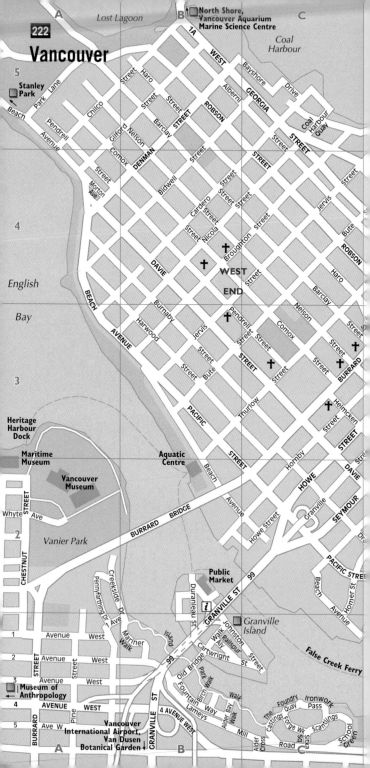

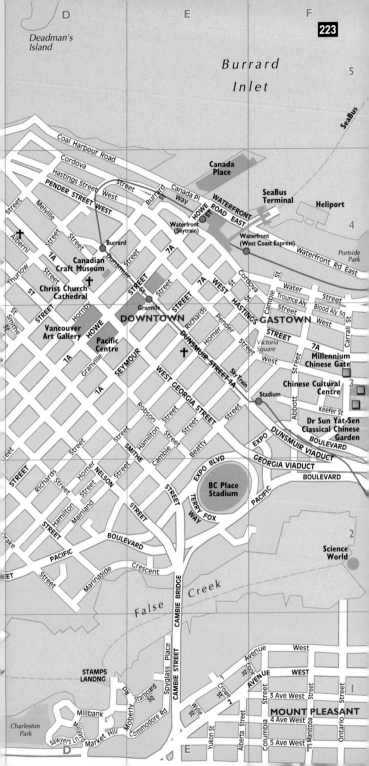

City Plan Street Indexes

QUÉBEC

OTTAWA

MONTRÉAL

Index

Picture credits

The Automobile Association wishes to thank the following photographers, libraries, associations and tourist organizations for their assistance in the preparation of this book.

Front and Back Cover: (t) **AA World Travel Library/ J Beazley**, (ct) **AA World Travel Library/N Sumner**, (cb), (b), Spine **AA World Travel Library/C Sawyer**.

1000 Islands International Tourism Council 94, 96b, 101, 102; **Alamy** 3(ii) (Dinodia Photo Library Pvt. Ltd), 13t (Bruce Coleman Brakefield), 13b (ImageState), 14bl (Robert E Barber), 15bl (Martin Harvey), 22b (xela), 163 (Dinodia Photo Library Pvt. Ltd), 173 (Peter Llewellyn), 178 (Brandon Cole Marine Photography), 179 (Chris Cheadle); **Calgary Stampede** 2(iv), 27, 71, 76; **Canadian Museum of Civilization** 30t (Spirit of Haida Gwaii, artist Bill Reid, catalogue no. 92-51, photographer Harry Foster), 30/1 (main builder Cesar Newashish, catalogue no. 111-P-21, photo Merle Toole); **Canadian Tourism Commission, Pierre St-Jacques** 24; **City of Saskatoon Imagebank** 86, 87; **Corbis** 14br, 15br, 32; **Dan Lavoie (Studio Odeyssée)** 20b; **Department of Tourism and Culture, Yukon Territorial Government** 29, 165, 166b, 167, 170, 171, 172, 191; **Festival International de Jazz de Montréal** 28. 28/9; **Getty Images** 10/11; **Getty Images/Hulton Collection** 16/17, 17t, 18t, 18b; **Kelly clark fotography:typical girl.com** 9b; **Michel Julien, ATR Gaspésie** 185, 186; **Musee Marguerite-Bourgeoys** 21; **Photodisc** 14/15; **RCMP** 73r; **John E. Sokolowski** 12; **Tourism Calgary** 26/7; **Tourisme Montréal, Stéphan Poulin** 120l, 122/3.

All remaining pictures are held in the Association's own library (AA World Travel Library) with contributions from the following photographers:

J Beazley 106; **P Bennett** 22t, 22/23, 57; **C Coe** 2(iii), 3(iii), 9t, 45, 52, 58, 60/1, 77, 164, 168l, 168c, 169, 177; **J Davison** 104, 105t, 105b, 184; **M Dent** 48, 50; **M Lynch** 148; **J F Pins** 2(vi), 6b, 7b, 20t, 25t, 98, 99, 103, 117, 120b, 124, 125, 126/7, 127, 128, 143t, 143b, 154/5, 158; **C Sawyer** 7t, 31t, 47, 49, 51, 54/5, 56t, 56b, 57, 62, 63, 64, 74cl, 180, 197l, 197r; **N Sumner** 2(i), 2(v), 3(i), 5t, 6/7, 8/9, 8, 25b, 93, 95t, 95b, 96t, 97t, 97b, 100, 107, 108/9, 110, 111, 118, 119, 121t, 121b, 129, 120, 131, 132, 133, 134, 141, 142, 144, 145, 146, 147, 149, 150, 151, 152, 153, 154, 156, 182, 183, 189, 190; **P Timmermans** 2(ii), 33, 46, 61cr, 65.

Acknowledgements

The author would like to thank the following for their invaluable assistance: Nim Singh (Canadian Tourism Commission), Kevin Johnston (Air Canada), all of the provincial tourist boards, Zoom Airlines, Westjet Airlines and the Westin Grand hotel in Vancouver.

Questionnaire

Dear Traveler

Your comments, opinions and recommendations are very important to us. So please help us to improve our travel guides by taking a few minutes to complete this simple questionnaire.

Send to: Spiral Guides, MailStop 66, 1000 AAA Drive, Heathrow, FL 32746–5063

Your recommendations...

We always encourage readers' recommendations for restaurants, nightlife or shopping – if your recommendation is added to the next edition of the guide, we will send you a FREE AAA Spiral Guide of your choice. Please state below the establishment name, location and your reasons for recommending it.

_____

_____

_____

_____

_____

Please send me AAA Spiral _____

(see list of titles inside the back cover)

About this guide...

Which title did you buy?

_____ **AAA Spiral**

Where did you buy it?_____

When? mm/ y y

Why did you choose a AAA Spiral Guide? _____

_____

_____

_____

Did this guide meet your expectations?

Exceeded ☐   Met all ☐   Met most ☐   Fell below ☐

Please give your reasons _____

_____

_____

_____

continued on next page...

Were there any aspects of this guide that you particularly liked?

____

Is there anything we could have done better?

____

About you...

Name (Mr/Mrs/Ms) ______________________________

Address ______________________________

______________________________ Zip ______________

Daytime tel nos. ______________________________

Which age group are you in?

Under 25 ☐ 25–34 ☐ 35–44 ☐ 45–54 ☐ 55–64 ☐ 65+ ☐

How many trips do you make a year?

Less than one ☐ One ☐ Two ☐ Three or more ☐

Are you a AAA member? Yes ☐ No ☐

Name of AAA club ______________________________

About your trip...

When did you book? m m/ y y When did you travel? m m/ y y

How long did you stay? ______________________________

Was it for business or leisure? ______________________________

Did you buy any other travel guides for your trip? ☐ Yes ☐ No

If yes, which ones? ______________________________

Thank you for taking the time to complete this questionnaire.

All information is for AAA internal use only and will NOT be distributed outside the organization to any third parties.